Accounts

Pippa Riley

Viva Books

New Delhi | Mumbai | Chennai | Kolkata | Bengaluru | Hyderabad | Kochi | Guwahati

First Indian Edition 2011

VIVA BOOKS PRIVATE LIMITED

- 4737/23 Ansari Road, Daryaganj, New Delhi 110 002
  E-mail: vivadelhi@vivagroupindia.net, Tel. 42242200
- 76, Service Industries, Shirvane, Sector 1, Nerul, Navi Mumbai 400 706
  E-mail: vivamumbai@vivagroupindia.net, Tel. 27721273, 27721274
- Jamals Fazal Chambers, 26 Greams Road, Chennai 600 006
  E-mail: vivachennai@vivagroupindia.net, Tel. 28290304, 28294241
- B-103, Jindal Towers, 21/1A/3 Darga Road, Kolkata 700 017
  E-mail: vivakolkata@vivagroupindia.net, Tel. 22836381, 22816713
- 7, Sovereign Park Apartments, 56-58, K. R. Road, Basavanagudi, Bengaluru 560 004
  E-mail: vivabangalore@vivagroupindia.net, Tel. 26607409, 26607410
- 101-102 Mughal Marc Aptt., 3-4-637 to 641, Narayanguda, Hyderabad 500 029
  E-mail: vivahyderabad@vivagroupindia.net, Tel. 27564481, 27564482
- First Floor, Beevi Towers, SRM Road, Kaloor, Kochi 682 018, Kerala
  E-mail: vivakochi@vivagroupindia.net, Tel: 0484-2403055, 2403056
- 232, GNB Road, Beside UCO Bank, Silpukhuri, Guwahati 781 003
  E-mail: vivaguwahati@vivagroupindia.net, Tel: 0361-2666386

Published by arrangement with

BPP Learning Media Ltd.
BPP House, Aldine Place
London W12 8AA

ISBN : 978-81-309-1752-8

Published by Vinod Vasishtha for Viva Books Private Limited, 4737/23, Ansari Road, Daryaganj, New Delhi - 110 002.

Printed and bound by Raj Press, R-3, Inderpuri, New Delhi - 110 012.

Contents

Introduction

Viva-BPP Learning Media's Business Essentials range is the ideal learning solution for students studying for business-related qualifications and degrees. The range provides concise and comprehensive coverage of the key areas that are essential to the business student.

Qualifications in business are traditionally very demanding. Students therefore need learning resources which go straight to the core of the topics involved, and which build upon students' pre-existing knowledge and experience. The BPP Learning Media Business Essentials range has been designed to meet exactly that need.

Features include:

- In-depth coverage of essential topics within business-related subjects
- Plenty of activities, quizzes and topics for discussion to help retain the interest of students and ensure progress
- Up-to-date practical illustrations and case studies that really bring the material to life
- A full index, with key terms highlighted in bold

Each chapter contains:

- An introduction and a list of specific study objectives
- Summary diagrams and signposts to guide you through the chapter
- A chapter roundup, quick quiz with answers and answers to activities

Titles in the Series

- Accounts
- Business Decision Making
- Business Environment
- Business Maths
- Business Strategy
- Economics
- Finance: Management Accounting and Financial Reporting
- Human Resource Development and Employee Relations
- Human Resource Management
- Management: Communications and Achieving Results
- Management: Leading People and Professional Development
- Managing Finance
- Marketing and Promotion
- Marketing and Sales Strategy
- Marketing Principles
- Organisations and Behaviour
- Research Project

Study Guide

This Course Book includes features designed specifically to make learning effective and efficient.

- Each chapter begins with a summary diagram which maps out the areas covered by the chapter. There are detailed summary diagrams at the start of each main section of the chapter. You can use the diagrams during revision as a basis for your notes.
- After the main summary diagram there is an introduction, which sets the chapter in context. This is followed by learning objectives, which show you what you will learn as you work through the chapter.
- Throughout the Course Book, there are special aids to learning. These are indicated by symbols in the margin:

Signposts guide you through the book, showing how each section connects with the next.

Definitions give the meanings of key terms. The *glossary* at the end of the book summarises these.

Activities help you to test how much you have learned. An indication of the time you should take on each is given. Answers are given at the end of each chapter.

Topics for discussion are for use in seminars. They give you a chance to share your views with your fellow students. They allow you to highlight holes in your knowledge and to see how others understand concepts. If you have time, try 'teaching' someone the concepts you have learned in a session. This helps you to remember key points and answering their questions will consolidate your knowledge.

Examples relate what you have learned to the outside world. Try to think up your own examples as you work through the Course Book.

Chapter roundups present the key information from the chapter in a concise format. Useful for revision.

- At the end of each chapter, there is a **chapter roundup** and a **quick quiz** with answers. Use these to revise and consolidate your knowledge. The chapter roundup summarises the chapter. The quick quiz tests what you have learned (the answers often refer you back to the chapter so you can look over subjects again).
- At the end of the book, there is an index.

Part A

Basic Accounting

Chapter 1:
INTRODUCTION TO ACCOUNTS

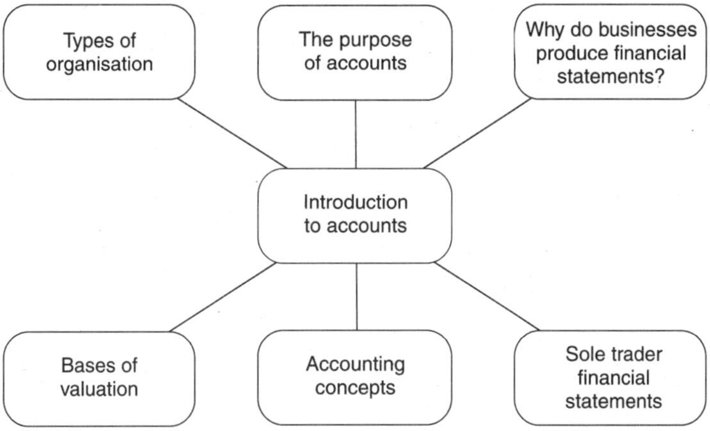

Introduction

If somebody were to present you with a set of accounts for a business, and ask you to tell them what they mean, you would probably feel rather intimidated. Accounting is an area in which many people believe only accountants should get involved!

In this Course Book we will cover quite a lot of ground in accounting, by the end of which you will not be an accountant – but you will feel more confident about the subject, and you will also appreciate the importance of understanding the subject yourself, rather than deferring to 'the professionals'.

The outcome for this first chapter is for you to be able to identify the basic components of a business's accounts, or financial statements. To do this you need to be aware of the different types of organisation that exist, and the basic characteristics of the profit-making businesses on which we will be concentrating in this Course Book. You will also understand the reasons why businesses produce financial statements, and what accounting concepts are followed in their preparation.

Your objectives

After completing this chapter you should be able to:

1. Identify different types of organisation
2. Identify the purpose of accounts
3. Explain why businesses produce financial statements
4. Set out the basic contents of a balance sheet and profit and loss account for a sole trader
5. Describe the concepts that underlie accounting
6. Describe three different bases of valuation used in accounting

1 TYPES OF ORGANISATION

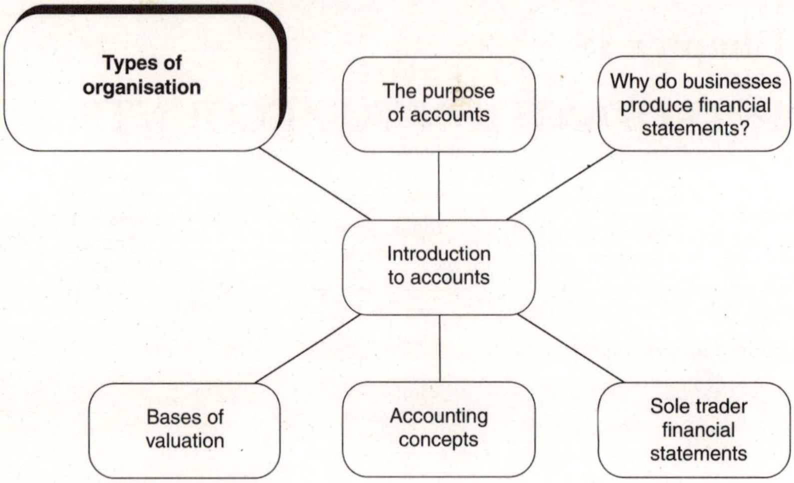

1.1 What is an organisation?

Here are some examples of organisations, categorised as to whether they exist to make profits for their owners (they are 'profit-oriented'), or to provide some sort of service (they are 'not-for-profit').

- A multinational car manufacturer (eg Ford) is profit-oriented
- An accountancy firm (eg KPMG) is profit-oriented
- A charity (eg UNICEF)
- A trade union
- A local authority
- A university
- A club

} all these are 'not-for profit', though they must still ensure they look after their money

Organisations of any type exist because they:

- Overcome people's individual limitations, whether physical or intellectual
- Enable people to specialise in what they do best
- Save time, because people can work together or do two aspects of a different task at the same time
- Accumulate and share knowledge (eg about how best to build cars)
- Enable people to pool their expertise
- Enable synergy: the combined output of two or more individuals working together exceeds their individual output ('None of us is as smart as all of us')

In brief, organisations enable people to be more productive.

Definition

> **Organisation**: 'A social arrangement for the controlled performance of collective goals, which has a boundary separating it from its environment'.

In this text we are concerned with organisations that exist to make a profit. We can broadly call these 'businesses'.

There are a number of different ways of looking at a business. Some ideas are listed below.

- A business is a **commercial or industrial concern** which exists to deal in the manufacture, re-sale or supply of goods and services.
- A business is an **organisation which uses economic resources** to create goods or services which customers will buy.
- A business is an **organisation providing jobs** for people.
- A business **invests money in resources** (for example it buys buildings, machinery and so on, it pays employees) in order to make even more money for its owners.

This last definition introduces the important idea of profit. Business organisations vary in character, size and complexity. They range from very small businesses (the local shopkeeper or plumber) to very large ones (ICI, IKEA, Corus). But the objective of earning profit is common to all of them.

Definition

> **Profit** is the amount by which income exceeds expenditure. When expenditure exceeds income, the business is running at a **loss**.

Measuring income, expenditure and profit is not such a straightforward problem as it may seem.

1.2 Types of business organisation

There are three main types of business organisation.

- Sole traders
- Partnerships
- Limited companies

> **Activity 1** **(10 minutes)**
>
> Accounts are the financial statements produced only by a large quoted company.
>
> Is this statement correct?
>
> A Yes
> B No

Sole traders are people who work for themselves. Examples include the local shopkeeper, a plumber and a hairdresser. Note that sole traders can employ people; the term 'sole trader' just refers to the **ownership** of the business.

Partnerships occur when two or more sole traders decide to share the risks and rewards of a business together. Examples include an accountancy practice, a medical practice and a legal practice.

Limited companies are incorporated to take advantage of 'limited liability' for their owners (shareholders). This means that, while sole traders and partners are personally responsible for the amounts owed by their businesses, the shareholders of a limited company are only responsible for the amount to be paid to the company for their shares.

In law sole traders and partnerships are not separate entities from their owners. However, a limited company is legally a separate entity from its owners and it can issue contracts in the company's name.

1.3 Advantages of trading as a limited company

(a) **Limited liability** makes investment less risky than investing in a sole trader or partnership. However, lenders to a small company may still ask for a shareholder's personal guarantee to secure any loans.

(b) It is **easier to raise finance** because of limited liability and there is no limit on the number of shareholders.

(c) A limited company has a **separate legal identity** from its shareholders. So a company continues to exist regardless of the identity of its owners. In contrast, a partnership ceases, and a new one starts, whenever a partner joins or leaves the partnership.

(d) There are **tax advantages** to being a limited company. The company is taxed as a separate entity from its owners and the tax rate on companies may be lower than the tax rate for individuals.

(e) It is relatively easy to **transfer shares** in a company from one owner to another. In contrast, it may be difficult to find someone to buy a sole trader's business or to buy a share in a partnership.

1.4 Disadvantages of trading as a limited company

(a) Limited companies have to **publish annual financial statements**. This means that anyone (including competitors) can see how well (or badly) they are doing. In contrast, sole traders and partnerships do not have to publish their financial statements.

(b) Limited company financial statements have to comply with **legal and accounting requirements**. In particular the financial statements have to comply with accounting standards. Sole traders and partnerships may choose to comply with accounting standards, but are not compelled to do so.

(c) The financial statements of larger limited companies have to be **audited**. This means that the financial statements are subject to an independent review to ensure that they comply with legal requirements and accounting standards. This can be inconvenient, time consuming and expensive.

(d) **Share issues** are regulated by law; for example, it is difficult to reduce share capital. Sole traders and partnership can increase or decrease capital as and when the owners wish.

2 THE PURPOSE OF ACCOUNTS

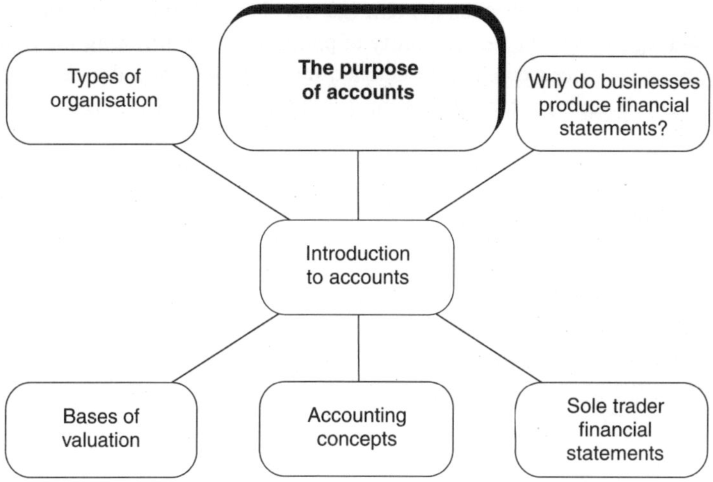

2.1 What are accounts?

Definition

> **Accounts** summarise a business's financial data.

Financial data is the name given to the actual transactions carried out by a business eg sales of goods, purchases of goods, payment of expenses.

These transactions are **recorded** and analysed in **books of prime entry**, and the totals are posted to the ledger accounts.

Finally, the transactions are **summarised** in the accounts (often known as the financial statements), that is the balance sheet and profit and loss account. We shall look at this process in Chapters 2-4.

2.2 Financial vs management accounts

Most businesses of any size prepare financial information for two quite distinct audiences. These take the form of financial and management accounts.

2.3 Financial accounts

So far in this chapter we have dealt with **financial** accounts. Financial accounting is mainly a method of reporting the results and financial position of a business. It is not primarily concerned with providing information for the more efficient running of the business. Although financial accounts are of interest to management, their principal function is to satisfy the information needs of persons not involved in running the business. They provide **historical** information.

2.4 Management accounts

The information needs of management go far beyond those of other users of accounts. Managers have the responsibility of planning and controlling the resources of the business, so they need much more detailed information. They also need to **plan for the future** (eg budgets, which represent the business's future plans, expressed in monetary terms).

Definition

> **Management accounting** is a management information system which analyses data to provide information as a basis for managerial action. The concern of a management accountant is to present accounting information in the form most helpful to management.

> **Activity 2** **(20 minutes)**
>
> They say that America is run by lawyers and the UK is run by accountants, but what do accountants do? Before moving on to the next section, think of any accountants you know and the kind of jobs they do.

3 WHY DO BUSINESSES PRODUCE FINANCIAL STATEMENTS?

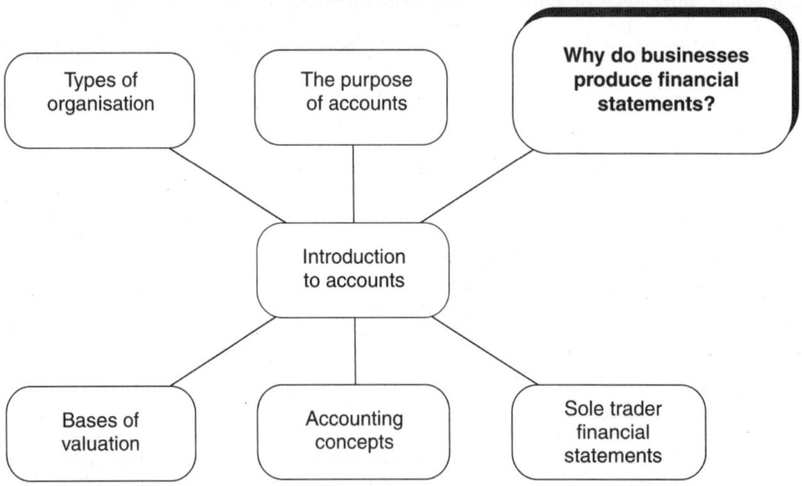

If a business is being run efficiently, why should it have to go through all the bother of accounting procedures in order to produce financial statements?

A business should produce information about its activities because there are various groups of people who want or need to know that information. This sounds rather vague: to make it clearer, we will study the classes of people who need information about a business. We need also to think about what information in particular is of interest to the members of each class.

Large businesses are of interest to a greater variety of people and so we will consider the case of a large public company whose shares can be purchased and sold on the Stock Exchange.

3.1 Users of financial statements and accounting information

The following people are likely to be interested in financial information about a large company with listed shares.

(a) **Managers of the company** appointed by the company's owners to supervise the day-to-day activities of the company. They need information about the company's financial situation as it is currently and as it is expected to be in the future. This is to enable them to manage the business efficiently and to make effective decisions.

(b) **Shareholders of the company,** ie the company's owners, want to assess how well the management is performing its stewardship function. They will want to know how profitably management is running the company's operations and how much profit they can afford to withdraw from the business for their own use.

(c) **Trade contacts,** including suppliers who provide goods to the company on credit and customers who purchase the goods or services provided by the company. **Suppliers** will want to know about the company's ability to pay its debts; **customers** need to know that the company is a secure source of supply and is in no danger of having to close down.

(d) **Providers of finance to the company**. These might include a bank which allows the company to operate an overdraft, or provides longer-term finance by granting a loan. The bank wants to ensure that the company is able to keep up interest payments, and eventually to repay the amounts advanced.

(e) **HM Revenue and Customs,** who will want to know about business profits in order to assess the tax payable by the company.

(f) **Employees of the company**. These should have a right to information about the company's financial situation, because their future careers and the size of their wages and salaries depend on it.

(g) **Financial analysts and advisers** need information for their clients or audience. For example, stockbrokers need information to advise investors; credit agencies want information to advise potential suppliers of goods to the company; and journalists need information for their reading public.

(h) **Government and their agencies**. Governments and their agencies are interested in the allocation of resources and therefore in the activities of enterprises. They also require information in order to provide a basis for national statistics.

(i) **The public**. Enterprises affect members of the public in a variety of ways. For example, they may make a substantial contribution to a local economy by providing employment and using local suppliers. Another important factor is the effect of an enterprise on the environment, for example as regards pollution.

Accounting information is summarised in financial statements to satisfy the **information needs** of these different groups. Not all needs, and not all users, will be equally satisfied.

3.2 Needs of different users

Managers of a business need the most information, to help them make their planning and control decisions. They obviously have 'special' access to information about the business, because they are able to demand whatever internally produced statements they require. When managers want a large amount of information about the costs and profitability of individual products, or different parts of their business, they can obtain it through its system of management accounting.

Activity 3 **(10 minutes)**

Which of the following statements is particularly useful for managers?

A Financial statements for the last financial year
B Tax records for the past five years
C Budgets for the coming financial year
D Bank statements for the past year

In addition to management information, financial statements are prepared (and perhaps published) for the benefit of other user groups, which may demand certain information.

(a) The **law** provides for the provision of some information. The Companies Act requires every company to publish accounting information for its shareholders; and companies must also file a copy of their financial statements with the Registrar of Companies, so that any member of the public who so wishes can look at them.

(b) **HM Revenue and Customs** will receive the information they need to make tax assessments.

(c) A **bank** might demand a forecast of a company's expected future cash flows as a pre-condition of granting an overdraft.

(d) The **professional accountancy bodies** have been jointly responsible for issuing **accounting standards** (known as FRSs or SSAPs) and some standards require companies to publish certain additional information. Accountants, as members of professional bodies, are placed under a strong obligation to ensure that company financial statements conform to the requirements of the standards.

(e) Some companies provide, voluntarily, specially prepared financial information for issue to their employees. These statements are known as **employee reports**.

4 SOLE TRADER FINANCIAL STATEMENTS

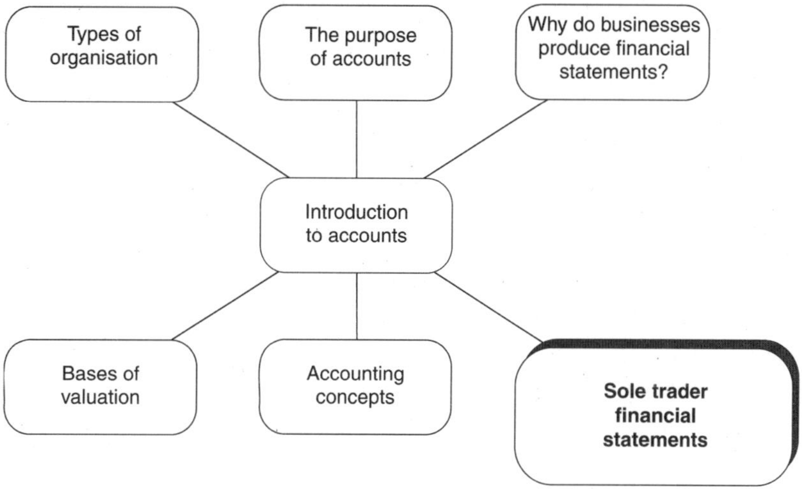

The two main financial statements are the balance sheet and the profit and loss account. Until we have covered how these are produced and what they contain, we shall concentrate exclusively in this text on the financial statements of sole traders.

4.1 Balance sheet

Definition

> The **balance sheet** is simply a list of all the assets owned and all the liabilities owed by a business as at a particular date. It is a snapshot of the financial position of the business at a particular moment in time.

4.1.1 Assets

Definition

> An **asset** is something valuable which a business owns or has the use of.

Examples of assets are factories, office buildings, warehouses, delivery vans, lorries, plant and machinery, computer equipment, office furniture, cash and goods held in store awaiting sale to customers.

Some assets are held and used in operations for a long time. An office building is occupied by administrative staff for years. A machine might have a productive life of many years before it wears out. These are called **fixed assets**. A charge is made against profits each year to reflect the fact that the asset has been used to generate profit. This is called **depreciation**.

Other assets are held for only a short time. The owner of a newsagent shop, for example, has to sell his newspapers on the same day that he gets them. This is an example of a **current asset.**

4.1.2 Liabilities

Definition

> A **liability** is something which is owed to somebody else.

Examples of liabilities are a bank loan or overdraft, amounts owed to a supplier, taxation owed to HM Revenue & Customs and amounts owed to the owners.

4.1.3 Capital or equity

Definition

> **Capital** is an investment of money in a business to earn profit.

Capital is the investment that the owner has made.

4.1.4 Sole trader balance sheet

In a balance sheet assets will always be equal to liabilities plus capital (or equity). A very simple balance sheet for a sole trader, Machek, is shown below.

MACHEK
BALANCE SHEET AS AT 30 MARCH 20X7

	£	£
Fixed assets – owned by the business		
Freehold premises		50,000
Fixtures and fittings		8,000
Motor vehicles		9,000
		67,000
Current assets – owned by the business		
Stocks	16,000	
Debtors (owed by customers)	500	
Cash	400	
	16,900	
Current liabilities – owed by the business		
Bank overdraft	2,000	
Creditors (owed to suppliers)	5,300	
	7,300	
Net current assets		9,600
Net assets		76,600

	£	£
Capital – Machek's ownership interest in the business		
Capital at 1 April 20X6		75,000
Profit for year (derived from profit and loss account)		10,400
Drawings by Machek		(8,800)
Capital at 31 March 20X7		76,600

We will be looking at a balance sheet in a lot more detail later.

4.2 Profit and loss account

Definition

> A **profit and loss account** is a record of income generated and expenditure incurred over a given period. The profit and loss account shows whether the business has had more income than expenditure (a profit) or *vice versa* (loss).

4.2.1 Revenue and expenses

Revenue is the income for a period (eg sales). The **expenses** are the costs of running the business for the same period. These expenses do **not** include amounts paid by the business to the owner. These are shown as **drawings** on the balance sheet.

4.2.2 Sole trader profit and loss account

The period of time chosen will depend on the purpose for which the statement is produced. The profit and loss account of a sole trader that is used to establish the owner's tax liability will usually be for the period of a **year**, commencing from the date of the previous year's statements. On the other hand, the sole trader or manager will want to keep a closer eye on profitability by making up **quarterly or monthly** statements.

Machek's simple profit and loss account for a sole trader is shown below.

MACHEK
PROFIT AND LOSS ACCOUNT FOR THE YEAR ENDED 30 APRIL 20X7

	£
Sales	150,000
Cost of sales	(75,000)
Gross profit	75,000
Other expenses	64,600
Net profit for the year (increase in Machek's capital – see balance sheet)	10,400

Once again, this example is given purely for illustrative purposes. We will be dealing with a profit and loss account in detail later, where we will also see how it fits in with the balance sheet.

4.3 Purpose of financial statements

Both the balance sheet and the profit and loss account are **summaries of accumulated data**. For example, the profit and loss account shows a figure for income earned from selling goods to customers. This is the total amount of income earned from all the individual sales made during the period.

The balance sheet and the profit and loss account form the basis of the financial statements of most businesses. For limited companies, other information by way of statements and notes may be required by law and/or accounting standards. For example a **cash flow statement** may be required. We will come back to this later in this Course Book.

5 ACCOUNTING CONCEPTS

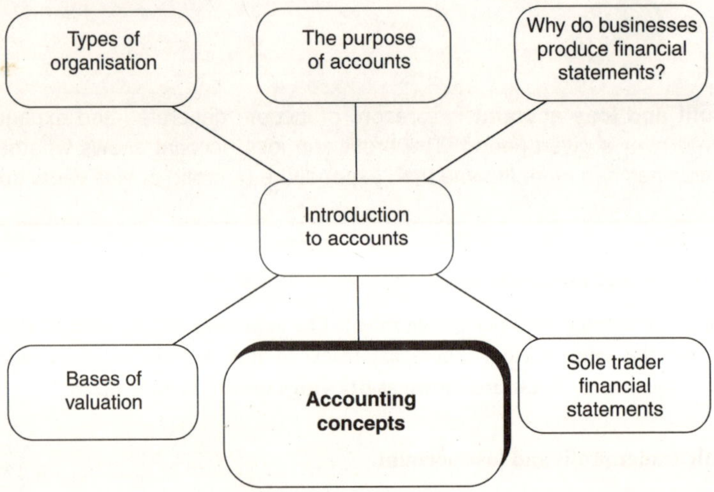

Accounting practice has developed gradually over a matter of centuries. Many of its procedures are operated automatically by people who have never questioned whether alternative methods exist which are just as valid. However, the procedures in common use imply the acceptance of certain concepts which are by no means self-evident; nor are they the only possible **concepts.** These concepts could be used to build up an accounting framework.

Our next step is to look at some of the more important concepts which are taken for granted in preparing financial statements which are intended to present a **true and fair view** of the entity's business and performance.

We shall single out the following concepts for discussion, though we shall look at some others in addition.

(a) Going concern
(b) Accruals (or matching)
(c) Prudence
(d) Consistency concept
(e) Comparability
(f) Offsetting

5.1 The going concern concept

Definition

> The **going concern concept** implies that the business will continue in operational existence for the foreseeable future, and that there is no intention to put the company into liquidation or to make drastic cutbacks to the scale of operations.

Financial statements **must** be prepared under the going concern basis unless the entity is being (or is going to be) liquidated or if it has ceased (or is about to cease) trading. The directors of a company must also disclose any significant doubts about the company's future if and when they arise.

The main significance of the going concern concept is that the assets of the business should not be valued at their 'break-up' value, which is the amount that they would sell for if they were sold off piecemeal and the business were thus broken up.

EXAMPLE: GOING CONCERN CONCEPT

Emma acquires a T-shirt making machine at a cost of £60,000. She expects to use it for six years, and then scrap it.

Using the going concern concept, it is presumed that the business will continue its operations and so the asset will live out its full six years in use. Emma will recognise a 'depreciation' charge of £10,000 each year, and the value of the asset in each year's balance sheet will be its cost less the accumulated amount of depreciation charged to date. After one year, the **net book value** of the asset would therefore be £(60,000 – 10,000) = £50,000, after two years it would be £40,000, after three years £30,000 etc, until it has been written down to a value of 0 after 6 years.

Now suppose that this asset has no other operational use outside the business, and in a forced sale it would only sell for scrap. After one year of operation its scrap value is, say, £8,000.

The net book value of the asset, applying the going concern concept, is £50,000 after one year, but its immediate sell-off value only £8,000. It can be argued that the asset is over-valued at £50,000 and that it should be written down to £8,000 in the balance sheet, with the balance of its cost treated as an expense. However, provided that the going concern concept is valid, so that the asset continues to be used and not sold, it is appropriate to value the asset at its net book value.

Activity 4 **(30 minutes)**

A retailer commences business on 1 January and buys stock of 20 washing machines, each costing £100. During the year he sells 17 machines at £150 each. How should the remaining machines be valued at 31 December if:

(a) He is forced to close down his business at the end of the year and the remaining machines will realise only £60 each in a forced sale?

(b) He intends to continue his business into the next year?

5.2 The accruals (or matching) concept

FRS 18 also stipulates that financial statements must be prepared under the accruals concept. This concept is a cornerstone of present day financial statements, so work through this section carefully so that you understand how it is applied during the preparation of accounts.

Definition

The **accruals concept** states that revenue and costs must be recognised as they are earned or incurred, not as cash is received or paid. They must be matched with one another so far as their relationship can be established or justifiably assumed, and dealt with in the profit and loss account of the period to which they relate.

If Emma makes 20 T-shirts at a cost of £100 and sells them for £200, she makes a profit of £100.

However, if Emma had only sold eighteen T-shirts, it would have been incorrect to charge her profit and loss account with the cost of twenty T-shirts, as she still has two T-shirts in stock. If she intends to sell them in June she is likely to make a profit on the sale. Therefore, only the purchase cost of eighteen T-shirts (£90) should be matched with her sales revenue, leaving her with a profit of £90.

Her balance sheet would therefore look like this.

	£
Assets	
Stock (at cost, ie 2 × £5)	10
Debtors (18 × £10)	180
	190
Liabilities	
Creditors	100
	90
Emma's capital (profit for the period)	90

Suppose Emma had decided to give up selling T-shirts, then the going concern concept would no longer apply and the value of the two T-shirts in the balance sheet would be a break-up valuation rather than cost. Similarly, if the two unsold T-shirts were now unlikely to be sold at more than their cost of £5 each (say, because of damage or a fall in demand) then they should be recorded on the balance sheet at their **net realisable value** (ie the likely eventual sales price less any expenses incurred to make them saleable, eg paint) rather than cost.

In this example, the concepts of going concern and accruals are linked. As the business is assumed to be a going concern, it is possible to carry forward the cost of the unsold T-shirts as a charge against profits of the next period.

5.3 The prudence concept

Definition

> **Prudence** is the inclusion of a degree of caution in the exercise of the judgements needed in making the estimates required under conditions of uncertainty, such that income, profit and assets are not overstated and expenses, losses and liabilities are not understated.

Prudence is a **desirable quality** of financial statements but it is *not* a bedrock. Businesses should not be over-pessimistic and **over-state** items in times of high profits in order to 'smooth' profits between periods of high and low profitability.

You should bear this in mind as you read through the explanation of prudence. On the one hand assets and profits should not be overstated, but a balance must be achieved to prevent the overstatement of liabilities or losses.

You may have wondered why the three washing machines in Activity 4 were stated in the balance sheet at their cost (£100 each) rather than their selling price (£150 each). This is an aspect of the prudence concept: to value the machines at £150 would be to anticipate making a profit before the profit had been realised, and while uncertainty still existed as to whether it would be realised.

The other aspect of the prudence concept is that where a **loss** is foreseen, it **should** be anticipated and taken into account immediately. If a business purchases stock for £1,200 but, because of a sudden slump in the market only £900 is likely to be realised when the stock is sold the prudence concept dictates that the stock should be valued at £900. It is not enough to wait until the stock is sold, and then recognise the £300 loss; it must be recognised as soon as it is foreseen.

A profit can be considered to be a **realised profit** when it is in the form of:

- Cash.
- Another asset which has a reasonably certain cash value. This includes amounts owing from debtors, provided that there is a reasonable certainty that the debtors will eventually pay up what they owe.

EXAMPLE: PRUDENCE CONCEPT

Mohammed begins trading on 1 January 20X5 and sells goods worth £100,000 during the year to 31 December. At 31 December there are debts outstanding of £15,000. Of these, Mohammed is now doubtful whether £6,000 will ever be paid.

Mohammed should make an **allowance for debtors** of £6,000. Sales for 20X5 will be shown in the profit and loss account at their full value of £100,000, but the allowance for debtors would be an expense of £6,000. Because there is some uncertainty that the sales will be realised in the form of cash, the prudence concept dictates that the £6,000 should not be included in Mohammed's profit for the year.

Activity 5 **(1 hour)**

Given that prudence is the main consideration, discuss under what circumstances, if any, revenue might be recognised at the following stages of a sale.

(a) Goods have been acquired by the business which it confidently expects to resell very quickly.

(b) A customer places a firm order for goods.

(c) Goods are delivered to the customer.

(d) The customer is invoiced for goods.

(e) The customer pays for the goods.

(f) The customer's cheque in payment for the goods has been cleared by the bank.

5.4 The consistency concept

Accounting is not an exact science. There are many areas in which judgement must be exercised in attributing money values to items appearing in accounts. Over the years certain procedures and principles have come to be recognised as good accounting practice, but within these limits there are often various acceptable methods of accounting for similar items.

Definition

The **consistency concept** states that similar items should be accorded similar accounting treatments.

In preparing financial statements consistency should be observed in two respects.

(a) Similar items within a single set of financial statements should be given similar accounting treatment.

(b) The same treatment should be applied from one period to another in accounting for similar items. This enables valid comparisons to be made from one period to the next and with information provided by other businesses (sometimes called the **comparability** concept).

5.5 No offsetting

'Assets and liabilities, and income and expenses, should be shown separately in the financial statement. They should not normally be 'offset' against each other, with only a 'net' figure reported.

5.6 Other accounting concepts

Certain other concepts are also applied when producing financial statements.

5.6.1 The entity concept

Accountants regard a business as a separate entity, distinct from its owners or managers. The concept applies whether the business is a limited company (and so recognised in law as a separate entity) or a sole tradership or partnership (in which case the business is not separately recognised by the law).

5.6.2 The materiality concept

Definition

> The **materiality concept** means that only items that are material in amount or in their nature will affect the true and fair view given by a set of accounts.

An error which is too trivial to affect anyone's understanding is referred to as **immaterial.** In preparing financial statements it is important to assess what is material and what is not, so that time and money are not wasted in the pursuit of excessive detail.

Determining whether or not an item is material is a **very subjective exercise**. There is no absolute measure of materiality. It is common to apply a convenient rule of thumb (for example, to define material items as those with a value greater than 5% of profit). However, some items are regarded as particularly sensitive by their **nature** and even a very small misstatement of such an item would be regarded as material. An example in the financial statements of a limited company might be the amount of remuneration paid to directors of the company.

The assessment of an item as material or immaterial may affect its treatment. For example, the profit and loss account of a business will show the expenses incurred grouped under suitable captions (heating and lighting expenses, rent and rates expenses etc); but in the case of very small expenses it may be appropriate to lump them together under a caption such as 'sundry expenses', because a more detailed breakdown would be inappropriate for such immaterial amounts.

EXAMPLE: MATERIALITY

(a) A balance sheet shows fixed assets of £2 million and stocks of £30,000. An error of £20,000 in the depreciation calculation might not be regarded as material, whereas an error of £20,000 in the stock valuation probably would be. In other words, the total of which the erroneous item forms part must be considered.

(b) If a business has a bank loan of £50,000 and a £55,000 balance on a savings account, it might well be regarded as a material misstatement if these two amounts were displayed on the balance sheet as 'cash at bank £5,000'. In other words, incorrect presentation may amount to material misstatement even if there is no monetary error.

Activity 6 **(20 minutes)**

Would you include the following items as fixed assets?

(a) A box file
(b) A forklift truck
(c) A small plastic display stand

5.6.3 The duality concept

Every transaction has two effects. This concept underpins double entry bookkeeping, and you will see it at work in your studies from Chapter 3 onwards.

5.6.4 Substance over form

Definition

Substance over form means that transactions should be accounted for and presented in accordance with their economic substance, not their legal form.

An example of substance over form is that of assets acquired on hire purchase. Legally the purchaser does not own the asset until the final instalment has been paid. However, the accounting treatment is to record a fixed asset at the start of the hire purchase agreement. The **substance** of the transaction is that the business owns the asset, even though its legal form shows that it does not.

5.6.5 Other qualities of useful accounting information

Below are some other qualities that accounting information should have if it is to be useful.

(a) **Relevance**. The information provided should satisfy the needs of information users.

(b) **Understandability**. Information may be difficult to understand because it is skimpy or incomplete, but too much detail is also a defect which can cause difficulties of understanding.

(c) **Reliability**. Information will be more reliable if it is independently verified. The law requires that the financial statements published by large limited companies should be verified by auditors, who must be independent of the company and must hold an approved qualification.

(d) **Completeness.** Accounts should present a rounded picture of the business's economic activities.

(e) **Fair presentation**. Financial statements should **present fairly** – give a **true and fair view** of – the financial position, financial performance and cash flows of a business. Compliance with accounting standards (FRSs and SSAPs) will usually achieve this.

(f) **Faithful representation.** The information gives full details of its effects on the financial statements and is only recognised if its financial effects are certain.

6 BASES OF VALUATION

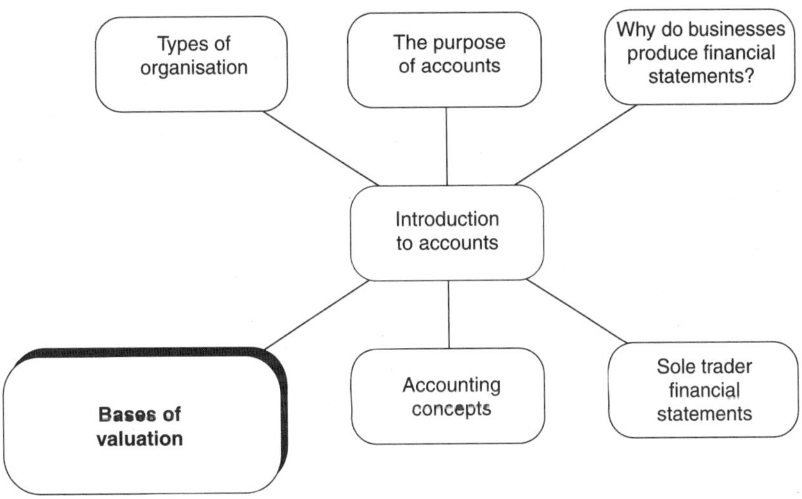

Items in the financial statements can be valued under a number of bases:

- Historical cost
- Replacement cost
- Net realisable value

6.1 Historical cost

A basic principle of accounting is that items are normally stated in accounts at **historical cost,** ie at the amount which the business paid to acquire them. An important advantage of this procedure is that objectivity is maximised: there is usually documentary evidence to prove the amount paid to purchase an asset or pay an expense.

Definition

> **Historical cost** means that transactions are recorded at their cost when they occurred.

In general, accountants prefer to deal with costs, rather than with 'values'. This is because valuations tend to be subjective and to vary according to what the valuation is for.

6.2 Replacement cost

Definition

> **Replacement cost** means the amount needed to replace an item with an identical item.

EXAMPLE: REPLACEMENT COST

Sonia bought a machine five years ago for £15,000. It is now worn out and needs replacing. An identical machine can be purchased for £20,000.

Historical cost is £15,000

Replacement cost is £20,000

6.3 Net realisable value

Definition

> **Net realisable value** is the expected selling price less any costs still to be incurred in getting the item ready for sale and then selling it.

EXAMPLE: NET REALISABLE VALUE

Sonia's machine from the example above can be restored to working order at a cost of £5,000. It can then be sold for £10,000. What is its net realisable value?

Net realisable value = £10,000 – £5,000
= £5,000

6.4 Advantages and disadvantages of historical cost accounting

The **advantage** of historical cost accounting is that the cost is known and can be proved (eg by the purchase invoice). There is no subjectivity or bias in the valuation.

There are a number of **disadvantages** and these usually arise in times of rising prices (inflation). When inflation is low, then historical cost accounting is usually satisfactory.

Chapter roundup

- Businesses of whatever size or nature exist to make a **profit**.
- **Financial accounting** is a way of recording, analysing and summarising financial data.
- You should be able to distinguish the following:
  - Financial accounting
  - Management accounting
- There are various groups of people who need information about the activities of a business.
- The two main financial statements are the balance sheet and the profit and loss account.
- Accounting practice recognises a number of concepts.
- Going concern and accruals are the two fundamental accounting concepts as identified by FRS 18 *Accounting policies*.
- Items in the financial statements can be valued under the following bases.
  - Historical cost
  - Replacement cost
  - Net realisable value

Quick quiz

1 What is financial accounting?

2 A business entity is owned and run by Alpha, Beta and Gamma.

What type of business is this an example of?

A Sole trader
B Partnership
C Limited company
D Don't know

3 Identify seven user groups who need accounting information.

4 What are the two main financial statements drawn up by accountants?

5 Which of the following is an example of a liability?

A Stock
B Debtors
C Plant and machinery
D Loan

6 Which FRS deals with accounting concepts?

7 Which of the following assumptions are included in FRS 18?

A Money measurement
B Objectivity
C Going concern
D Business entity

8 Define 'going concern'.

9 What is meant by the prudence concept?

10 Only items which have a monetary value can be included in accounts. Which of the following is a basis of valuation?

A Historical cost
B Money measurement
C Realisation
D Business entity

11 Suggest four possible values which might be attributed to an asset in the balance sheet of a business.

12 Making an allowance for debtors is an example of which concept?

A Accruals
B Going concern
C Materiality
D Prudence

Answers to quick quiz

1 A way of recording, analysing and summarising financial data.

2 B. A partnership, as it is owned and run by three people.

3 See section 3.

4 The profit and loss account and the balance sheet.

5 D. A loan. The rest are all assets.

6 FRS 18 *Accounting Policies*.

7 C Only going concern is included in FRS 18, the others are assumptions and concepts generally used in accountancy, but not mentioned in FRS 18.

8 The assumption that a business will continue in operation for the foreseeable future, without going into liquidation or materially scaling down its operations.

9 Prudence means to be cautious when exercising judgement. In particular profits should not be recognised until realised, but a loss should be recognised as soon as it is foreseen.

10 A This is the only valuation basis.

11
- Historical cost
- Replacement value
- Net realisable value
- Economic value

12 D Prudence

Answers to activities

1 The correct answer is B. Financial accounting is carried out by all businesses, no matter what their size or structure.

2 Obviously the answer to this activity depends on your own situation and how many accountants you know! What the activity should have drawn out is that accountants actually have quite a wide range of responsibilities, from recording transactions through preparing financial statements and budgets, to advising on improving business operations and making major transactions, such as takeovers.

3 The correct answer is C. Managers need to look forward and make plans to keep the business profitable. Therefore the most useful information for them would be the budgets – which are plans for the future expressed in monetary terms – for the coming financial year.

4 (a) If the business is to be closed down, the remaining three machines must be valued at the amount they will realise in a forced sale, ie 3 × £60 = £180.

(b) If the business is regarded as a going concern, the stock unsold at 31 December will be carried forward into the following year, when the cost of the three machines will be matched against the eventual sale proceeds in computing that year's profits. The three machines will therefore appear in the balance sheet at 31 December at cost, 3 × £100 = £300.

5 (a) A sale must never be recognised before the goods have even been ordered by a customer. There is no certainty about the value of the sale, nor when it will take place, even if it is virtually certain that goods will be sold.

(b) A sale must never be recognised when the customer places an order. Even though the order is for a specific quantity of goods at a specific price, it is not yet certain that the sale transaction will go through. The customer may cancel the order, the supplier might be unable to deliver the goods as ordered or it may be decided that the customer is not a good credit risk.

(c) A sale will be recognised when delivery of the goods is made only when the sale is for cash, and so the cash is received at the same time.

(d) The critical event for a credit sale is usually the despatch of an invoice to the customer. There is then a legally enforceable debt, payable on specified terms, for a completed sale transaction.

(e) The critical event for a cash sale is when delivery takes place and when cash is received; both take place at the same time.

It would be too cautious or 'prudent' to wait for cash payment for a credit sale transaction before recognising the sale, unless the customer is a high credit risk and there is a serious doubt about his ability or intention to pay.

(f) It would again be over-cautious to wait for clearance of the customer's cheques before recognising sales revenue. Such a precaution would only be justified in cases where there is a very high risk of the bank refusing to honour the cheque.

6 (a) No. You would write it off to the profit and loss account as an expense.

(b) Yes. You would treat the forklift as a fixed asset (you would **capitalise** it) and charge depreciation on it.

(c) Your answer depends on the size of the business and whether writing off the item has a material effect on its profits. A larger organisation might well write this item off under the heading of marketing expenses, while a small one would capitalise it and depreciate it over time. This is because the item would be material to the small business but not to the large one.

Chapter 2:
RECORDING TRANSACTIONS

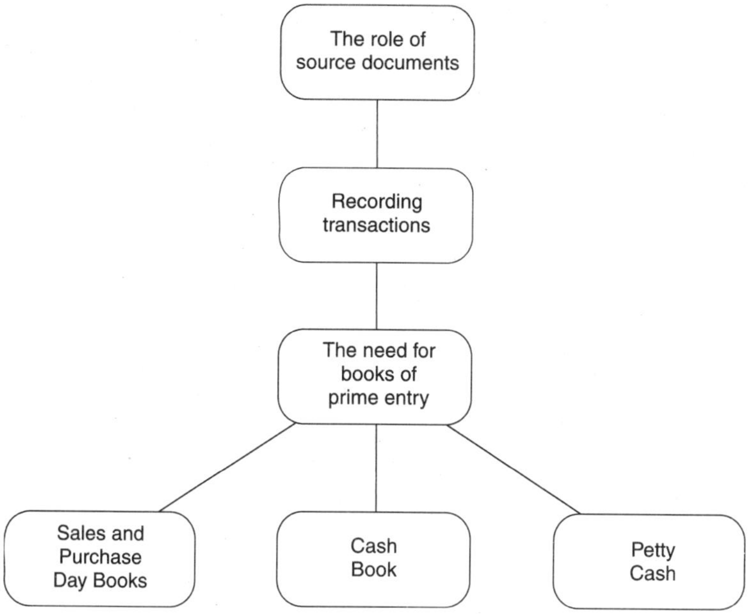

Introduction

From your study of the first chapter you should have grasped some important points about the nature and purpose of accounting.

- Most businesses provide products and services in the hope of making a profit for their owners, by receiving payment in money for those goods and services.
- The role of the accounting system is to record these monetary effects and create information about them.

You should also, by now, understand the basic principles underlying the balance sheet and profit and loss account and have an idea of what they look like.

We now turn our attention to the process by which a business transaction works its way through to the financial statements.

It is usual to record a business transaction on a **document**. Such documents include invoices, orders, credit notes and goods received notes, all of which will be discussed in Section 1 of this chapter. In terms of the accounting system these are known as **source documents**. The information on them is processed by the system by, for example, aggregating (adding together) or classifying.

Records of source documents are kept in 'books of prime entry', which, as the name suggests, are the first stage at which a business transaction enters into the accounting system. The various types of books of prime entry are discussed in Sections 2 to 4. We will also look at the treatment of petty cash in Section 5.

In the next chapter we consider what happens to transactions after the books of prime entry stage.

Your objectives

After completing this chapter you should be able to:

1. Understand the role and types of source documents
2. Identify the reasons why books of prime entry are used
3. Use the sales and purchase day books, the cash book and the petty cash book

1 THE ROLE OF SOURCE DOCUMENTS

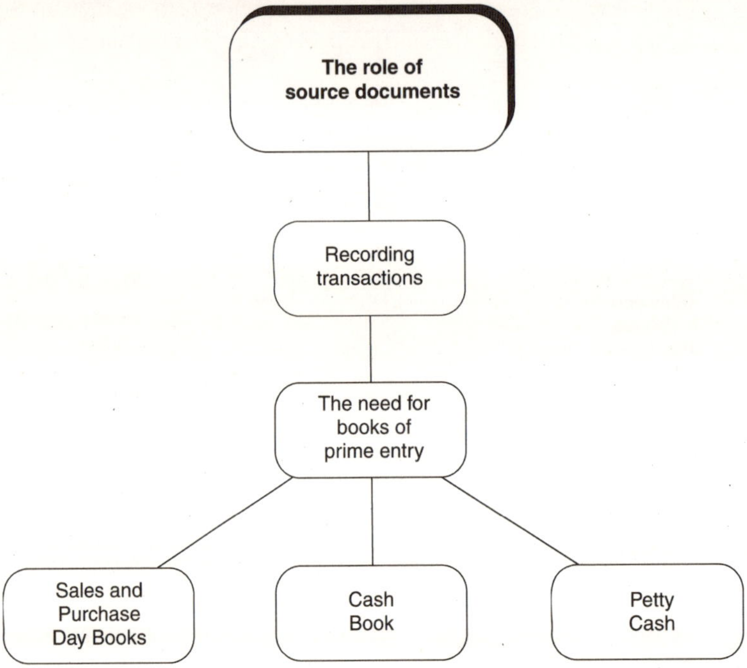

Business transactions are recorded on source documents. Examples include sales and purchase orders, invoices and credit notes.

1.1 Types of source document

Whenever a business transaction takes place, involving sales or purchases, receiving or paying money, or owing or being owed money, it is usual for the transaction to be recorded on a document. These documents are the source of all the information recorded by a business.

Documents used to record the business transactions in the 'books of account' of the business include the following.

- **Quotation.** A business makes a written offer to a customer to produce or deliver goods or services for a certain amount of money.
- **Sales order**. A customer writes out or signs an order for goods or services he requires.
- **Purchase order**. A business orders from another business goods or services, such as material supplies.
- **Goods received note.** A list of goods that a business has received from a supplier. This is usually prepared by the business's own warehouse or goods receiving area.
- **Goods despatched note.** A list of goods that a business has sent out to a customer.
- **Invoice**. This is discussed further below.
- **Statement.** A document sent out by a supplier to a customer listing all invoices, credit notes and payments received from the customer.
- **Credit note.** A document sent by a supplier to a customer in respect of goods returned or overpayments made by the customer. It is a 'negative' invoice.
- **Debit note.** A document sent by a customer to a supplier in respect of goods returned or an overpayment made. It is a formal request for the supplier to issue a credit note.
- **Remittance advice.** A document sent with a payment, detailing which invoices are being paid and which credit notes offset.
- **Receipt.** A written confirmation that money has been paid. This is usually in respect of cash sales, eg a till receipt from a cash register.

1.2 Invoices

Definition

> An **invoice** relates to a sales order or a purchase order.

When a business sells goods or services on credit to a customer – that is, when there is a time-lag between delivering the goods and receiving payment – it sends out an invoice. The details on the invoice should match up with the details on the sales order. The invoice is a request for the customer to pay what he owes.

When a business buys goods or services on credit it receives an invoice from the supplier. The details on the invoice should match up with the details on the purchase order.

The invoice is primarily a **demand for payment**, but it is used for other purposes as well, as we shall see. Because it has several uses, an invoice is often produced on multi-part stationery, or photocopied, or carbon-copied. The top copy will go to the customer and other copies will be used by various people within the business.

1.2.1 What does an invoice show?

Most invoices are numbered, so that the business can keep track of all the invoices it sends out. Information usually shown on an invoice includes the following.

(a) Name and address of the seller and the purchaser

(b) Date of the sale

(c) Description of what is being sold

(d) Quantity and unit price of what has been sold (eg 20 pairs of shoes at £25 a pair)

(e) Details of trade discount, if any (eg 10% reduction in cost if buying over 100 pairs of shoes). We shall look at discounts in a later chapter

(f) Total amount of the invoice including (in the UK) any details of VAT

(g) Sometimes, the date by which payment is due, and other terms of sale

1.2.2 Uses of multi-part invoices

As stated above invoices may be used for different purposes.

- Top copy to customer as a request for payment
- Second copy to accounts department to match to eventual payment
- Third copy to ware house to generate a despatch of goods, as evidenced by a goods despatched note.
- Fourth copy stapled to sales order and kept in sales department as a record of sales.

Businesses design their own invoices and there may be other copies for other departments. Not all businesses will need four part invoices. A very small business may use the customer copy of the invoice as a despatch note as well. In addition, the sales invoice may be stapled to the sales order and both documents passed to the accounts department.

1.3 Credit notes

EXAMPLE: CREDIT NOTES

Student Supplies Ltd sent out an invoice to the county council for 450 rulers delivered to the local primary school. The typist accidentally typed in a total of £162.10, instead of £62.10. The county council has been *overcharged* by £100. What is Student Supplies to do?

Alternatively, suppose that when the primary school received the rulers, it found that they had all been broken in the post and that it was going to send them back. Although the county council has received an invoice for £62.10, it has no intention of paying it, because the rulers were useless. Again, what is Student Supplies to do?

The answer is that the supplier (in this case, Student Supplies) sends out a **credit note**. A credit note is sometimes printed in red to distinguish it from an invoice. Otherwise, it will be made out in much the same way as an invoice, but with less detail and 'Credit Note Number' instead of 'Invoice Number'.

Definition

A **credit note** is a document relating to returned goods or refunds when a customer has been overcharged. It can be regarded as a 'negative invoice'.

1.4 Goods received notes

Definition

Goods received notes (GRNs) record a receipt of goods, most commonly in a warehouse. They may be used in addition to suppliers' advice notes.

Often the accounts department will require to see the relevant GRN before paying a supplier's invoice. Even where GRNs are not routinely used, the details of a consignment from a supplier which arrives without an advice note must always be recorded.

Activity 1 **(5 minutes)**

Fill in the blanks.

'Student Supplies Ltd sends out a .... to a credit customer in order to correct an error where a customer has been overcharged on an ....

2 THE NEED FOR BOOKS OF PRIME ENTRY

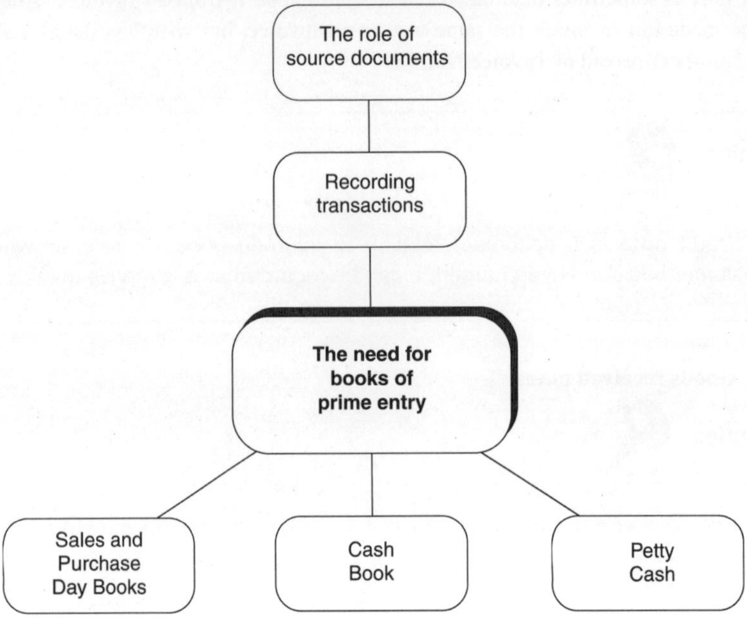

We have seen that in the course of business, source documents are created. The details on these source documents need to be summarised, as otherwise the business might forget to ask for some money, or forget to pay some, or even accidentally pay something twice. In other words, it needs to keep records of source documents – of transactions – so that it can keep tabs on what is going on. Such records are made in **books of prime entry**.

Definition

> **Books of prime entry** are books in which we first record transactions.

The main books of prime entry are as follows.

(a) Sales day book
(b) Purchase day book
(c) Sales returns day book
(d) Purchases returns day book
(e) Journal (described in the next chapter)
(f) Cash book
(g) Petty cash book

It is worth bearing in mind that, for convenience, this chapter describes books of prime entry as if they are actual books. Nowadays, books of prime entry are not books at all, but rather files hidden in the memory of a computer. However, the principles remain the same whether they are manual or computerised.

3 SALES AND PURCHASE DAY BOOKS

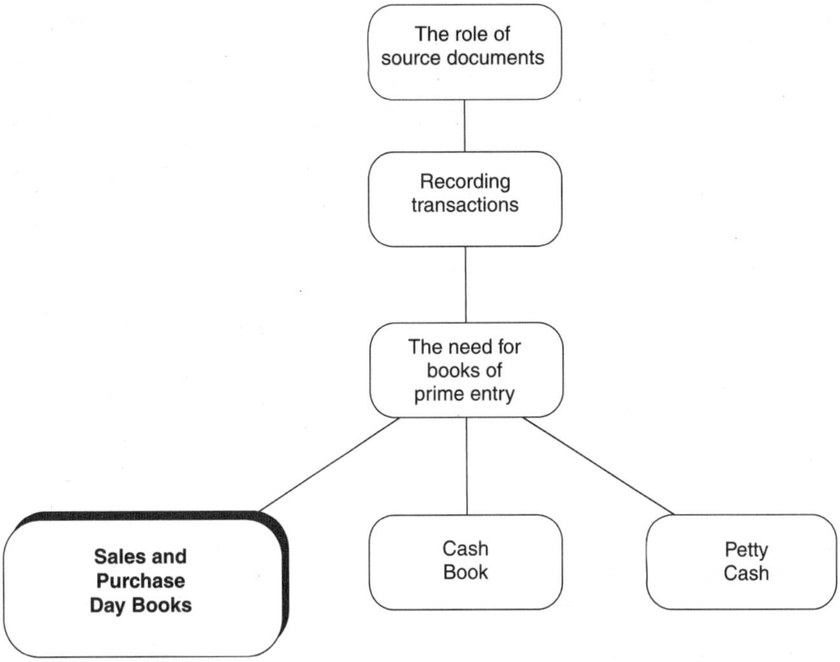

Definition

Day books are the books of prime entry for sales and purchases.

3.1 The sales day book

Definition

The **sales day book** is the book of prime entry for credit sales.

The **sales day book** is used to keep a list of all invoices sent out to customers each day. An extract from a sales day book might look like this.

SALES DAY BOOK

Date	*Invoice*	*Customer*	*Total amount invoiced*
20X0			£
Jan 10	247	Jones & Co	105.00
	248	Smith Ltd	86.40
	249	Alex & Co	31.80
	250	Enor College	1,264.60
			1,487.80

Most businesses 'analyse' their sales. For example, suppose that the business sells boots and shoes, and that the sale to Smith was entirely boots, the sale to Alex was entirely shoes, and the other two sales were a mixture of both.

Then the sales day book might look like this.

SALES DAY BOOK

Date	*Invoice*	*Customer*	*Total amount invoiced*	*Boot sales*	*Shoe sales*
20X0			£	£	£
Jan 10	247	Jones & Co	105.00	60.00	45.00
	248	Smith Ltd	86.40	86.40	
	249	Alex & Co	31.80		31.80
	250	Enor College	1,264.60	800.30	464.30
			1,487.80	946.70	541.10

This sort of analysis gives the managers of the business useful information which helps them to decide how best to run the business.

3.2 The purchase day book

A business also keeps a record in the purchase day book of all the invoices it receives.

Definition

The **purchase day book** is the book of prime entry for credit purchases.

An extract from a purchase day book might look like this.

PURCHASE DAY BOOK

Date	*Supplier*	*Total amount invoiced*	*Purchases*	*Electricity etc*
20X8		£	£	£
Mar 15	Cook & Co	315.00	315.00	
	W Butler	29.40	29.40	
	EEB	116.80		116.80
	Show Fair Ltd	100.00	100.00	
		561.20	444.40	116.80

Points to note:

(a) There is no 'invoice number' column, because the purchase day book records other people's invoices, which have all sorts of different numbers.

(b) Like the sales day book, the purchase day book analyses the invoices which have been sent in. In this example, three of the invoices related to goods which the business intends to re-sell (called simply 'purchases') and the fourth invoice was an electricity bill.

3.3 The sales returns day book

When customers return goods for some reason, the credit notes sent out are recorded in the sales return day book. An extract from the sales returns day book might look like this:

SALES RETURNS DAY BOOK

Date	*Customer and goods*	*Amount*
20X8		£
30 April	Owen Plenty	
	3 pairs 'Texas' boots	135.00

Definition

The **sales returns day book** is the book of prime entry for credit notes sent to customers.

Not all sales returns day books analyse what goods were returned, but it makes sense to keep as complete a record as possible. Where a business has very few sales returns, it may record a credit note as a negative entry in the sales day book.

3.4 The purchase returns day book

The purchase returns day book is kept to record credit notes received in respect of goods which the business sends back to its suppliers. If the business receives a cash refund from the supplier, this is recorded in the cash book (see later) not the purchase returns day book.

An extract from the purchase returns day book might look like this:

PURCHASE RETURNS DAY BOOK

Date	*Supplier and goods*	*Amount*
20X8		£
29 April	Boxes Ltd	
	300 cardboard boxes	46.60

Definition

The **purchase returns day book** is the book of prime entry for credit notes received from suppliers.

Once again, a business with very few purchase returns may record a credit note received as a negative entry in the purchase day book.

4 CASH BOOK

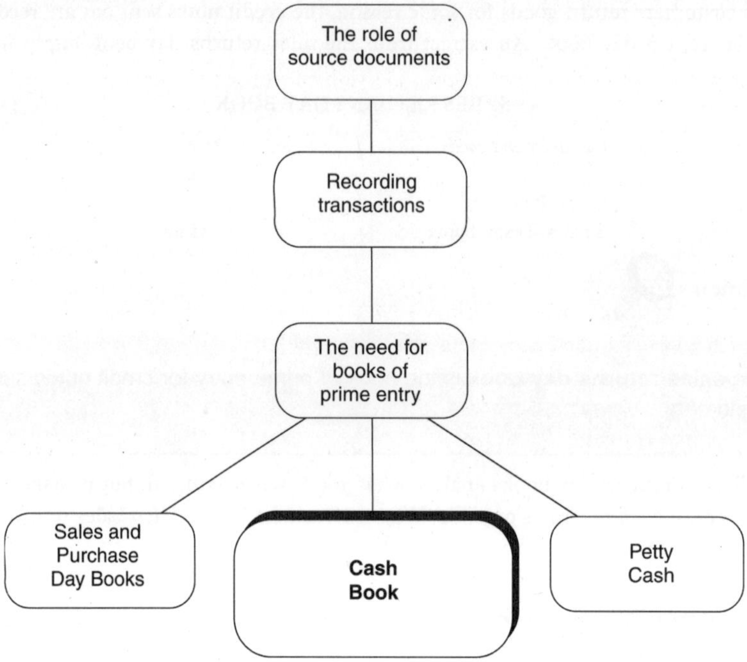

The cash book is a day book used to keep a cumulative record of money received and money paid out by the business. The cash book deals with money paid into and out of the business **bank account**. This could be money received on the business premises in notes, coins and cheques. There are also receipts and payments made by bank transfer, standing order, direct debit and, in the case of bank interest and charges, directly by the bank.

Some cash, in notes and coins, is usually kept on the business premises in order to make occasional payments for odd items of expense. This cash is usually accounted for separately in a **petty cash book** (which we will look at shortly).

One side of the cash book is used to record receipts of cash, and the other side is used to record payments. The best way to see how the cash book works is to follow through an example.

Definition

> The **cash book** is the book of prime entry for amounts paid into and out of the bank account.

EXAMPLE: CASH BOOK

At the beginning of 1 September, Robin Plenty had £900 in the bank. During 1 September 20X7, Robin Plenty had the following receipts and payments.

(a) Cash sale – receipt of £80
(b) Payment from credit customer Hay £400 less discount allowed £20
(c) Payment from credit customer Been £720
(d) Payment from credit customer Seed £150 less discount allowed £10
(e) Cheque received for cash to provide a short-term loan from Len Dinger £1,800
(f) Second cash sale – receipts of £150
(g) Cash received for sale of machine £200
(h) Payment to supplier Kew £120
(i) Payment to supplier Hare £310
(j) Payment of telephone bill £400
(k) Payment of gas bill £280
(l) £100 in cash withdrawn from bank for petty cash
(m) Payment of £1,500 to Hess for new plant and machinery

If you look through these transactions, you will see that seven of them are receipts and six of them are payments.

The receipts part of the cash book for 1 September would look like this.

CASH BOOK (RECEIPTS)

Date	*Narrative*	*Reference*	*Total*
20X7			£
1 Sept	Opening balance b/d		900
	Cash sale		80
	Debtor: Hay		380
	Debtor: Been		720
	Debtor: Seed		140
	Loan: Len Dinger		1,800
	Cash sale		150
	Sale of fixed asset		200
			4,370
2 Sept	New opening balance b/d*		1,660

* 'b/d' = brought down (ie brought forward)

Points to note:

(a) There is space on the right-hand side so that the receipts can be analysed under various headings - for example, 'receipts from debtors', 'cash sales' and 'other receipts'.

(b) The cash received in the day amounted to £3,470. Added to the £900 opening balance at the start of the day, this comes to £4,370. But this is not the amount to be shown on the closing balance to the next day, because first we have to subtract all the payments made during 1 September.

The payments part of the cash book for 1 September would look like this.

CASH BOOK (PAYMENTS)

Date	*Narrative*	*Reference*	*Total*
20X7			£
1 Sept	Creditor: Kew		120
	Creditor: Hare		310
	Telephone		400
	Gas bill		280
	Petty cash		100
	Machinery purchase		1,500
	Closing balance c/d		1,660
			4,370

As you can see, this is very similar to the receipts part of the cash book. But note the following.

(a) The analysis on the right would be under headings like 'payments to creditors', 'payments into petty cash', 'wages' and 'other payments'.

(b) Payments during 1 September totalled £2,710. We know that the total of receipts was £4,370. That means that there is a closing balance of £4,370 – £2,710 = £1,660 to be 'carried down' to the start of the next day. As you can see this 'closing balance carried down' (c/d) is noted at the end of the payments column, so that the receipts and payments totals show the same figure of £4,370 at the end of 1 September. And if you look to the receipts part of this example, you can see that £1,660 has been brought down ready for the next day.

With analysis columns completed, the cash book given in the examples above might look as follows.

CASH BOOK (RECEIPTS SECTION)

Date	*Narrative*	*Total*	*Debtors*	*Cash sales*	*Other*
20X7		£	£	£	£
1 Sept	Balance b/d	900			
	Cash sale	80		80	
	Debtor – Hay	380	380		
	Debtor – Been	720	720		
	Debtor – Seed	140	140		
	Loan – Len Dinger	1,800			1,800
	Cash sale	150		150	
	Sale of fixed asset	200			200
		4,370	1,240	230	2,000

CASH BOOK (PAYMENTS SECTION)

Date	*Narrative*	*Total*	*Creditors*	*Petty cash*	*Wages*	*Other*
20X7		£	£	£	£	£
1 Sept	Creditor – Kew	120	120			
	Creditor – Hare	310	310			
	Telephone	400				400
	Gas bill	280				280
	Petty cash	100		100		
	Machinery purchase	1,500				1,500
	Balance c/d	1,660				
		4,370	430	100	–	2,180

5 PETTY CASH

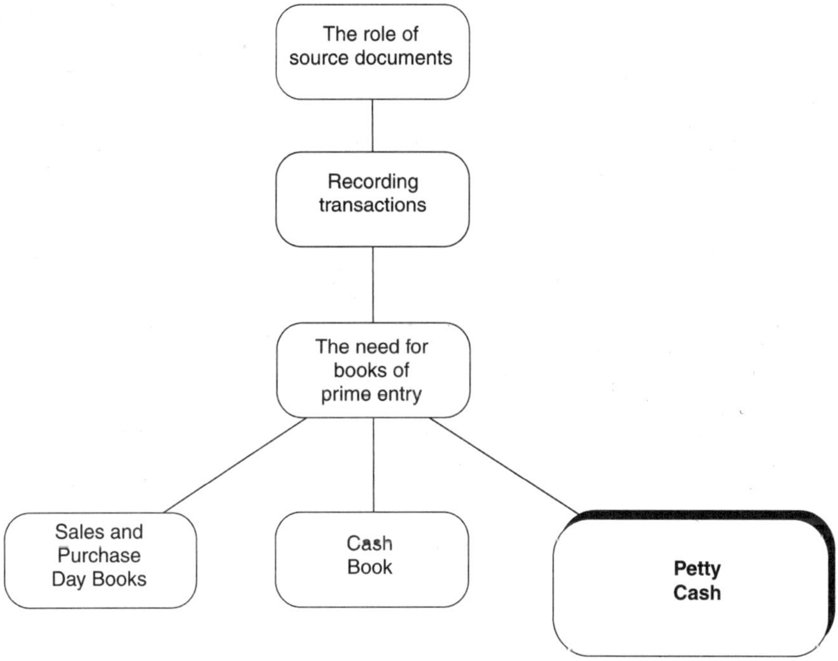

5.1 What is petty cash?

Most businesses keep a small amount of cash on the premises to make occasional small payments in cash, eg staff refreshments, postage stamps, taxi fares, etc. This is often called the cash float or **petty cash** account. The cash float can also be the resting place for occasional small receipts, eg cash paid by a visitor to make a phone call, etc.

5.2 Security

As you will appreciate, keeping cash (even in small amounts) on the premises is a security risk. Therefore a petty cash system is usually subject to strict controls.

- Payment is only made in respect of **authorised** claims.
- All claims are supported by **evidence**.

In addition, the business may use the **imprest system** (see Section 5.4 below).

5.2.1 Authorisation

An employee must complete a **petty cash voucher** detailing the expenses claimed. Usually receipts must be attached to the voucher (see below: evidence). The completed voucher then needs to be signed by (say) the employee's manager to **authorise** payment. Some times the petty cashier may be authorised to sign vouchers for small amounts (eg £5 or less) if these are supported by receipts.

5.2.2 Evidence

All petty cash vouchers must have receipts for the expenditure attached, as **evidence** that the employee has really incurred that cost. Sometimes receipts may not be available (eg taxi fares) and the employer may then have systems in place to authorise claims without evidence.

5.3 The petty cash book

Definition

> A **petty cash book** is a cash book for small payments.

Although the amounts involved are small, petty cash transactions still need to be recorded; otherwise the cash float could be abused for personal expenses or even stolen.

There are usually more payments than receipts, and petty cash must be 'topped up' from time to time with cash from the business bank account. A typical layout follows.

PETTY CASH BOOK

Receipts	*Date*	*Narrative*	*Total*	*Milk*	*Postage*	*Travel*	*Other*
£	20X7		£	£	£	£	£
250	1 Sept	Bal b/d					
		Milk bill	25	25			
		Postage stamps	5		5		
		Taxi fare	10			10	
		Flowers for sick staff	15				15
		Bal c/d	195				
250			250	25	5	10	15

5.4 Imprest system

Under what is called the **imprest system,** the amount of money in petty cash is kept at an agreed sum or 'float' (say £250). Expense items are recorded on vouchers as they occur, so that at any time:

	£
Cash still held in petty cash	195
Plus voucher payments (25 + 5 + 10 + 15)	55
Must equal the agreed sum or float	250

The total float is made up regularly (to £250, or whatever the agreed sum is) by means of a cash payment from the bank account into petty cash. The amount of the 'top-up' into petty cash will be the total of the voucher payments since the previous top-up.

Definition

The **imprest system** makes a refund of the total paid out in a period.

Activity 2 **(20 minutes)**

State which books of prime entry the following transactions would be entered into.

(a) Your business pays A Brown (a supplier) £450.00.

(b) You send D Smith (a customer) an invoice for £650.

(c) Your accounts manager asks you for £12 urgently in order to buy some envelopes.

(d) You receive an invoice from A Brown for £300.

(e) You pay D Smith £500.

(f) F Jones (a customer) returns goods to the value of £250.

(g) You return goods to J Green to the value of £504.

(h) F Jones pays you £500.

Another book of prime entry is the **journal** which is considered in the next chapter.

Chapter roundup

- Business transactions are recorded on **source documents**. Examples include sales and purchase orders, invoices and credit notes.
- Books of prime entry record the source documents.
- The main books of prime entry are as follows.
  - Sales day book
  - Purchase day book
  - Sales returns day book
  - Purchases returns day book
  - Journal (described in the next chapter)
  - Cash book
  - Petty cash book
- Day books are the books of prime entry for sales and purchases.
- The cash book is the book of prime entry for the bank account.
- Most businesses keep petty cash on the premises, which is topped up from the main bank account. Under the imprest system, the petty cash is kept at an agreed sum, so that each topping up is equal to the amount paid out in the period.

Quick quiz

1 Name four pieces of information normally shown on an invoice.

2 Which of the following is not a book of prime entry?

A Sales invoice
B Purchase day book
C Sales day book
D Journal

3 Which of the following is a source document for petty cash?

A Purchase invoice
B Quotation
C Sales invoice
D Receipt and claim form

4 What is the purchase returns day book used to record?

A Supplier's invoices
B Customer's invoices
C Details of goods returned to suppliers
D Details of goods returned by customers

5 What is the difference between the cash book and the petty cash book?

6 Petty cash is controlled under an imprest system. The imprest amount is £100. During a period, payments totalling £53 have been made. How much needs to be reimbursed at the end of the period to restore petty cash to the imprest account?

A £100
B £53
C £47
D £50

7 All petty cash claims are automatically paid from petty cash.

Is this statement:

A True
B False

Answers to quick quiz

1 **Four** from the following

- Invoice number
- Seller's name and address
- Purchaser's name and address
- Date of sale
- Description of goods or services
- Quantity and unit price
- Trade discount (if any)
- Total amount, including sales tax (if any)
- Any special terms

2 A Sales invoice is a source document

3 D The claim form and receipt form the source document for the petty cash system.

4 C Supplier's invoices (A) are recorded in the purchase day book, customer's invoices (B) are recorded in the sales day book and goods returned by customers (D) are recorded in the sales returns day book.

5 The cash book records amounts paid into or out of the bank account. The petty cash book records payments of small amounts of cash.

6 B Under the imprest system, a reimbursement is made of the amount of the vouchers (or payments made) for the period.

7 B Only **authorised** and **evidenced** petty cash claims are paid out of petty cash.

Answers to activities

1 Credit note; invoice.

2 (a) Cash book
(b) Sales day book
(c) Petty cash book
(d) Purchases day book
(e) Cash book
(f) Sales returns day book
(g) Purchase returns day book
(h) Cash book

Chapter 3:

ACCOUNTING FUNDAMENTALS: LEDGER ACCOUNTS AND DOUBLE ENTRY

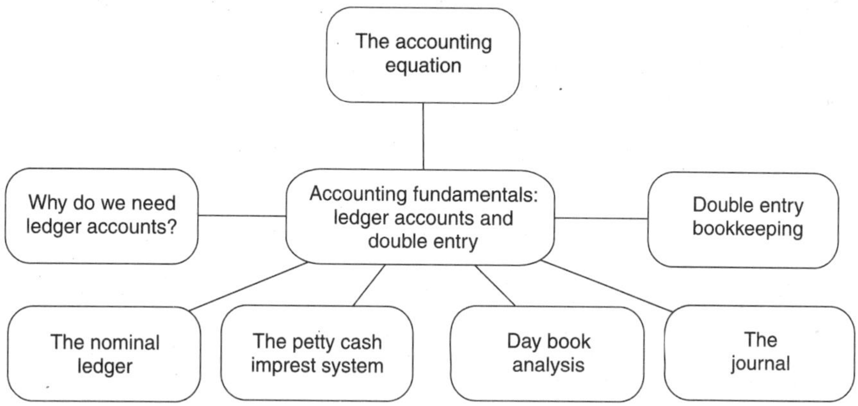

Introduction

In the previous chapter we saw how to organise transactions into lists (ie entered into books of prime entry). It is not easy, however, to see how a business is doing from the information scattered throughout these books of prime entry. The lists need to be summarised. This is **ledger accounting,** which we look at in Sections 1 and 2.

The summary is produced in the nominal ledger by a process you may have heard of known as **double entry bookkeeping**. This is the cornerstone of accounts preparation and is surprisingly simple, once you have grasped the rules. We will look at the essentials in Sections 3 and 4.

In Section 5, we will deal with the final book of prime entry: **the journal**.

We will then look in detail at posting transactions from the day books to the ledgers in Sections 6 and 7.

Your objectives

After completing this chapter you should be able to:

1 Identify the purpose of ledger accounts and the nominal ledger

2 State and use the accounting equation and the business equation

3 Understand the principles of debits and credits (double entry bookkeeping)

4 Write up ledger accounts for a range of transactions

5 Analyse and post day books to the nominal ledger

6 Use the journal

7 Operate petty cash as an imprest system

1 WHY DO WE NEED LEDGER ACCOUNTS?

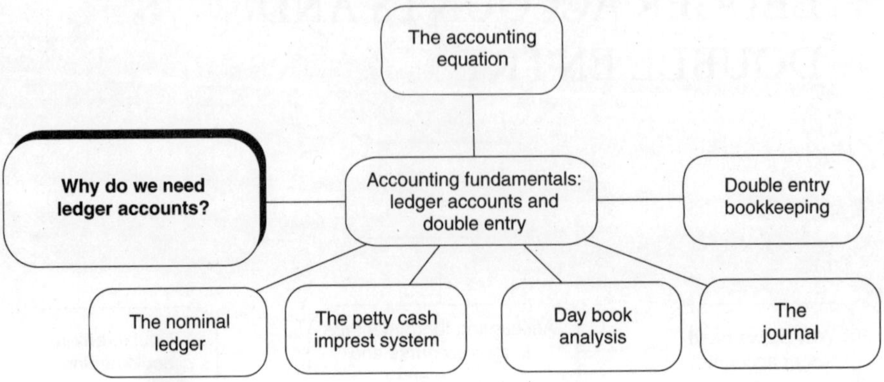

Definition

> **Ledger accounts** are a summary of the books of prime entry.

A business is continually making transactions (eg buying and selling) and it is common sense that it should keep a record of the transactions that it makes, the assets it acquires and liabilities it incurs. When the time comes to prepare a profit and loss account and a balance sheet, the relevant information can be taken from those records.

The **records of transactions, assets and liabilities** should be:

(a) **Dated** and in **chronological order**, so that transactions can be related to a particular period of time.

(b) Built up in **cumulative totals**. For example, a business may build up the total of its sales:

 (i) Day by day (eg total sales on Monday, total sales on Tuesday)
 (ii) Week by week
 (iii) Month by month
 (iv) Year by year

We have already seen the first step in this process, which is to list all the transactions in various books of prime entry. Now we must turn our attention to the method used to summarise these records: **ledger accounting** and **double entry**.

2 THE NOMINAL LEDGER

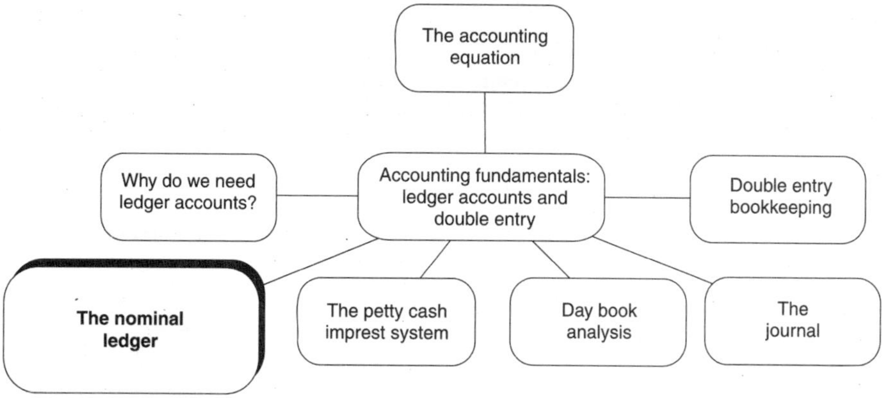

Definition

> The **nominal ledger** is an accounting record which summarises the financial affairs of a business. In some businesses it is called the general ledger; the two terms are inter-changeable

The information contained in the books of prime entry (see Chapter 2) is **summarised** and **posted** to accounts in the nominal ledger.

It contains details of assets, liabilities and capital, income and expenditure and so profit and loss. It consists of a large number of different accounts, each account having its own purpose or 'name' and an identity or code.

There may be various subdivisions, whether for convenience, ease of handling, confidentiality, security, or to meet the needs of computer software design. For example, the ledger may be split alphabetically, with different clerks responsible for sections A-F, G-M, N-R and S-Z. This can help to stop fraud, as there would have to be collusion between the different section clerks.

Examples of accounts in the nominal ledger include the following.

(a) Plant and machinery at cost (fixed asset)
(b) Motor vehicles at cost (fixed asset)
(c) Plant and machinery, provision for depreciation (liability)
(d) Motor vehicles, provision for depreciation (liability)
(e) Proprietor's capital (liability)
(f) Stocks – raw materials (current asset)
(g) Stocks – finished goods (current asset)
(h) Total debtors (current asset)
(i) Total creditors (current liability)
(j) Wages and salaries (expense item)
(k) Rent and rates (expense item)
(l) Advertising expenses (expense item)
(m) Bank charges (expense item)
(n) Motor expenses (expense item)

(o) Telephone expenses (expense item)
(p) Sales (income or revenue item)
(q) Total cash or bank overdraft (current asset or liability)

In the financial statements, the revenue and expenditure accounts will help to form the profit and loss account; while the asset and liability accounts go into the balance sheet.

2.1 The format of a ledger account

If a ledger account were to be kept in an actual book rather than as a computer record, it might look like this:

ADVERTISING EXPENSES

Date	*Narrative*	*Reference*	£	*Date*	*Narrative*	*Reference*	£
20X6							
15 April	JFK Agency for quarter to 31 March	PL 348	2,500				

For the rest of this chapter, we will assume that a manual system is being used in order to illustrate fully the workings of the ledger accounts. However, a computerised system performs the same functions.

There are two sides to the account, and an account heading on top, and so it is convenient to think in terms of 'T' accounts.

(a) On top of the account is its name.
(b) There is a left hand side, or **debit side**.
(c) There is a right hand side, or **credit side**.

NAME OF ACCOUNT

DEBIT SIDE	£	CREDIT SIDE	£

3 THE ACCOUNTING EQUATION

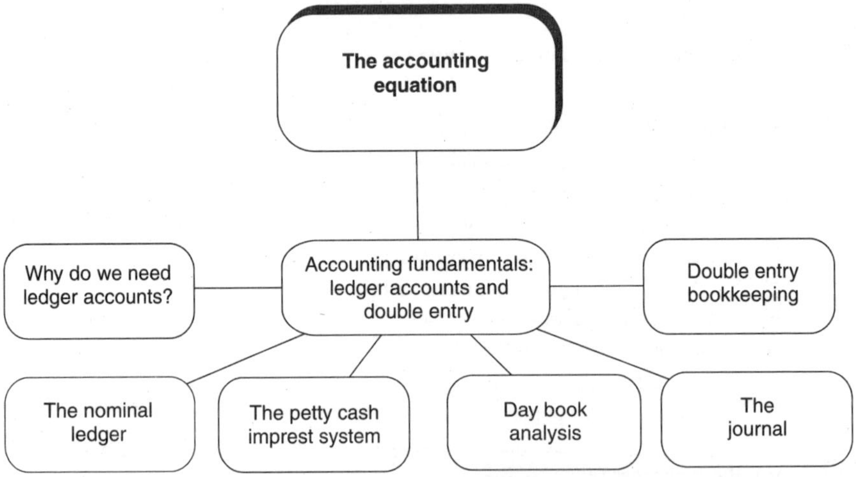

3.1 The basic accounting equation

Definition

> **Accounting equation**: The assets of a business must be equal to its liabilities plus capital.

We will start by showing how to account for a business's transactions from the time that trading first begins. We will use an example to illustrate the 'accounting equation', ie the rule that the assets of a business will at all times equal its liabilities plus capital. This is also known as **the balance sheet equation**.

EXAMPLE: THE ACCOUNTING EQUATION

Courtney Spice starts a business. The business begins by owning the cash that Courtney put into it, £2,500. The business is a separate entity in accounting terms and so it owes the money to Courtney as **capital**.

Definition

> In accounting, **capital** is an investment of money (funds) with the intention of earning a return. A sole trader invests capital with the intention of earning profit. As long as that money is invested, accountants will treat the capital as money owed to the sole trader by the business.

When Courtney Spice sets up her business:

Capital invested	=	£2,500
Cash	=	£2,500

You can think of capital invested as a form of liability, because it is an amount owed by the business to its owner(s). Adapting this to the idea that liabilities and assets are always equal amounts, we can state the accounting equation as follows.

Assets = Capital + Liabilities

For Courtney Spice, as at 1 July 20X6:

£2,500 (cash) = £2,500 + £0

EXAMPLE CONTINUED: DIFFERENT TYPES OF ASSET

Courtney Spice uses some of the money invested to purchase a market stall from Noel Jarvis, who is retiring from his fruit and vegetables business. The cost of the stall is £1,800.

She also purchases some herbs and spices from a trader in the Albert Square wholesale market, at a cost of £650.

This leaves £50 in cash, after paying for the stall and goods for resale, out of the original £2,500. Courtney kept £30 in the bank and drew out £20 in small change to use as a float. She was now ready for her first day of market trading on 3 July 20X6.

The assets and liabilities of the business have now altered, and at 3 July, before trading begins, the state of her business is as follows.

Assets	£	=	*Capital*	+	*Liabilities*
Stall	1,800	=	£2,500	+	£0
Herbs and spices	650				
Cash at bank	30				
Cash in hand	20				
	2,500				

The stall and the herbs and spices are physical items, but they must be given a money value. This money value is usually what they cost the business (the **historical cost**).

EXAMPLE CONTINUED: MAKING A PROFIT

Let us now suppose that on 3 July Courtney has a very successful day. She is able to sell all of her herbs and spices, for £900. All of her sales are for cash.

Since Courtney has sold goods costing £650 to earn revenue of £900, we can say that she has **earned a profit of £250 on the day's trading.**

Profits belong to the owners of a business. In this case, the £250 belongs to Courtney Spice. However, so long as the business retains the profits, and does not pay anything out to its owner, the **retained profit** are accounted for as an addition to the sole trader's capital.

Assets		=	*Capital*		+	*Liabilities*
	£			£		
Stall	1,800		Original investment	2,500		
Herbs and spices	0					
Cash in hand and at bank						
(30+20+900)	950		Retained profit	250		
	2,750	=		2,750	+	£0

We can rearrange the accounting equation to help us to calculate the capital balance.

Assets – liabilities	=	Capital, which is the same as
Net assets	=	Capital

At the beginning and then at the end of 3 July 20X6 Courtney Spice's financial position was as follows.

	Net Assets	*Capital*
At the beginning of the day:	£(2,500 – 0) = £2,500 =	£2,500
At the end of the day:	£(2,750 – 0) = £2,750 =	£2,750

There has been an increase of £250 in net assets, which is the amount of profits earned during the day.

3.2 Drawings

Definition

> **Drawings** are amounts of money taken out of a business by its owner.

Since Courtney Spice has made a profit of £250 from her first day's work, she might well feel fully justified in drawing some of the profits out of the business. After all, business owners, like everyone else, need income for living expenses. We will suppose that Courtney decides to pay herself £180, in 'wages'.

The payment of £180 is probably regarded by Courtney as a fair reward for her day's work, and she might think of the sum as being in the nature of wages. However, the £180 is not an expense to be deducted before the figure of net profit is arrived at. In other words, it would be incorrect to calculate the net profit earned by the business as follows.

	£
Profit on sale of herbs and spices etc	250
Less 'wages' paid to Courtney	180
Net profit earned by business (incorrect)	70

This is because any amounts paid by a business to its proprietor are treated by accountants as withdrawals of profit (the usual term is **appropriations of profit**), and not as expenses incurred by the business. In the case of Courtney's business, the true position is that the net profit earned is the £250 surplus on sale of flowers.

	£
Net profit earned by business	250
Less profit withdrawn by Courtney	180
Net profit retained in the business	70

Profits are capital as long as they are retained in the business. Once they are **appropriated,** the business suffers a reduction in capital.

The drawings are taken in cash, and so the business loses £180 of its cash assets. After the drawings have been made, the accounting equation would be restated.

(a)	*Assets*		=	*Capital*		+	*Liabilities*
		£			£		
	Stall	1,800		Original investment	2,500		
	Herbs and spices	0		Retained profit	70		
	Cash (950-180)	770					
		2,570			2,570	+	£0

(b)	Alternatively	*Net assets*		*Capital*
		£(2,570 – 0)	=	£2,570

The increase in net assets since trading operations began is now only £(2,570 – 2,500) = £70, which is the amount of the retained profits.

Activity 1 **(5 minutes)**

Which of the following is correct?

A Capital = assets + liabilities
B Capital = liabilities – assets
C Capital = assets – liabilities
D Capital + assets = liabilities

3.3 The business equation

The preceding example has attempted to show that the amount of profit earned can be related to the increase in the net assets of the business, and the drawings of profits by the sole trader.

Definition

Business equation:

Profit (P) = Increase in net assets (I) + drawings (D) – capital introduced (C_i)

In our example of Courtney Spice's business on 3 July 20X6, after drawings have been taken:

Profit = £ 70 + £180 – £0 = £250

EXAMPLE CONTINUED: BUSINESS EQUATION

The next market day is on 10 July, and Courtney gets ready by purchasing more herbs and spices for cash, at a cost of £740. She was not feeling well, however, because of a heavy cold, and so she decided to accept the offer of help for the day from her cousin Bianca. Bianca would be paid a wage of £40 at the end of the day.

Trading on 10 July was again very brisk, and Courtney and Bianca sold all their goods for £1,100 cash. Courtney paid Bianca her wage of £40 and drew out £200 for herself.

Required

(a) State the accounting equation before trading began on 10 July.

(b) State the accounting equation at the end of 10 July, after paying Bianca:

(i) But before drawings are taken out.
(ii) After drawings have been made.

(c) State the business equation to compute profits earned on 10 July.

You are reminded that the accounting equation for the business at the end of transactions for 3 July is given in Paragraph 3.2.

SOLUTION

(a) After the purchase of the goods for £740.

Assets		=	*Capital*	+	*Liabilities*
	£				
Stall	1,800				
Goods	740				
Cash (770 – 740)	30				
	2,570	=	£ 2,570	+	£0

(b) (i) On 10 July, all the goods are sold for £1,100 cash, and Bianca is paid £40. The profit for the day is £320.

	£	£
Sales		1,100
Less cost of goods sold	740	
Bianca's wage	40	
		780
Profit		320

Assets		=	*Capital*		+	*Liabilities*
	£			£		
Stall	1,800		At beginning of 10 July	2,570		
Goods	0		Profits earned on 10 July	320		
Cash						
(30+ 1,100 – 40)	1,090					
	2,890	=		2,890	+	£0

(ii) After Courtney has taken drawings of £200 in cash, retained profits will be only £(320 - 200) = £120.

Assets		=	*Capital*		+	*Liabilities*
	£			£		
Stall	1,800		At beginning of 10 July	2,570		
Goods	0		Retained profits for 10 July	120		
Cash						
(1,090 – 200)	890					
	2,690			2,690	+	£0

(c) The increase in net assets on 10 July, after drawings have been taken, is as follows.

	£
Net assets at end of 10 July	2,690
Net assets at beginning of 10 July	2,570
Increase in net assets	120

The business equation is:

$$P = I + D - C_i$$
$$= £120 + £200 - £0$$
$$= £320$$

This confirms the calculation of profit made in b(i).

It is very important that you understand the principles described so far. Do not read on until you are confident that you understand the solution to this example.

3.4 Creditors and debtors

Definition

> A **creditor** is a person to whom a business owes money. A creditor is a liability.

A **trade creditor** is a person to whom a business owes money for debts incurred in the course of trading operations. In an examination question, this term might refer to debts still outstanding which arise from the purchase from suppliers of materials, components or goods for resale.

A business does not always pay immediately for goods or services it buys. It is a common business practice to make purchases on credit, with a promise to pay within 30 days, or two months or three months of the date of the bill or 'invoice' for the goods. For example, if A buys goods costing £2,000 on credit from B, B might send A an invoice for £2,000, dated say 1 March, with credit terms that payment must be made within 30 days. If A then delays payment until 31 March, B will be a creditor of A between 1 and 31 March, for £2,000.

A creditor is a **liability** of a business.

Definition

> Just as a business might buy goods on credit, so too might it sell goods to customers on credit. A customer who buys goods without paying cash for them straight away is a **debtor**.

For example, suppose that C sells goods on credit to D for £6,000 on terms that the debt must be settled within two months of the invoice date 1 October. If D does not pay the £6,000 until 30 November, D will be a debtor of C for £6,000 from 1 October until 30 November.

A debtor is an asset of a business. When the debt is finally paid, the debtor 'disappears' as an asset, to be replaced by 'cash at bank and in hand'.

EXAMPLE CONTINUED: LIABILITIES

The example of Courtney Spice's market stall will be continued further, by looking at the consequences of the following transactions in the week to 17 July 20X6. (See Paragraph 3.3 (b)(ii) for the situation as at the end of 10 July.)

(a) Courtney Spice realises that she is going to need more money in the business and so she makes the following arrangements.

 (i) She invests immediately a further £250 of her own capital.

(ii) She persuades her Uncle Felix to lend her £500 immediately. Uncle Felix tells her that she can repay the loan whenever she likes, but in the meantime, she must pay him interest of £5 per week each week at the end of the market day. They agree that it will probably be quite a long time before the loan is eventually repaid.

(b) She is very pleased with the progress of her business, and decides that she can afford to buy a second hand van to pick up herbs and spices from her supplier and bring them to her stall in the market. She finds a car dealer, Laurie Loader, who agrees to sell her a van on credit for £700. Courtney agrees to pay for the van after 30 days' trial use.

(c) During the week before the next market day (which is on 17 July), Courtney's Uncle Grant telephones her to ask whether she would be interested in selling him some spice racks and herb chopping boards as presents for his friends. Courtney tells him that she will look for a supplier. After some investigations, she buys what Uncle Grant has asked for, paying £300 in cash to the supplier. Uncle Grant accepts delivery of the goods and agrees to pay £350 to Courtney for them, but he asks if she can wait until the end of the month for payment. Courtney agrees.

(d) The next market day approaches, and Courtney buys herbs and spices costing £800. Of these purchases £750 are paid in cash, with the remaining £50 on seven days' credit. Courtney decides to use Bianca's services again as an assistant on market day, at an agreed wage of £40.

(e) For the third market day running, on 17 July, Courtney succeeds in selling all her goods earning revenue of £1,250 (all in cash). She decides to take out drawings of £240 for her week's work. She also pays Bianca £40 in cash. She decides to make the interest payment to her Uncle Felix the next time she sees him.

(f) We shall ignore any van expenses for the week, for the sake of relative simplicity.

Required

(a) State the business equation:

(i) After Courtney and Uncle Felix have put more money into the business and after the purchase of the van.

(ii) After the sale of goods to Uncle Grant.

(iii) After the purchase of goods for the weekly market.

(iv) At the end of the day's trading on 17 July, and after drawings have been appropriated out of profit.

(b) State the business equation showing profit earned during the week ended 17 July.

Activity 2 **(5 minutes)**

Before you look through the solution, can you state the formula for the business equation?

Solution

There are a number of different transactions to account for here. This solution deals with them one at a time in chronological order. (In practice, it would be possible to do one set of calculations which combines the results of all the transactions, but we shall defer such 'shortcut' methods until later.)

(a) (i) *The addition of Courtney's extra capital and Uncle Felix's loan*

An investment analyst might define the loan of Uncle Felix as a capital investment on the grounds that it will probably be for the long term. Uncle Felix is not the owner of the business, however, even though he has made an investment of a loan in it. He would only become an owner if Courtney offered him a partnership in the business, and she has not done so. To the business, Uncle Felix is a long-term creditor, and it is more appropriate to define his investment as a liability of the business and not as business capital.

The accounting equation after £(250 + 500) = £750 cash is put into the business will be:

Assets		= *Capital*		+ *Liabilities*	
	£		£		£
Stall	1,800	As at end of 10 July	2,690	Loan	500
Goods	0	Additional capital put in	250		
Cash (890+750)	1,640				
	3,440 =		2,940 =		500

The purchase of the van (cost £700) is on credit.

Assets		= *Capital*		+ *Liabilities*	
	£		£		£
Stall	1,800	As at end of 10 July	2,690	Loan	500
Van	700	Additional capital	250	Creditor	700
Cash	1,640				
	4,140 =		2,940 +		1,200

(ii) *The sale of goods to Uncle Grant on credit (£350) which cost the business £300 (cash paid)*

Assets		= *Capital*		+ *Liabilities*	
	£		£		£
Stall	1,800	As at end of 10 July	2,690	Loan	500
Van	700	Additional capital	250	Creditor	700
Debtors	350	Profit on sale to			
Cash (1,640 – 300)	1,340	Uncle Grant	50		
	4,190 =		2,990 +		1,200

(iii) *After the purchase of goods for the weekly market (£750 paid in cash and £50 of purchases on credit)*

Assets		= *Capital*		+ *Liabilities*	
	£		£		£
Stall	1,800	As at end of 10 July	2,690	Loan	500
Van	700			Creditor for van	700
Goods	800	Additional capital	250	Creditor for goods	50
Debtors	350	Profit on sale to			
Cash (1,340 – 750)	590	Uncle Grant	50		
	4,240 =		2,990 +		1,250

(iv) *After market trading on 17 July*

Sales of goods costing £800 earned revenues of £1,250. Bianca's wages were £40 (paid), Uncle Felix's interest charge is £5 (not paid yet) and drawings out of profits were £240 (paid). The profit for 17 July may be calculated as follows, taking the full £5 of interest as a cost on that day.

	£	£
Sales		1,250
Cost of goods sold	800	
Wages	40	
Interest	5	
		845
Profit earned on 17 July		405
Profit on sale of goods to Uncle Grant		50
Profit for the week		455
Drawings appropriated out of profits		240
Retained profit		215

Assets		= *Capital*		+ *Liabilities*	
	£		£		£
Stall	1,800	As at end of 10 July	2,690	Loan	500
Van	700	Additional capital	250	Creditor for van	700
Stocks	0			Creditor for goods	50
Debtors	350				
Cash (590+ 1,250 – 40 – 240)	1,560	Profits retained	215	Creditor for interest payment	5
	4,410 =		3,155 +		1,255

(b) The increase in the net assets of the business during the week was as follows.

	£
Net assets as at the end of 17 July £(4,410 – 1,255)	3,155
Net assets as at the end of 10 July (as above)	2,690
Increase in net assets	465

The business equation for the week ended 17 July is as follows.

(Remember that extra capital of £250 was invested by the proprietor.)

$$
\begin{aligned}
P &= I + D - C_i \\
&= £465 + £240 - £250 \\
&= £455
\end{aligned}
$$

This confirms the calculation of profit above in (a)(iv).

In the example above, we have 'matched' the income earned with the expenses incurred in earning it. So in part (a)(iv), we included all the costs of the goods sold of £800, even though £50 had not yet been paid in cash. Also the interest of £5 was deducted from income, even though it had not yet been paid. This is the **accrual concept** in action.

Activity 3 **(10 minutes)**

Calculate the profit for the year ended 31 December 20X1 from the following information.

	1 January 20X1		*31 December 20X1*	
	£	£	£	£
Assets				
Property	20,000		20,000	
Machinery	6,000		9,000	
Debtors	4,000		8,000	
Cash	1,000		1,500	
		31,000		38,500
Liabilities				
Overdraft	6,000		9,000	
Creditors	5,000		3,000	
		(11,000)		(12,000)
Net assets		20,000		26,500
Drawings during the year				£4,500
Additional capital introduced by the sole trader during the year				£5,000

4 DOUBLE ENTRY BOOKKEEPING

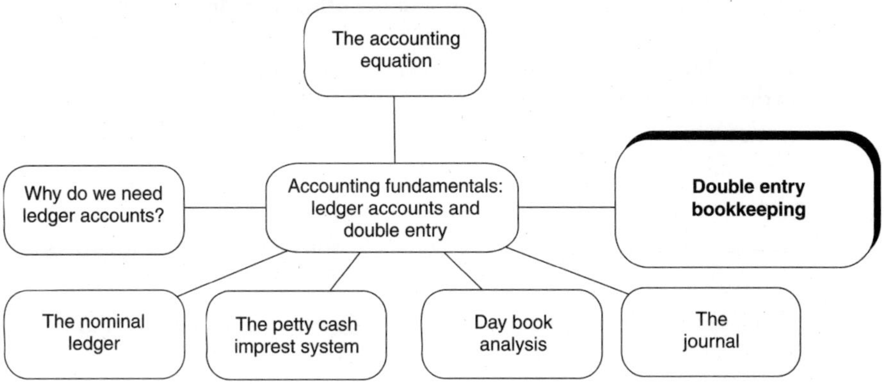

4.1 Dual effect (duality concept)

Central to this process is the idea that every transaction has two effects, the **dual effect** (or **duality concept**, as seen in Chapter 1). This feature is not something peculiar to businesses. If you were to purchase a car for £1,000 cash for instance, you would be affected in two ways.

(a) You own a car worth £1,000.
(b) You have £1,000 less cash.

If instead you got a bank loan to make the purchase:

(a) You own a car worth £1,000.
(b) You owe the bank £1,000.

A month later if you pay a garage £50 to have the exhaust replaced:

(a) You have £50 less cash.
(b) You have incurred a repairs expense of £50.

Ledger accounts, with their debit and credit sides, are kept in a way which allows the two-sided nature of business transactions to be recorded. This system of accounting is known as the '**double entry**' system of bookkeeping, so called because **every transaction is recorded twice** in the accounts.

4.2 The rules of double entry bookkeeping

A debit entry will:

- *increase an asset*
- *decrease a liability*
- *increase an expense*

A credit entry will:

- *decrease an asset*
- *increase a liability*
- *increase income*

The basic rule which must always be observed is that **every financial transaction gives rise to two accounting entries, one a debit and the other a credit.** The total value of debit entries in the nominal ledger is therefore always equal at any time to the total value of credit entries. Which account receives the credit entry and which receives the debit depends on the nature of the transaction.

Definitions

- An **increase** in an **expense** (eg a purchase of stationery) or an **increase in an asset** (eg a purchase of office furniture) is a **debit**.
- An **increase** in **income** (eg a sale) or an **increase** in a **liability** (eg buying goods on credit) is a **credit**.
- A **decrease** in an **asset** (eg making a cash payment) is a **credit**.
- A **decrease** in a **liability** (eg paying a creditor) is a **debit**.

This can be illustrated by the 'T' accounts below.

ASSET

DEBIT	CREDIT
Increase	Decrease

LIABILITY

DEBIT	CREDIT
Decrease	Increase

CAPITAL

DEBIT	CREDIT
Decrease	Increase

Income increases profit, which increases capital, so:

INCOME

DEBIT	CREDIT
Decrease	Increase

EXPENSES

DEBIT	CREDIT
Increase	Decrease

Have a go at the activity below before you learn about this topic in detail.

Activity 4 **(30 minutes)**

Complete the following table relating to the transactions of a bookshop. (The first two are done for you.)

(a) Purchase of books on credit

(i) creditors increase	CR	creditors	(increase in liability)
(ii) purchases expense increases	DR	purchases	(item of expense)

(b) Purchase of cash register

(i) own a cash register	DR	fixed assets	(increase in asset)
(ii) cash at bank decreases	CR	cash at bank	(decrease in asset)

(c) Payment received from a debtor

(i) debtors decrease
(ii) cash at bank increases

(d) Purchase of van

(i) own a van
(ii) cash at bank decreases

4.3 Double entry and cash transactions

How did you get on? Students coming to the subject for the first time often have difficulty in knowing where to begin. A good starting point is the cash account, ie the nominal ledger account in which receipts and payments of cash are recorded. (This is different to the *cash book* which is a book of prime entry and the totals are posted to the *cash account*). The rule to remember about the cash account is as follows.

(a) A cash **payment** is a **credit** entry in the cash account. Here the **asset is decreasing**. Cash may be paid out, for example, to pay an expense (such as rates) or to purchase an asset (such as a machine). The matching debit entry is therefore made in the appropriate expense account or asset account.

(b) A cash **receipt** is a **debit** entry in the cash account. Here the **asset is increasing**. Cash might be received, for example, by a retailer who makes a cash sale. The credit entry would then be made in the sales account.

This is the opposite way round to the entries on a bank statement. Can you think why?

Cash at bank is an asset in your hands as the **bank owes you** the money. From the **bank's point of view the amount is a liability**. The **bank owes you the balance on your account**. You are a creditor and so your positive balance is a credit balance on your bank statement.

Definition

Double entry bookkeeping is the method by which a business records financial transactions. An account is maintained for every supplier, customer, asset, liability, and income and expense. Every transaction is recorded twice so that for every *debit* there is an equal, corresponding *credit*.

EXAMPLE: DOUBLE ENTRY FOR CASH TRANSACTIONS

In the cash book of a business, the following transactions have been recorded.

(a) A cash sale (ie a receipt) of £2
(b) Payment of a rent bill totalling £150
(c) Buying some goods for cash at £100
(d) Buying some shelves for cash at £200

How would these four transactions be posted to the ledger accounts? For that matter, which ledger accounts should they be posted to? Don't forget that each transaction will be posted twice, in accordance with the rule of double entry.

SOLUTION

(a) The two sides of this transaction are:

(i) Cash is received (debit entry in the cash account).
(ii) Sales increase by £2 (credit entry in the sales account).

CASH AT BANK ACCOUNT

	£		£
Sales a/c	2		

SALES ACCOUNT

	£		£
		Cash at bank a/c	2

(Note how the entry in the cash account is cross-referenced to the sales account and vice-versa. This enables a person looking at one of the ledger accounts to trace where the other half of the double entry can be found.)

(b) The two sides of this transaction are:

(i) Cash is paid (credit entry in the cash account).
(ii) Rent expense increases by £150 (debit entry in the rent account).

CASH AT BANK ACCOUNT

	£		£
		Rent a/c	150

RENT ACCOUNT

	£		£
Cash at bank a/c	150		

(c) The two sides of this transaction are:

(i) Cash is paid (credit entry in the cash account).
(ii) Purchases increase by £100 (debit entry in the purchases account).

CASH AT BANK ACCOUNT

	£		£
		Purchases a/c	100

PURCHASES ACCOUNT

	£		£
Cash at bank a/c	100		

(d) The two sides of this transaction are:

(i) Cash is paid (credit entry in the cash at bank account).

(ii) Assets – in this case, shelves – increase by £200 (debit entry in shelves account).

CASH AT BANK ACCOUNT

	£		£
		Shelves a/c	200

SHELVES (ASSET) ACCOUNT

	£		£
Cash at bank a/c	200		

If all four of these transactions related to the same business, the cash at bank account of that business would end up looking as follows.

CASH AT BANK ACCOUNT

	£		£
Sales a/c	2	Rent a/c	150
		Purchases a/c	100
		Shelves a/c	200

4.4 Double entry for credit transactions

Not all transactions are settled immediately in cash. A business might purchase goods or fixed assets from its suppliers on credit terms, so that the suppliers would be creditors of the business until settlement was made in cash. Equally, the business might grant credit terms to its customers who would then be debtors of the business. Clearly no entries can be made in the cash book when a credit transaction occurs, because initially no cash has been received or paid. Where then can the details of the transactions be entered?

The solution to this problem is to use **debtors and creditors accounts**. When a business acquires goods or services on credit, the credit entry is made in an account designated 'creditors' instead of in the cash account. The debit entry is made in the appropriate expense or asset account, exactly as in the case of cash transactions. Similarly, when a sale is made to a credit customer the entries made are a debit to the total debtors account (instead of cash account) and a credit to sales account.

EXAMPLE: CREDIT TRANSACTIONS

Recorded in the sales day book and the purchase day book are the following transactions.

(a) The business sells goods on credit to a customer Mr A for £2,000.

(b) The business buys goods on credit from a supplier B Ltd for £100.

How and where are these transactions posted in the ledger accounts?

SOLUTION

(a) DEBTORS ACCOUNT

	£		£
Sales a/c	2,000		

SALES ACCOUNT

	£		£
		Debtors account	2,000

(b) CREDITORS ACCOUNT

	£		£
		Purchases a/c	100

PURCHASES ACCOUNT

	£		£
Creditors a/c	100		

4.5 When cash is paid to creditors or by debtors

What happens when a credit transaction is eventually settled in cash? Suppose that, in the example above, the business paid £100 to B Ltd one month after the goods were acquired. The two sides of this new transaction are:

(a) Cash is paid (credit entry in the cash account)

(b) The amount owing to creditors is reduced (debit entry in the creditors account).

CASH AT BANK ACCOUNT

	£		£
		Creditors a/c (B Ltd)	100

CREDITORS ACCOUNT

	£		£
Cash at bank a/c	100		

If we now bring together the two parts of this example, the original purchase of goods on credit and the eventual settlement in cash, we find that the accounts appear as follows.

CASH AT BANK ACCOUNT

	£		£
		Creditors a/c	100

PURCHASES ACCOUNT

	£		£
Creditors a/c	100		

CREDITORS ACCOUNT

	£		£
Cash at bank a/c	100	Purchases a/c	100

The two entries in the creditors account cancel each other out, indicating that no money is owing to creditors any more. We are left with a credit entry of £100 in the cash account and a debit entry of £100 in the purchases account. These are exactly the entries which would have been made to record a *cash* purchase of £100 (compare example above). This is what we would expect: after the business has paid off its creditors it is in exactly the position of a business which has made cash purchases of £100, and the accounting records reflect this similarity.

Similar reasoning applies when a customer settles his debt. In the example above when Mr A pays his debt of £2,000 the two sides of the transaction are:

(a) Cash is received (debit entry in the cash at bank account)

(b) The amount owed by debtors is reduced (credit entry in the debtors account).

CASH AT BANK ACCOUNT

	£		£
Debtors a/c	2,000		

DEBTORS ACCOUNT

	£		£
		Cash at bank a/c	2,000

The accounts recording this sale to, and payment by, Mr A now appear as follows.

CASH AT BANK ACCOUNT

	£		£
Debtors a/c	2,000		

SALES ACCOUNT

	£		£
		Debtors a/c	2,000

DEBTORS ACCOUNT

	£		£
Sales a/c	2,000	Cash at bank a/c	2,000

The two entries in the debtors account cancel each other out; while the entries in the cash account and sales account reflect the same position as if the sale had been made for cash (see above).

Now try the following activities.

Activity 5 **(30 minutes)**

See if you can identify the debit and credit entries in the following transactions.

(a) Bought a machine on credit from A, cost £8,000.
(b) Bought goods on credit from B, cost £500.
(c) Sold goods on credit to C, value £1,200.
(d) Paid D (a creditor) £300.
(e) Collected £180 from E, a debtor.
(f) Paid wages £4,000.
(g) Received rent bill of £700 from landlord G.
(h) Paid rent of £700 to landlord G.
(i) Paid insurance premium £90.
(j) Received a credit note for £450 from supplier H.
(k) Sent out a credit note for £200 to customer I.

Activity 6 **(1 hour)**

See now whether you can record the ledger entries for the following transactions. Ron Knuckle set up a business selling keep fit equipment, trading under the name of Buy Your Biceps Shop. He put £7,000 of his own money into a business bank account (transaction A) and in his first period of trading, the following transactions occurred.

Transaction		£
B	Paid rent of shop for the period	3,500
C	Purchased equipment (stocks) on credit	5,000
D	Raised loan from bank	1,000
E	Purchase of shop fittings (for cash)	2,000
F	Sales of equipment: cash	10,000
G	Sales of equipment: on credit	2,500
H	Payments to trade creditors	5,000
I	Payments from debtors	2,500
J	Interest on loan (paid)	100
K	Other expenses (all paid in cash)	1,900
L	Drawings	1,500

All stocks purchased during the period was sold, and so there were no closing stocks of equipment.

Try to do as much of this activity as you can by yourself before reading the answer. Use accounts for cash, debtors, creditors, purchases, shop fittings, sales, loan, rent, bank interest and other expenses and capital, plus a separate drawings account. Start with cash.

5 THE JOURNAL

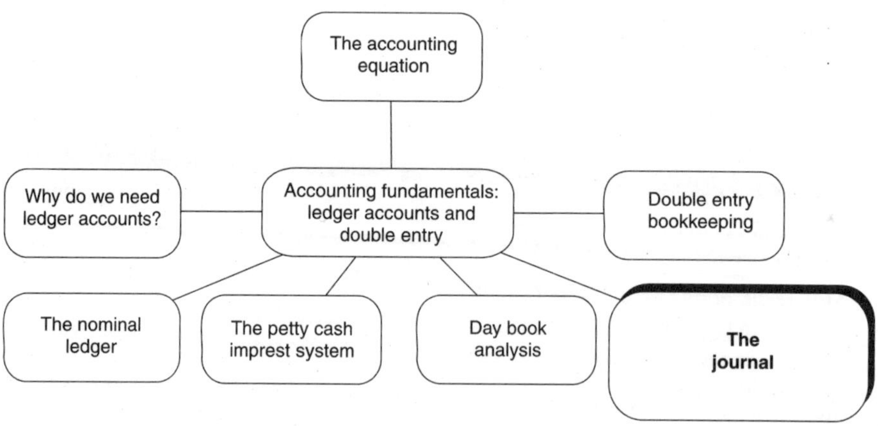

Definition

> The **journal** keeps a record of unusual movement between accounts. It is used to record any double entries made which do not arise from the other books of prime entry. For example, journal entries are made when errors are discovered and need to be corrected.

5.1 Format of a journal entry

Whatever type of transaction is being recorded, the **format of a journal entry** is:

Date	*Debit*	*Credit*
	£	£
Account to be debited	X	
Account to be credited		X
(Narrative to explain the transaction)		

(Remember: in due course, the ledger accounts will be written up to include the transactions listed in the journal.)

A **narrative explanation** must accompany each journal entry. It is required for audit and control, to indicate the purpose and authority of every transaction which is not first recorded in a book of prime entry.

EXAMPLE: JOURNAL ENTRIES

The following is a summary of the transactions of 'Hair by Fiona' hairdressing business of which Fiona Middleton is the sole proprietor.

1 January	Put in cash of £2,000 as capital
	Purchased brushes and combs for cash £50
	Purchased hair driers from Gilroy Ltd on credit £150
30 January	Paid three months rent to 31 March £300
	Collected and paid in takings £600
31 January	Gave Mrs Sullivan a perm, highlights etc on credit £80

Show the transactions by means of journal entries.

SOLUTION

JOURNAL

		£	£
1 January	DEBIT Cash at bank	2,000	
	CREDIT Fiona Middleton – capital account		2,000
	Initial capital introduced		
1 January	DEBIT Brushes and combs account	50	
	CREDIT Cash at bank		50
	The purchase for cash of brushes and combs as fixed assets		

		£	£
1 January	DEBIT Hair dryer account	150	
	CREDIT Sundry creditors account *		150
	The purchase on credit of hair driers as fixed assets		
30 January	DEBIT Rent account	300	
	CREDIT Cash at bank		300
	The payment of rent to 31 March		
30 January	DEBIT Cash at bank	600	
	CREDIT Sales (or takings account)		600
	Cash takings		
31 January	DEBIT Debtors account	80	
	CREDIT Sales account (or takings account)		80
	The provision of a hair-do on credit		

* *Note*. Creditors who have supplied fixed assets are included amongst sundry creditors, as distinct from creditors who have supplied raw materials or goods for resale, who are trade creditors.

5.2 General entries and the correction of errors

Journals can be used to adjust figures at the end of the accounting period. For example, loan interest paid on the last day of the accounting period.

	Debit	*Credit*
31 December 20X6		
Interest expense	800	
Interest payable		800
Being interest paid to bank		

The journal is most commonly used to record corrections to errors that have been made in writing up the nominal ledger accounts. Errors corrected by the journal must be **capable of correction by means of a double entry** in the ledger accounts. In other words the error must not have caused total debits and total credits to be unequal. Special rules apply when errors are made which break the rule of double entry; these are outside the scope of this Course Book.

There are several types of error which can occur.

Errors may occur because an invoice has accidentally been posted to the wrong account. For example, the fee for stationery has been posted to the computer supplies account.

The journal to correct this would be

	Debit	*Credit*
31 December 20X6		
Stationery	800	
Computer supplies		800
Being invoice posted to the wrong account		

Another common error is to transpose the figures and post the wrong amount. This will be corrected as follows:

	Debit	*Credit*
31 December 20X6		
Sales	121	
Debtors		121
Being incorrect figure posted to sales		

6 DAY BOOK ANALYSIS

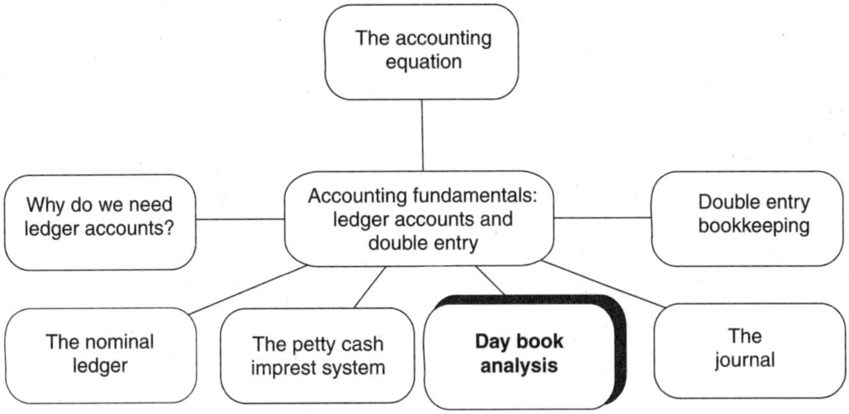

Entries in the day books are totalled and analysed before posting to the nominal ledger.

6.1 Sales day book

In the previous chapter, we used the following example of four transactions entered into the sales day book.

SALES DAY BOOK

Date	*Invoice*	*Customer*	*Total amount invoiced*	*Boot sales*	*Shoe sales*
20X0			£	£	£
Jan 10	247	Jones & Co	105.00	60.00	45.00
	248	Smith Ltd	86.40	86.40	
	249	Alex & Co	31.80		31.80
	250	Enor College	1,264.60	800.30	464.30
			1,487.80	946.70	541.10

We have already seen that in theory these transactions are posted to the ledger accounts as follows.

DEBIT	Debtors account	£1,487.80	
CREDIT	Sales account		£1,487.80

However, a total sales account is not very informative, particularly if the business sells lots of different products. So, using our example, the business might open up a 'sale of shoes' account and a 'sale of boots' account, then at the end of the day, the ledger account postings are:

		£	£
DEBIT	Debtors account	1,487.80	
CREDIT	Sale of shoes account		541.10
	Sale of boots account		946.70

That is why the analysis of sales is kept. Exactly the same reasoning lies behind the analyses kept in other books of prime entry.

6.2 Sales returns day book

We will now look at the sales returns day book.

SALES RETURNS DAY BOOK

Date	*Credit note*	*Customer and goods*	*Amount*
20X8			£
30 April	CR008	Owen Plenty 3 pairs 'Texas' boots	135.00

This will be posted as follows.

		£	£
DEBIT	Sales returns – boots	135.00	
CREDIT	Debtors		135.00

6.3 Purchase day book and purchases returns day book

The purchase day book and purchases returns day book in Chapter 4 can be posted in a similar way.

6.3.1 Purchases

		£	£
DEBIT	Purchases	444.40	
	Electricity	116.80	
CREDIT	Creditors		561.20

6.3.2 Purchase return

		£	£
DEBIT	Creditors	46.60	
CREDIT	Purchases returns		46.60

7 THE PETTY CASH IMPREST SYSTEM

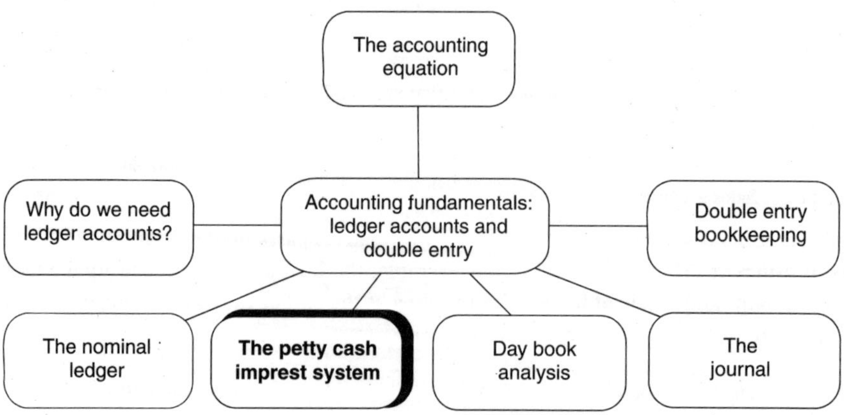

In Chapter 2, we saw how the petty cash book was used to operate the imprest system. It is now time to see how the double entry works.

A business starts off a cash float on 1.3.20X7 with £250. This will be a payment from cash at bank to petty cash, ie:

DEBIT	Petty cash	£250	
CREDIT	Cash at bank		£250

Five payments were made out of petty cash during March 20X7. The petty cash book might look as follows.

Receipts	*Date*	*Narrative*	*Total*	*Payments* *Postage*	*Travel*
£			£	£	£
250.00	1.3.X7	Cash			
	2.3.X7	Stamps	12.00	12.00	
	8.3.X7	Stamps	10.00	10.00	
	19.3.X7	Travel	16.00		16.00
	23.3.X7	Travel	5.00		5.00
	28.3.X7	Stamps	11.50	11.50	
250.00			54.50	33.50	21.00

At the end of each month (or at any other suitable interval) the total credits in the petty cash book are **posted** to ledger accounts. For March 20X7, £33.50 would be debited to postage account, and £21.00 to travel account. The total expenditure of £54.50 is credited to the petty cash account. The cash float would need to be topped up by a payment of £54.50 from the main cash book, ie:

		£	£
DEBIT	Petty cash	54.50	
CREDIT	Cash		54.50

So the rules of double entry have been satisfied, and the petty cash book for the month of March 20X7 will look like this.

Receipts	*Date*	*Narrative*	*Total*	*Payments* *Postage*	*Travel*
£			£	£	£
250.00	1.3.X7	Cash			
	2.3.X7	Stamps	12.00	12.00	
	8.3.X7	Stamps	10.00	10.00	
	19.3.X7	Travel	16.00		16.00
	23.3.X7	Travel	5.00		5.00
	28.3.X7	Stamps	11.50	11.50	
	31.3.X7	Balance c/d	195.50		
250.00			250.00	33.50	21.00
195.50	1.4.X7	Balance b/d			
54.50	1.4.X7	Cash			

As you can see, the cash float is back up to £250 on 1.4.X7, ready for more payments to be made.

The petty cash account in the ledger will appear as follows.

PETTY CASH

		£			£
1.3.X7	Cash	250.00	31.3.X7	Payments	54.50
1.4.X7	Cash	54.50	1.4.X7	Balance c/d	250.00
		304.50			304.50
1.4.X7	Balance b/d	250.00			

Activity 7 **(10 minutes)**

Summit Glazing operates an imprest petty cash system. The imprest amount is £150.00. At the end of the period the totals of the four analysis columns in the petty cash book were as follows.

	£
Column 1	23.12
Column 2	6.74
Column 3	12.90
Column 4	28.50

How much cash is required to restore the imprest amount?

Chapter roundup

- Ledger accounts are a summary of the books of prime entry.
- The assets of a business must be equal to the liabilities (accounting equation).
- The business equation gives a definition of profits earned.
- Creditors are liabilities. Debtors are assets.
- **Double entry bookkeeping** is the method used to transfer our weekly/monthly totals from our books of prime entry into the nominal ledger.
- A debit entry will:
  - increase an asset
  - decrease a liability
  - increase an expense

  A credit entry will:
  - decrease an asset
  - increase a liability
  - increase income
- Some accounts in the nominal ledger represent the total of very many smaller balances. For example, the **debtors account** represents all the balances owed by individual customers of the business while the **creditors account** represents all money owed by the business to its suppliers.
- You should remember that one of the books of prime entry from the previous chapter was the **journal**.
- Entries in the day books are totalled and analysed before posting to the nominal ledger.
- In the last chapter, we saw how the petty cash book was used to operate the impress system. It is now time to see how the **double entry** works.

Quick quiz

1 What is the double entry to record a cash sale of £50?

2 What is the double entry to record a credit sale of £50?

A Debit cash £50, credit sales £50
B Debit debtors £50, credit sales £50
C Debit sales £50, credit debtors £50
D Debit sales £50, credit cash £50

3 What is the double entry to record a purchase of office chairs for £1,000?

A Debit fixed assets £1,000, credit cash £1,000
B Debit cash £1,000, credit purchases £1,000

4 What is the double entry to record a credit sale of £500 to A?

A Debit debtors £500, credit sales £500
B Debit sales ledger (A's account) £500, credit sales £500

5 Name one reason for making a journal entry.

Answers to quick quiz

1

		£	£
DEBIT	Cash a/c	50	
CREDIT	Sales a/c		50

2 B

3 A

4 A The sales ledger is a memorandum account and not part of the double entry system.

5 Most commonly to correct an error, although it can be used to make any entry that is not recorded in a book of prime entry (eg prepayments, accrued expenses, depreciation).

Answers to activities

1 The correct answer is C. As assets = liabilities + capital, then capital = assets – liabilities

2 $P = I + D - C_i$

3 The increase in net assets during the year was £(26,500 - 20,000) = £6,500.

$$P = I + D - C_i$$
$$= £6{,}500 + £4{,}500 - £5{,}000$$
$$= \underline{\underline{£6{,}000}}$$

4 (c) Payment received from a debtor

(i) debtors decrease	CREDIT	debtors	(decrease in asset)
(ii) cash at bank increases	DEBIT	cash at bank	(increase in asset)

(d) Purchase of van

(i) own a van	DEBIT	fixed assets	(increases in asset)
(ii) cash at bank decreases	CREDIT	cash at bank	(decrease in asset)

5

			£	£
(a)	DEBIT	Machine account (fixed asset)	8,000	
	CREDIT	Creditors		8,000
(b)	DEBIT	Purchases account	500	
	CREDIT	Creditors		500
(c)	DEBIT	Debtors	1,200	
	CREDIT	Sales		1,200
(d)	DEBIT	Creditors	300	
	CREDIT	Cash at bank		300
(e)	DEBIT	Cash at bank	180	
	CREDIT	Debtors		180

			£	£
(f)	DEBIT	Wages account	4,000	
	CREDIT	Cash at bank		4,000
(g)	DEBIT	Rent account	700	
	CREDIT	Creditors		700
(h)	DEBIT	Creditors	700	
	CREDIT	Cash at bank		700
(i)	DEBIT	Insurance costs	90	
	CREDIT	Cash at bank		90
(j)	DEBIT	Creditors	450	
	CREDIT	Purchase returns		450
(k)	DEBIT	Sales returns	200	
	CREDIT	Debtors		200

6

CASH AT BANK

	£		£
Capital – Ron Knuckle (A)	7,000	Rent (B)	3,500
Bank loan (D)	1,000	Shop fittings (E)	2,000
Sales (F)	10,000	Trade creditors (H)	5,000
Debtors (I)	2,500	Bank loan interest (J)	100
		Incidental expenses (K)	1,900
		Drawings (L)	1,500

CAPITAL (RON KNUCKLE)

	£		£
		Cash at bank (A)	7,000

BANK LOAN

	£		£
		Cash at bank (D)	1,000

PURCHASES

	£		£
Trade creditors (C)	5,000		

TRADE CREDITORS

	£		£
Cash at bank (H)	5,000	Purchases (C)	5,000

RENT

	£		£
Cash at bank (B)	3,500		

FIXED ASSETS

	£		£
Cash at bank (E)	2,000		

SALES

	£		£
		Cash at bank (F)	10,000
		Debtors (G)	2,500

DEBTORS

	£		£
Sales (G)	2,500	Cash at bank (I)	2,500

BANK LOAN INTEREST

	£		£
Cash at bank (J)	100		

OTHER EXPENSES

	£		£
Cash at bank (K)	1,900		

DRAWINGS ACCOUNT

	£		£
Cash at bank (L)	1,500		

(a) If you want to make sure that this solution is complete, you should go through the transactions A to L and tick off each of them twice in the ledger accounts, once as a debit and once as a credit. When you have finished, all transactions in the 'T' account should be ticked, with only totals left over.

(b) In fact, there is an easier way to check that the solution to this sort of problem does 'balance' properly, which we will meet in the next chapter.

(c) On asset and liability accounts, the debit or credit balance represents the amount of the asset or liability outstanding at the period end. For example, on the cash account, debits exceed credits by £6,500 and so there is a debit balance of cash in hand of £6,500. On the capital account, there is a credit balance of £7,000 and so the business owes Ron £7,000.

(d) The balances on the revenue and expenses accounts represent the total of each revenue or expense for the period. For example, sales for the period total £12,500.

7 £71.26. This is the total amount of cash that has been used.

Part B

Preparing Financial Statements

Chapter 4:

PREPARING A PROFIT AND LOSS ACCOUNT AND BALANCE SHEET

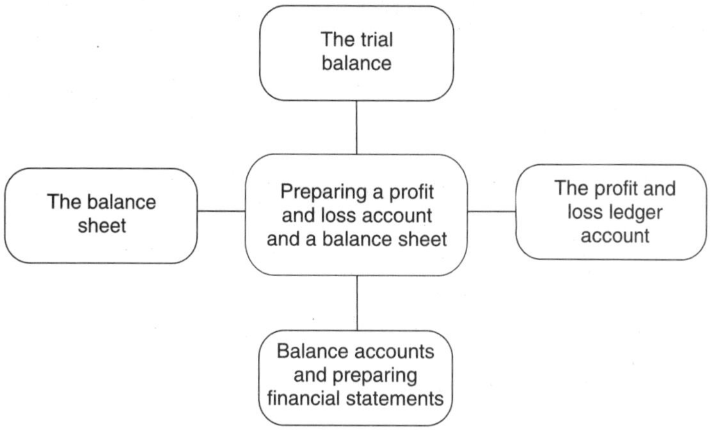

Introduction

In the previous chapter you learned the principles of double entry and how to post to the ledger accounts. The next step in our progress towards the financial statements is the **trial balance**.

Before transferring the relevant balances at the year end to the profit and loss account and putting closing balances carried forward into the balance sheet, it is usual to test the accuracy of double entry bookkeeping records by preparing a trial balance. This is done by listing all the balances on every account, with one column for debit balances and one for credit balances. Because of the self-balancing nature of the system of double entry the **total of the debit balances should be exactly equal to the total of the credit balances.**

In very straightforward circumstances, where no complications arise and where the records are complete, it is possible to prepare financial statements directly from a trial balance. This is covered in Section 4.

Your objectives

After completing this chapter you should be able to:

1 Calculate balances on ledger accounts

2 Draw up a trial balance

3 Prepare a profit and loss account and balance sheet from a trial balance

1 THE TRIAL BALANCE

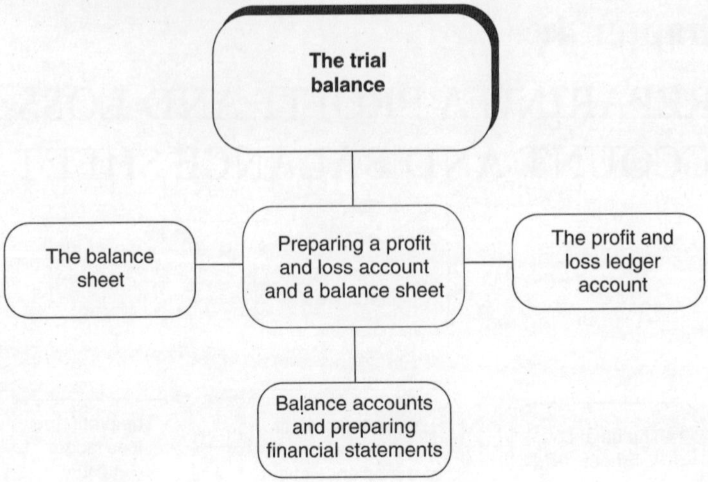

A technique which shows up the more obvious mistakes in double entry bookkeeping is to prepare a **trial balance.**

Definition

A **trial balance** is a list of ledger balances shown in debit and credit columns.

1.1 The first step

Before you draw up a trial balance, you must have a collection of ledger accounts. For the sake of convenience, we will use the accounts of Ron Knuckle, which we drew up in the previous chapter.

CASH AT BANK

	£		£
Capital: Ron Knuckle	7,000	Rent	3,500
Bank loan	1,000	Shop fittings	2,000
Sales	10,000	Trade creditors	5,000
Debtors	2,500	Bank loan interest	100
		Other expenses	1,900
		Drawings	1,500

CAPITAL (RON KNUCKLE)

	£		£
		Cash at bank	7,000

BANK LOAN

	£		£
		Cash at bank	1,000

PURCHASES

	£		£
Trade creditors	5,000		

TRADE CREDITORS

	£		£
Cash at bank	5,000	Purchases	5,000

RENT

	£		£
Cash at bank	3,500		

SHOP FITTINGS

	£		£
Cash at bank	2,000		

SALES

	£		£
		Cash at bank	10,000
		Debtors	2,500

DEBTORS

	£		£
Sales	2,500	Cash at bank	2,500

BANK LOAN INTEREST

	£		£
Cash at bank	100		

OTHER EXPENSES

	£		£
Cash at bank	1,900	Purchases	5,000

DRAWINGS

	£		£
Cash at bank	1,500	Purchases	5,000

The next step is to 'balance' each account.

1.2 Balancing ledger accounts

At the end of an accounting period, a **balance is struck** on each account in turn. This means that all the debits on the account are totalled and so are all the credits.

- If the **total debits exceed the total credits** there is said to be a **brought down debit balance on the account**
- If the **credits exceed the debits** then the account has a **brought down credit balance.**

In our simple example, there is very little balancing to do.

(a) Both the creditors account and the debtors account balance off to zero.
(b) The cash at bank account has a debit balance of £6,500.
(c) The total on the sales account is £12,500, which is a credit balance.

CASH AT BANK

	£		£
Capital: Ron Knuckle	7,000	Rent	3,500
Bank loan	1,000	Shop fittings	2,000
Sales	10,000	Trade creditors	5,000
Debtors	2,500	Bank loan interest	100
		Other expenses	1,900
		Drawings	1,500
			14,000
		Balancing figure c/d – the amount of cash left over after payments have been made	6,500
	20,500		20,500
Balance b/d (debit balance)	6,500	Bank loan interest	100

CREDITORS

	£		£
Cash at bank	5,000	Purchases	5,000

SALES

	£		£
Balance c/d	12,500	Cash at bank	10,000
		Debtors	2,500
			12,500
		Balance b/d (debit balance)	12,500

DEBTORS

	£		£
Sales	2,500	Cash at bank	2,500

Otherwise, the accounts have only one entry each, so there is no totalling to do to arrive at the balance on each account.

1.3 Collecting the balances

If the basic principle of double entry has been correctly applied throughout the period it will be found that the credit balances equal the debit balances in total. This can be illustrated by collecting together the balances on Ron Knuckle's accounts.

	Debit	*Credit*
	£	£
Cash at bank	6,500	
Capital		7,000
Bank loan		1,000
Purchases	5,000	
Creditors	–	–
Rent	3,500	
Shop fittings	2,000	
Sales		12,500
Debtors	–	–
Bank loan interest	100	
Other expenses	1,900	
Drawings	1,500	
	20,500	20,500

This list of balances is called the **trial balance**. It does not matter in what order the various accounts are listed. It is just a method used to test the accuracy of the double entry bookkeeping.

1.4 What if the trial balance shows unequal debit and credit balances?

If the two columns of the trial balance are not equal, there must be an error in recording the transactions in the accounts. A trial balance, however, will not disclose the following types of errors, so even if the trial balance balances there may still be undiscovered errors.

(a) The **complete omission** of a transaction, because neither a debit nor a credit is made.

(b) The posting of a debit or credit to the correct side of the ledger, but to a **wrong account**.

(c) **Compensating errors** (eg an error of £100 is exactly cancelled by another £100 error elsewhere).

(d) **Errors of principle,** eg cash received from debtors being debited to the debtors account and credited to cash instead of the other way round.

EXAMPLE: TRIAL BALANCE

As at 30.3.20X7, your business has the following balances on its ledger accounts.

Accounts	*Balance*
	£
Bank loan	12,000
Cash at bank	11,700
Capital	13,000
Business rates	1,880
Creditors	11,200
Purchases	12,400
Sales	14,600
Other creditors	1,620
Debtors	12,000
Bank loan interest	1,400
Other expenses	11,020
Vehicles	2,020

On 31.3.20X7 year the business made the following transactions.

(a) Bought materials for £1,000, half for cash and half on credit.

(b) Made £1,040 sales, £800 of which was for credit.

(c) Paid wages to shop assistants of £260 in cash.

You are required to draw up a trial balance showing the balances as at the end of 31.3.X7.

Solution

First it is necessary to put the original balances into a trial balance – ie decide which are debit and which are credit balances.

Account	*Dr*	*Cr*
	£	£
Bank loan		12,000
Cash at bank	11,700	
Capital		13,000
Business rates	1,880	
Creditors		11,200
Purchases	12,400	
Sales		14,600
Other creditors		1,620
Debtors	12,000	
Bank loan interest	1,400	
Other expenses	11,020	
Vehicles	2,020	
	52,420	52,420

Now we must take account of the effects of the three transactions which took place on 31.3.X7.

			£	£
(a)	DEBIT	Purchases	1,000	
	CREDIT	Cash at bank		500
		Creditors		500
(b)	DEBIT	Cash at bank	240	
		Debtors	800	
	CREDIT	Sales		1,040
(c)	DEBIT	Other expenses	260	
	CREDIT	Cash at bank		260

When these figures are included in the trial balance, it becomes:

Account	*Dr*	*Cr*
	£	£
Bank loan		12,000
Cash at bank (11,700 + 240 – 500 – 260)	11,180	
Capital		13,000
Business rates	1,880	
Creditors (11,200 + 500)		11,700
Purchases (12,400 + 1,000)	13,400	
Sales (14,600 + 1,040)		15,640
Other creditors		1,620
Debtors (12,000 +800)	12,800	
Bank loan interest	1,400	
Other expenses (11,020 + 260)	11,280	
Vehicles	2,020	
	53,960	53,960

Before moving on, try this activity to make sure you have understood the basics.

Activity 1 **(30 minutes)**

Here is a list of balances. Arrange them into debit and credit columns as in a trial balance.

LIST OF BALANCES AS AT 31 JULY 20X2

		£
Cash at bank		215
Bank		96
Capital		250
Rent		30
Carriage		23
Creditors:	B Jackson	130
	G Mitchell	186
	D Wickes	64
Debtors:	D Cotton	129
	C Beale	26
Purchases		459
Sales		348

2 THE PROFIT AND LOSS LEDGER ACCOUNT

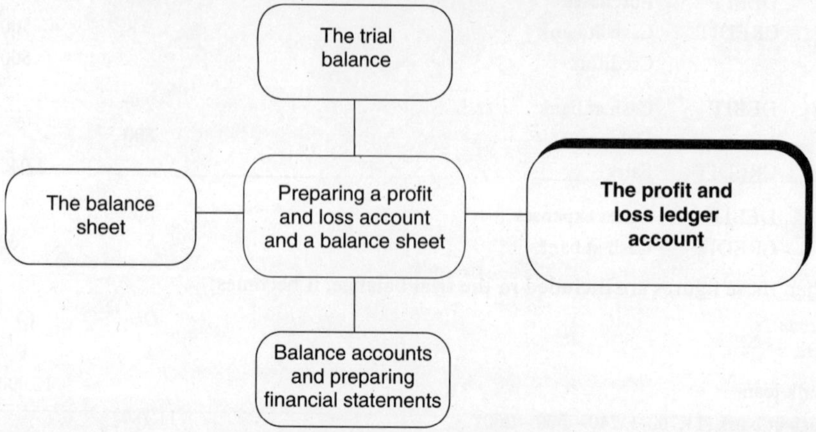

The first step in the process of preparing the financial statements is to open up another ledger account, called the **profit and loss ledger account**. In it a business summarises its results for the period by gathering together all the ledger account balances relating to income and expenses. This account is still part of the double entry system, so the basic rule of double entry still applies: every debit must have an equal and opposite credit entry.

This profit and loss ledger account we have opened up is **not** the financial statement we are aiming for, even though it has the same name. The difference between the two is not very great, because they contain the same information. However, the financial statement lays it out differently and may be much less detailed.

So what do we do with this new ledger account? The first step is to look through the original ledger accounts and identify which ones relate to income and expenses. In the case of Ron Knuckle, the income and expense accounts consist of purchases, rent, sales, bank loan interest, and other expenses.

The balances on these accounts are transferred to the new profit and loss ledger account. For example, the balance on the purchases account is £5,000 DR. To balance this to zero, we write in £5,000 CR. But to comply with the rule of double entry, there has to be a debit entry somewhere, so we write £5,000 DR in the profit and loss ledger account. Now the balance on the purchases account has been moved to the profit and loss ledger account.

If we do the same thing with all the income and expense accounts of Ron Knuckle, the result is as follows.

PURCHASES

	£		£
Trade creditors	5,000	P & L a/c	5,000

RENT

	£		£
Cash at bank	3,500	P & L a/c	3,500

SALES

	£		£
P & L a/c	12,500	Cash at bank	10,000
		Debtors	2,500
	12,500		12,500

BANK LOAN INTEREST

	£		£
Cash at bank	100	P & L a/c	100

OTHER EXPENSES

	£		£
Cash at bank	1,900	P & L a/c	1,900

PROFIT AND LOSS ACCOUNT

	£		£
Purchases	5,000	Sales	12,500
Rent	3,500		
Bank loan interest	100		
Other expenses	1,900		

(Note that the profit and loss ledger account has not yet been balanced off but we will return to that later.)

If you look at the items we have gathered together in the profit and loss ledger account, they should strike a chord in your memory. They are the same items that we need to draw up the profit and loss account in the form of a financial statement. With a little rearrangement they could be presented as follows.

RON KNUCKLE: PROFIT AND LOSS ACCOUNT

	£	£
Sales		12,500
Cost of sales (= purchases in this case)		(5,000)
Gross profit		7,500
Expenses		
Rent	3,500	
Bank loan interest	100	
Other expenses	1,900	
		(5,500)
Net profit		2,000

3 THE BALANCE SHEET

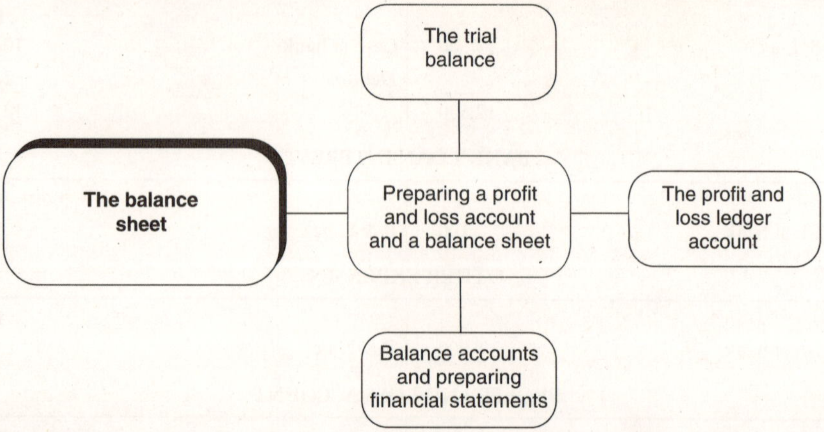

Look back at the ledger accounts of Ron Knuckle. Now that we have dealt with those relating to income and expenses, which ones are left? The answer is that we still have to find out what to do with cash, capital, bank loan, creditors, shop fittings, debtors and the drawings account.

Are these the only ledger accounts left? No: don't forget there is still the last one we opened up, called the **profit and loss ledger account**. The balance on this account represents the profit earned by the business, and if you go through the arithmetic, you will find that it has a credit balance – a profit – of £2,000. (Not surprisingly, this is the figure that is shown in the profit and loss account financial statement.)

These remaining accounts must also be balanced and ruled off, but since they represent assets and liabilities of the business (not income and expenses) their balances are not transferred to the profit and loss ledger account. Instead they are **carried down** in the books of the business. This means that they become opening balances for the next accounting period and indicate the value of the assets, liabilities and capital at the end of one period and the beginning of the next.

The conventional method of ruling off a ledger account at the end of an accounting period is illustrated by the bank loan account in Ron Knuckle's books.

BANK LOAN ACCOUNT

	£		£
Balance carried down (c/d)	1,000	Cash at bank	1,000
		Balance brought down (b/d)	1,000

Ron Knuckle therefore begins the new accounting period with a credit balance of £1,000 on this account. A **credit balance brought down** denotes a **liability**. An **asset** would be represented by a **debit balance brought down**.

One further point is worth noting before we move on to complete this example. You will remember that a proprietor's capital comprises any cash introduced by him, plus any profits made by the business, less any drawings made by him. At the stage we have now reached, these three elements are contained in different ledger accounts: cash introduced of £7,000 appears in the capital account; drawings of £1,500 appear in the drawings account; and the profit made by the business is represented by the £2,000 credit balance on the profit and loss ledger account. It is convenient to gather together all these amounts into one **capital account**, in the same way as we earlier gathered together income and expense accounts into one profit and loss ledger account.

If we go ahead and gather the three amounts together, the results are as follows.

DRAWINGS

	£		£
Cash at bank	1,500	Capital a/c	1,500

PROFIT AND LOSS ACCOUNT

	£		£
Purchases	5,000	Sales	12,500
Rent	3,500		
Bank loan interest	100		
Other expenses	1,900		
Capital a/c	2,000		
	12,500		12,500

CAPITAL

	£		£
Drawings	1,500	Cash at bank	7,000
Balance c/d	7,500	P & L a/c	2,000
	9,000		9,000
		Balance b/d	7,500

A rearrangement of these balances will complete Ron Knuckle's simple balance sheet:

RON KNUCKLE
BALANCE SHEET AT END OF FIRST TRADING PERIOD

	£	£
Fixed assets		
Shop fittings		2,000
Current assets		
Cash	6,500	
Current liabilities		
Bank loan	(1,000)	
Net current assets		5,500
Net assets		7,500
Sole trader's capital		7,500

When a balance sheet is drawn up for an accounting period which is not the first one, then it ought to show the capital at the start of the accounting period and the capital at the end of the accounting period. This will be illustrated in the next activity.

4 BALANCING ACCOUNTS AND PREPARING FINANCIAL STATEMENTS

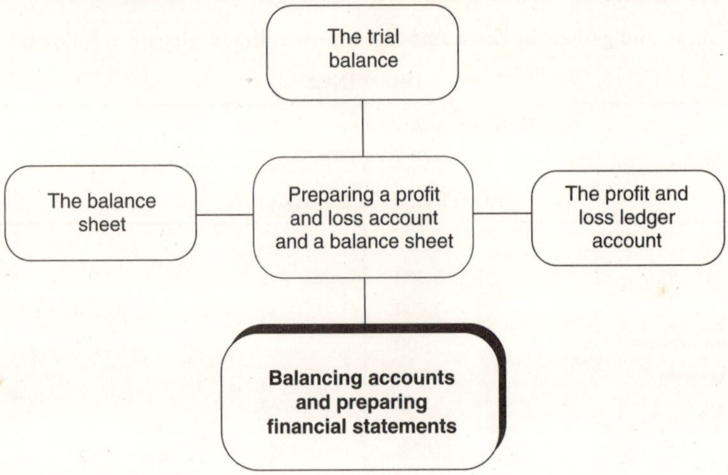

The activity which follows is **by far the most important in this book so far**. It uses all the accounting steps from entering up ledger accounts to preparing the financial statements. It is very important that you try the activity by yourself: if you do not, you will be missing out a vital part of this Course Book.

Activity 2 **(1 hour)**

A business (Ardwa Enterprises) is established with capital of £2,000, and this amount is paid into a business bank account by the Stefano Ardwa. During the first year's trading, the following transactions occurred:

	£
Purchases of goods for resale, on credit	4,300
Payments to creditors	3,600
Sales, all on credit	5,800
Receipts from debtors	3,200
Fixed assets purchased for cash	1,500
Other expenses, all paid in cash	900

The bank has provided an overdraft facility of up to £3,000.

Prepare the ledger accounts including a profit and loss ledger account for the year and a profit and loss account and balance sheet as at the end of the year.

Helping hand

You should attempt this activity on your own, but if you are daunted by the prospect, here are some tips to get you started.

The first thing to do is to open ledger accounts so that the transactions can be entered up. The relevant accounts which we need for this example are: cash; capital; creditors; purchases; fixed assets; sales; debtors; other expenses.

The next step is to work out the double entry for each transaction. Normally you would write them straight into the accounts, but to make this example easier to follow, they are first listed below.

	Transaction	DR	CR
(a)	Establishing business (£2,000):	DR Cash	CR Capital
(b)	Purchases (£4,300) :	DR Purchases	CR Creditors
(c)	Payments to creditors (£3,600) :	DR Creditors	CR Cash
(d)	Sales (£5,800) :	DR Debtors	CR Sales
(e)	Payments by debtors (£3,200) :	DR Cash	CR Debtors
(f)	Fixed assets (£1,500) :	DR Fixed assets	CR Cash
(g)	Other (cash) expenses (£900):	DR Other expenses	CR Cash

Activity 3 **(10 minutes)**

Alpha has the following opening balances on its ledger accounts.

	£
Fixtures	5,000
Debtors	2,000
Bank account	1,000
Loan	3,000

(a) What is the figure for total assets?

A £6,000
B £5,000
C £8,000
D £3,000

(b) What is the figure for capital?

A £6,000
B £5,000
C £8,000
D £3,000

Chapter roundup

- A trial balance is a means of checking that the total debits equal total credits.
- This time, the profit and loss ledger account is a new ledger account, not the financial statement.
- The remaining ledger accounts form the balance sheet.
- You can now prepare basic financial statements.

Quick quiz

1 What is the purpose of a trial balance?

2 A trial balance may still balance if some of the balances are wrong.

Is this statement correct?

A Yes
B No

3 In a period, sales are £140,000, purchases £75,000 and other expenses £25,000. What is the figure for net profit to be transferred to the capital account?

A £40,000
B £65,000
C £75,000
D £140,000

4 The balance on an expense account will go to the P & L ledger account. However, the balance on a liability account is written off to capital.

Is this statement correct?

A Yes
B No

Answers to quick quiz

1 To test the accuracy of the double entry bookkeeping.

2 A It could be the result of an error of omission, posting to a wrong account, a compensating error or an error of principle.

3 A PROFIT AND LOSS ACCOUNT

	£		£
Purchases	75,000	Sales	140,000
Gross profit c/d	65,000		
	140,000		140,000
Other expenses	25,000	Gross profit b/d	65,000
Net profit – to capital a/c	40,000		
	65,000		65,000

B is the **gross** profit figure, while C is the figure for purchases and D sales.

4 B When an expense account is balanced off, the balance is transferred to the income and expense account. When a liability account is balanced off, the balance is carried forward to the next accounting period.

Answers to activities

1 TRIAL BALANCE AS AT 31 JULY 20X2

		Dr	*Cr*
		£	£
Cash at bank		215	
Bank		96	
Capital			250
Rent		30	
Carriage		23	
Creditors	– B Jackson		130
	– G Mitchell		186
	– D Wickes		64
Debtors	– D Cotton	129	
	– C Beale	26	
Purchases		459	
Sales			348
		978	978

2 After the first stage, the ledger accounts will look like this:

CASH AT BANK

	£		£
Capital	2,000	Creditors	3,600
Debtors	3,200	Fixed assets	1,500
		Other expenses	900

CAPITAL

	£		£
		Cash	2,000

CREDITORS

	£		£
Cash at bank	3,600	Purchases	4,300

PURCHASES

	£		£
Creditors	4,300		

FIXED ASSETS

	£		£
Cash at bank	1,500		

SALES

	£		£
		Debtors	5,800

DEBTORS

	£		£
Sales	5,800	Cash at bank	3,200

OTHER EXPENSES

	£		£
Cash at bank	900		

The next thing to do is to extract a balance on all these accounts. It is at this stage that you could, if you wanted to, draw up a trial balance to make sure the double entries are accurate. There is not very much point in this simple example, but if you did draw up a trial balance, it would look like this.

	Dr £	*Cr* £
Cash at bank		800
Capital		2,000
Creditors		700
Purchases	4,300	
Fixed assets	1,500	
Sales		5,800
Debtors	2,600	
Other expenses	900	
	9,300	9,300

After balancing the accounts, the trading and profit and loss account should be opened. Into it should be transferred all the balances relating to income and expenses (ie purchases, other expenses, and sales). At this point, the ledger accounts will be:

CASH AT BANK

	£		£
Capital	2,000	Trade creditors	3,600
Debtors	3,200	Fixed assets	1,500
Balance c/d	800	Other expenses	900
	6,000		6,000
		Balance b/d	800*

* A credit balance b/d means that this cash item is a liability, not an asset. This indicates a bank overdraft of £800, with cash income of £5,200 falling short of cash payments of £6,000 by this amount.

CAPITAL

	£		£
Balance c/d	2,600	Cash at bank	2,000
		P & L a/c	600
	2,600		2,600

CREDITORS

	£		£
Cash at bank	3,600	Purchases	4,300
Balance c/d	700		
	4,300		4,300
		Balance b/d	700

PURCHASES

	£		£
Creditors	4,300	P&L a/c	4,300

FIXED ASSETS

	£		£
Cash at bank	1,500	Balance c/d	1,500
Balance b/d	1,500		

SALES

	£		£
P&L a/c	5,800	Debtors	5,800

DEBTORS

	£		£
Sales	5,800	Cash at bank	3,200
		Balance c/d	2,600
	5,800		5,800
Balance b/d	2,600		

OTHER EXPENSES

	£		£
Cash at bank	900	P & L a/c	900

PROFIT AND LOSS ACCOUNT

	£		£
Purchases	4,300	Sales	5,800
Gross profit c/d	1,500		
	5,800		5,800
Other expenses	900	Gross profit b/d	1,500
Capital (net profit)	600		
	1,500		1,500

So the profit and loss account financial statement will be as follows.

ARDWA ENTERPRISES PROFIT AND LOSS ACCOUNT FOR THE ACCOUNTING PERIOD

	£
Sales	5,800
Cost of sales (purchases)	(4,300)
Gross profit	1,500
Expenses	(900)
Net profit	600

Listing and then rearranging the balances on the ledger accounts gives the balance sheet as follows:

ARDWA ENTERPRISES
BALANCE SHEET AS AT THE END OF THE PERIOD

	£	£
Fixed assets		1,500
Current assets		
Debtors	2,600	
Current liabilities		
Bank overdraft	800	
Creditors	700	
	1,500	
Net current assets (2,600 – 1,500)		1,100
Net assets		2,600
Capital		
At start of period		2,000
Net profit for period		600
At end of period		2,600

3 (a) C Assets = 5,000 + 2,000 + 1,000
= 8,000

(b) B Capital = assets – liabilities
= (5,000 + 2,000 + 1,000) – 3,000
= 5,000

Chapter 5:

FIXED ASSETS

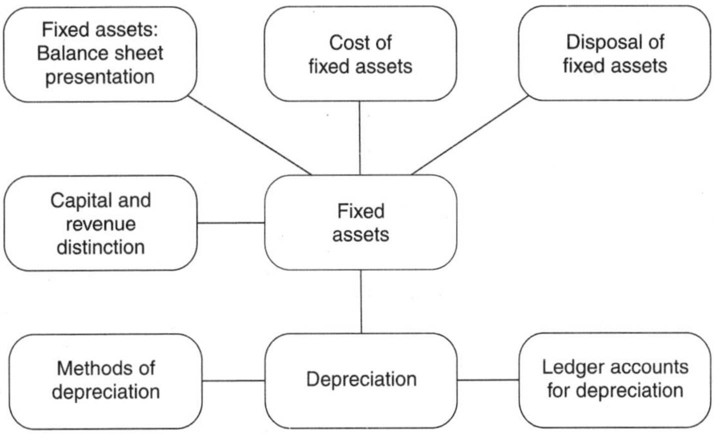

Introduction

Now that we have got to the position that we can read and summarise transactions in a basic balance sheet and profit and loss account, it is time to look in a little more detail at some of the items that appear in the balance sheet beginning with an analysis of fixed assets.

You should by now be familiar with the distinction between **fixed and current assets**, a fixed asset being one bought for ongoing use in the business. If you are unsure of this, look back to Chapter 1 to refresh your memory.

Fixed assets might be held and used by a business for a number of years, but they wear out or lose their usefulness in the course of time. Nearly every fixed asset has a **limited** life. The process by which this is recognised in the accounts is **depreciation**, and this is discussed in Section 3.

Section 6 deals with **disposals** of fixed assets. A profit may arise on the sale of a fixed asset if too much depreciation has been charged.

Your objectives

After completing this chapter you should be able to:

1 Distinguish between capital and revenue items

2 Account for the cost of fixed assets

3 Calculate and account for depreciation and disposal of fixed assets

1 CAPITAL AND REVENUE DISTINCTION

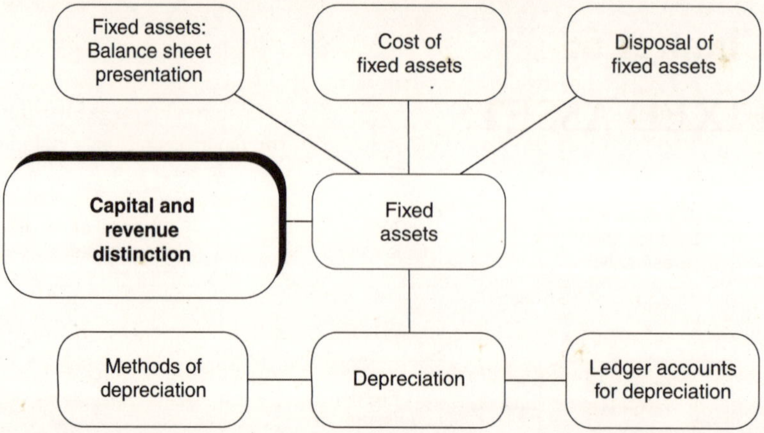

Before we start properly on fixed assets, you need to be familiar with an important distinction, the distinction between **capital and revenue expenditure**.

1.1 Capital and revenue expenditure

Definitions

Capital expenditure is expenditure which results in the acquisition of fixed assets, or an improvement in their earning capacity.

(a) Capital expenditure is not charged as an expense in the profit and loss account, although a depreciation charge will usually be made to write off the capital expenditure gradually over time. Depreciation charges are expenses in the profit and loss account.

(b) Capital expenditure on fixed assets results in the appearance of a fixed asset in the balance sheet of the business.

Revenue expenditure is expenditure which is incurred for either of the following reasons.

(a) For the purpose of the trade of the business. This includes expenditure classified as selling and distribution expenses, administration expenses and finance charges.

(b) To maintain the existing earning capacity of fixed assets.

Revenue expenditure is charged to the profit and loss account of a period, if it relates to the trading activity and sales of that particular period.

EXAMPLE: TRADING ITEMS

A business buys ten widgets for £200 (£20 each) and sells eight of them during an accounting period. It has two widgets left at the end of the period. The full £200 is revenue expenditure but only £160 is a cost of goods sold during the period. The remaining £40 (cost of two units) will be included in the balance sheet as a current asset valued at £40.

EXAMPLE: FIXED ASSETS AND MAINTENANCE

A business purchases a building for £30,000. It then adds an extension to the building at a cost of £10,000. The building needs to have a few broken windows mended, its floors polished and some missing roof tiles replaced. These cleaning and maintenance jobs cost £900.

The original purchase (£30,000) and the cost of the extension (£10,000) are capital expenditure, because they are incurred to acquire and then improve a fixed asset. The other costs of £900 are revenue expenditure, because these merely maintain the building and thus the 'earning capacity' of the building.

1.2 Capital and revenue income

Definitions

> **Capital income** is the proceeds from the disposal of fixed assets. The profits (or losses) from the disposal of fixed assets are included in the profit and loss account of a business, for the accounting period in which the disposal takes place.
>
> **Revenue income** is income derived from the following sources:
>
> (a) The sale of trading assets or provision of services;
>
> (b) Interest received from the business's savings.

1.3 Capital transactions

The categorisation of capital and revenue items given above does not mention raising additional capital from the owner(s) of the business, or raising and repaying loans. These are transactions which:

(a) Add to the cash assets of the business, thereby creating a corresponding liability or capital.

(b) When a loan is repaid, reduce the liabilities (loan) and the assets (cash) of the business.

None of these transactions would be reported through the profit and loss account.

1.4 Why is the distinction between capital and revenue items important?

Revenue expenditure results from the **purchase of goods and services** that will:

(a) Be used fully in the accounting period in which they are purchased, and so be a cost or expense in the profit and loss account.

(b) Result in a current asset as at the end of the accounting period because the goods or services have not yet been consumed or made use of. The current asset would be shown in the balance sheet and is not yet a cost or expense in the profit and loss account.

Capital expenditure results in the **purchase or improvement of fixed assets**, which are assets that will provide benefits to the business in more than one accounting period, and which are not acquired with a view to being resold in the normal course of trade. The cost of purchased fixed assets is not charged in full to the profit and loss account of the period in which the purchase occurs. Instead, the fixed asset is gradually depreciated over a number of accounting periods, under the **accruals concept**, so as to match the cost with revenues earned by the asset over time.

Since revenue items and capital items are accounted for in different ways, the correct and consistent calculation of profit for any accounting period depends on the correct and consistent classification of items as revenue or capital.

Activity 1 **(30 minutes)**

State whether each of the following items should be classified as 'capital' or 'revenue' expenditure or income for the purpose of preparing the profit and loss account and the balance sheet of a business.

(a) The purchase of premises on a 100-year lease (leasehold premises).

(b) The annual depreciation of leasehold premises.

(c) Solicitors' fees in connection with the purchase of leasehold premises.

(d) The costs of adding extra memory to a mainframe computer used by the business.

(e) Computer repairs and maintenance costs.

(f) Profit on the disposal of an office building.

(g) Revenue from sales paid for by credit card.

(h) The cost of new machinery.

(i) Customs duty charged on the machinery to its purchaser when imported into the country.

(j) The 'carriage' costs paid by the purchaser of transporting the new machinery from the supplier's factory to its premises.

(k) The cost of installing the new machinery in the purchaser's premises.

(l) The wages of the machine operators.

2 COST OF FIXED ASSETS

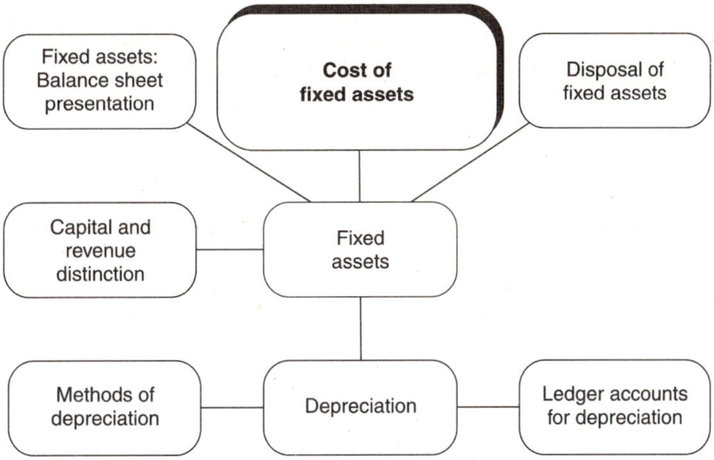

According to FRS 15 *Tangible Fixed Assets* the cost of a fixed asset should include its purchase price and any costs directly attributable to bringing the asset into working condition for its intended use.

Examples of directly attributable costs are:

- **Acquisition costs**, eg stamp duty, import duties
- Cost of **site preparation** and clearance
- Initial **delivery and handling** costs
- **Installation** costs
- **Professional fees** eg legal fees

Any abnormal costs, such as those arising from design error, industrial disputes or idle capacity are not directly attributable costs and therefore should not be capitalised as part of the cost of the asset.

To record the asset's cost, the double entry is very simple:

		£	£
DEBIT	Fixed asset cost	X	
CREDIT	Cash or creditors		X

3 DEPRECIATION

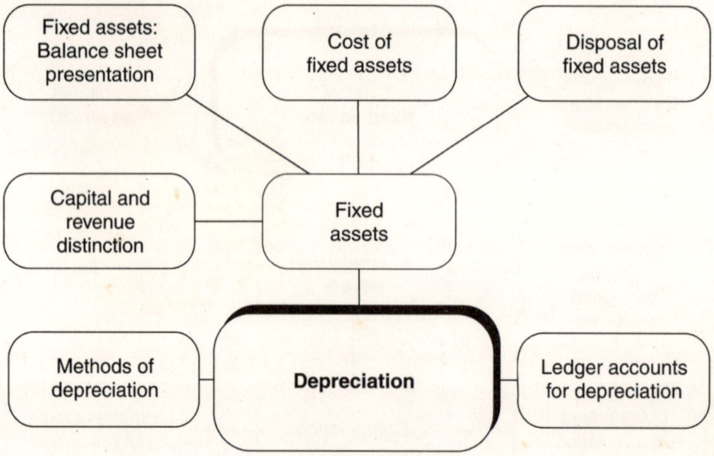

A fixed asset is acquired for use within a business with a view to earning profits. Its life extends over more than one accounting period, and so it earns profits over more than one period. In contrast, a current asset is used and replaced many times within the period eg stock is sold and replaced, debtors increase with sales and decrease with payments received.

With the exception of land held on freehold or very long leasehold, **every fixed asset eventually wears out over time**. Machines, cars and other vehicles, fixtures and fittings, and even buildings do not last for ever. When a business acquires a fixed asset, it will have some idea about how long its useful life will be, and it might decide:

(a) To keep on using the fixed asset until it becomes completely worn out, useless, and worthless.

(b) To dispose of the fixed asset at the end of its useful life, either by selling it as a second-hand item or as scrap.

Since a fixed asset has a cost, and a limited useful life, and its value declines, it follows that a charge should be made in the profit and loss account to reflect the use that is made of the asset by the business. This charge is called **depreciation**.

3.1 What is depreciation?

Suppose that a business buys a machine for £40,000. Its expected life is four years, and at the end of that time it is expected to be worthless.

Since the fixed asset is used to make profits for four years, it would be reasonable to charge the cost of the asset over those four years (perhaps by charging £10,000 per annum) so that at the end of the four years the total cost of £40,000 would have been charged against profits.

Definition

> **Depreciation is a means of spreading the cost of a fixed asset over its useful life**, and so matching the cost against the full period during which it earns profits for the business. Depreciation charges are an example of the application of the accruals concept to calculate profits.

Depreciation has two important aspects.

(a) Depreciation is a **measure of the wearing out** or depletion of a fixed asset through use, time or obsolescence.

(b) Depreciation charges should be **spread fairly** over a fixed asset's life, and so allocated to the accounting periods which are expected to benefit (ie make profits) from the asset's use.

The need to depreciate fixed assets arises from the accruals concept. If money is expended in purchasing an asset then the amount expended must at some time be charged against profits. If the asset is one which contributes to an enterprise's revenue over a number of accounting periods it would be inappropriate to charge any single period (for example, the period in which the asset was acquired) with the whole of the expenditure. Instead, some method must be found of spreading the cost of the asset over its useful economic life.

3.2 The total charge for depreciation: the depreciable amount

Definition

> The total amount to be charged over the life of a fixed asset (**'the depreciable amount'**) is usually its cost less any expected 'residual' sales value or disposal value at the end of the asset's life.

A fixed asset costing £20,000, which has an expected life of five years and an expected residual value of nil, should be depreciated by £20,000 in total over the five year period.

A fixed asset costing £20,000, which has an expected life of five years and an expected residual value of £3,000, should be depreciated by £17,000 in total over the five years.

3.3 Depreciation in the accounts of a business

When a fixed asset is depreciated, two things must be accounted for.

(a) The **charge for depreciation** is a **cost or expense** of the accounting period. Depreciation is an expense in the profit and loss account.

(b) At the same time, the fixed asset is wearing out and diminishing in value, so the value of the fixed asset in the balance sheet must be reduced by the amount of depreciation charged. The balance sheet value of the fixed asset will be its '**net book value**', which is the cost less total depreciation charged in the books of account of the business.

The amount of depreciation will build up (or 'accumulate') over time, as more depreciation is charged in each successive accounting period. This is called **accumulated depreciation**.

EXAMPLE: ACCUMULATED DEPRECIATION AND NET BOOK VALUE

If a fixed asset costing £40,000 has an expected life of four years and an estimated residual value of nil, it might be depreciated by £10,000 per annum.

	Depreciation charge for the year (P & L a/c)	*Accumulated depreciation at end of year*	*Cost of the asset*	*Net book value at end of year*
	(A)	*(B)*	*(C)*	*(C – B)*
	£	£	£	£
At beginning of its life	–	–	40,000	40,000
Year 1	10,000	10,000	40,000	30,000
Year 2	10,000	20,000	40,000	20,000
Year 3	10,000	30,000	40,000	10,000
Year 4	10,000	40,000	40,000	0

So each year £10,000 depreciation is charged as an expense in the profit and loss account. Also each year, the net book value (NBV) recorded in the balance sheet reduces by £10,000 until the NBV reaches the residual value (nil in this case).

3.4 Depreciation is not a cash expense

Depreciation spreads the cost of a fixed asset (less its estimated residual value) over the asset's life. The cash payment for the fixed asset will be made when, or soon after, the asset is purchased. Therefore, annual depreciation of the asset in subsequent years is **not a cash expense.**

For example, a business purchased some shop fittings for £6,000 on 1 July 20X5 and paid for them in cash on that date.

Subsequently, depreciation may be charged at £600 pa for ten years. So each year £600 is deducted from profits and the net book value of the fittings goes down, but no actual cash is being paid. The cash was all paid on 1 July 20X5. So annual depreciation is not a cash expense, but rather an allocation of the original cost to later years.

4 METHODS OF DEPRECIATION

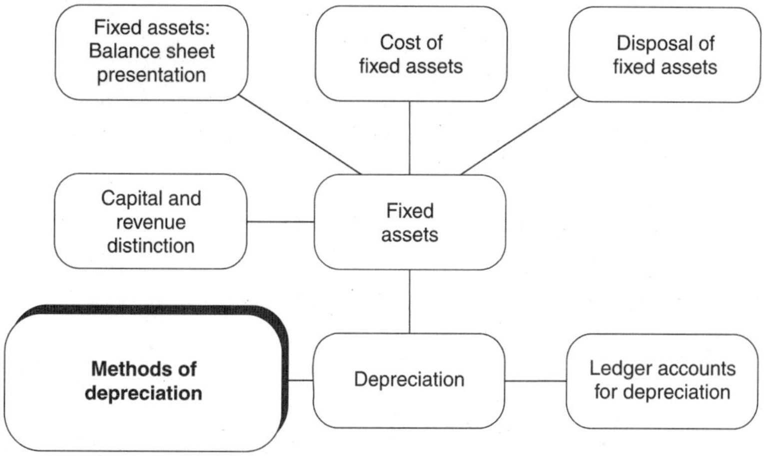

The most common methods of depreciation are:

- Straight line method
- Reducing balance method

4.1 Straight line depreciation

This is the most commonly used method of all. The total depreciable amount is charged in **equal instalments to each accounting period** over the expected useful life of the asset. So the net book value of the fixed asset declines at a steady rate, or in a 'straight line' over time.

The annual depreciation charge is calculated as:

$$\frac{\text{Cost of asset minus residual value}}{\text{Expected useful life of the asset}}$$

EXAMPLE: STRAIGHT LINE DEPRECIATION

(a) A fixed asset costing £20,000 with an estimated life of ten years and no residual value would be depreciated at the rate of:

$$\frac{£20{,}000}{10\text{ years}} = £2{,}000 \text{ per annum}$$

(b) A fixed asset costing £60,000 has an estimated life of five years and a residual value of £7,000. The annual depreciation charge using the straight line method would be:

$$\frac{£(60{,}000 - 7{,}000)}{5\text{ years}} = £10{,}600 \text{ per annum}$$

The net book value of this fixed asset would be:

	After 1 year	*After 2 years*	*After 3 years*	*After 4 years*	*After 5 years*
	£	£	£	£	£
Cost of the asset	60,000	60,000	60,000	60,000	60,000
Accumulated depreciation	10,600	21,200	31,800	42,400	53,000
Net book value	49,400	38,800	28,200	17,600	7,000*

* ie its estimated residual value.

Since the depreciation charge per annum is the same amount every year with the straight line method, it is often convenient to state that depreciation is charged at the rate of x per cent per annum on the cost of the asset. In the example above, the depreciation charge per annum is 10% of cost (ie 10% of £20,000 = £2,000).

The straight line method of depreciation is a fair allocation of the total depreciable amount between the different accounting periods, provided the business enjoys equal benefits from the use of the asset in every period throughout its life. An example of this could be shelving (fixtures and fittings) used in the accounts department.

4.1.1 Assets acquired in the middle of an accounting period

A business can purchase new fixed assets at any time during the course of an accounting period, so it is fair to charge a reduced amount for depreciation in the period when the purchase occurs.

EXAMPLE: ASSETS ACQUIRED IN THE MIDDLE OF AN ACCOUNTING PERIOD

A business which has an accounting year from 1 January to 31 December purchases a new fixed asset on 1 April 20X1, at a cost of £24,000. The expected life of the asset is 4 years, and its residual value is nil. What should the depreciation charge be for 20X1?

The annual depreciation charge will be $\frac{24{,}000}{4 \text{ years}}$ = £6,000 per annum

However, since the asset was acquired on 1 April 20X1, the business has only benefited from the use of the asset for 9 months instead of a full 12 months. It is therefore fair to charge depreciation in 20X1 of only:

9/12 × £6,000 = £4,500

In practice, many businesses ignore the niceties of part-year depreciation, and charge a full year's depreciation on fixed assets in the year of their purchase and/or disposal, regardless of the time of year they were acquired.

4.2 Reducing balance depreciation

The **reducing balance method** of depreciation calculates the depreciation charge in a period as a **fixed percentage of the net book value of the asset at the end of the**

accounting period. This means that the annual depreciation charge declines over the asset's life.

EXAMPLE: REDUCING BALANCE DEPRECIATION

A business purchases a fixed asset at a cost of £10,000. Its expected useful life is 3 years and its estimated residual value is £2,160. The business wishes to use the reducing balance method to depreciate the asset, and calculates that the rate of depreciation should be 40% of the reducing balance (NBV) of the asset. (The method of deciding that 40% is a suitable annual percentage is a problem of mathematics, not accounting, and is not described here.)

The total depreciable amount is £(10,000 – 2,160) = £7,840, but remember that the percentage is applied to the net book value, not to the depreciable amount.

The depreciation charge per annum and the net book value of the asset as at the end of each year will be as follows:

	NBV	*Accumulated depreciation*
	£	£
Asset at cost	10,000	
Depreciation in year 1 (40% × £10,000)	(4,000)	4,000
Net book value at end of year 1	6,000	
Depreciation in year 2		
(40% × £6,000)	(2,400)	2,400
Net book value at end of year 2	3,600	6,400
Depreciation in year 3 (40% × £3,600)	(1,440)	1,440
Net book value at end of year 3	2,160	7,840

With the reducing balance method, the annual charge for depreciation is higher in the earlier years of the asset's life, and lower in the later years. In the example above, the annual charges for years 1, 2 and 3 are £4,000, £2,400 and £1,440 respectively. The reducing balance method, therefore, is used when it is considered fair to allocate a greater proportion of the total depreciable amount to the earlier years and a lower proportion to later years, on the assumption that the benefits obtained by the business from using the asset decline over time. An example of this could be machinery in a factory, where productivity falls as the machine gets older.

4.3 Applying a depreciation method consistently

It is up to the business concerned to decide which method of depreciation to apply to its fixed assets. Once that decision has been made, however, it should not be changed - the chosen method of depreciation should be applied **consistently from year to year**. This is an instance of the consistency concept, which we looked at in Chapter 1.

Similarly, it is up to the business to decide what a sensible life span for a fixed asset should be. Again, once that life span has been chosen, it should not be changed unless something unexpected happens to the fixed asset.

It is permissible for a business to depreciate different categories of fixed assets in different ways. For example, if a business owns three cars, then each car would normally be depreciated in the same way (eg by the straight line method); but another category of fixed asset, say photocopiers, can be depreciated using a different method (eg by the reducing balance method).

Activity 2 **(30 minutes)**

A lorry bought for a business cost £17,000. It is expected to last for five years and then be sold for scrap proceeds of £2,000.

Required

Work out the depreciation to be charged each year under:

(a) The straight line method
(b) The reducing balance method using a rate of 35%

5 LEDGER ACCOUNTS FOR DEPRECIATION

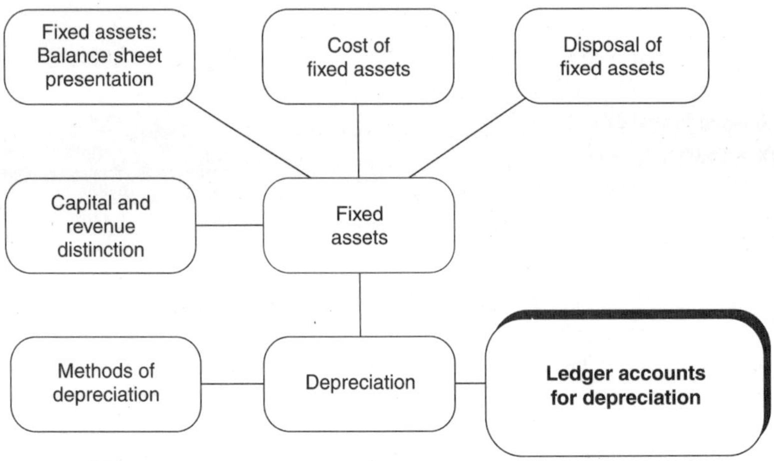

Definition

Accumulated depreciation is the amount set aside as a charge for the wearing out of fixed assets.

There are two basic aspects of accumulated depreciation to remember:

(a) A depreciation charge is made in the **profit and loss account** in each accounting period for every depreciable fixed asset. Nearly all fixed assets are depreciable, the most important exception being freehold land.

(b) The total accumulated depreciation on a fixed asset builds up in the **balance sheet** as the asset gets older. The depreciation accumulates until the fixed asset is fully depreciated.

The ledger accounting entries for depreciation are as follows.

(a) There is an accumulated depreciation account for each separate category of fixed assets, for example, plant and machinery, buildings, fixtures and fittings.

(b) The depreciation charge for an accounting period is a charge against profit. It is an increase in the accumulated depreciation and is accounted for as follows:

DEBIT	P & L account (depreciation expense)
CREDIT	Accumulated depreciation account

with the depreciation charge for the period.

(c) The balance on the account is the **total accumulated depreciation**. This is always a credit balance brought down in the ledger account for depreciation.

(d) The fixed asset cost accounts are unaffected by depreciation. Fixed assets are recorded in these accounts at cost.

(e) In the balance sheet of the business, the total balance on the **accumulated depreciation** account is netted off against the value of **fixed asset cost** accounts (ie fixed assets at cost) to derive the **net book value** of the fixed assets.

EXAMPLE: ACCOUNTING FOR DEPRECIATION

Brian Box set up his own computer software business on 1 March 20X6. He purchased a computer system on credit from a manufacturer, at a cost of £16,000. The system has an expected life of three years and a residual value of £2,500. Using the straight line method of depreciation, the fixed asset cost account, accumulated depreciation account and P & L account (extract) and balance sheet (extract) would be as follows, for each of the next three years ended 28 February 20X7, 20X8 and 20X9.

FIXED ASSET COST – COMPUTER EQUIPMENT

	Date		£	*Date*		£
(a)	1.3.X6	Creditor	16,000	28.2.X7	Balance c/d	16,000
(b)	1.3.X7	Balance b/d	16,000	28.2.X8	Balance c/d	16,000
(c)	1.3.X8	Balance b/d	16,000	28.2.X9	Balance c/d	16,000
(d)	1.3.X9	Balance b/d	16,000			

In theory, the fixed asset has completed its expected useful life. However, until it is sold off or scrapped, the asset will still appear in the balance sheet at cost (less accumulated depreciation) and it should remain in the ledger account for computer equipment until it is eventually disposed of.

ACCUMULATED DEPRECIATION

	Date		£	*Date*		£
(a)	28.2.X7	Balance c/d	4,500	28.2.X7	P & L account	4,500
(b)	28.2.X8	Balance c/d	9,000	1.3.X7	Balance b/d	4,500
				28.2.X8	P & L account	4,500
			9,000			9,000
(c)	28.2.X9	Balance c/d	13,500	1.3.X8	Balance b/d	9,000
				28.2.X9	P & L account	4,500
			13,500			13,500
				1.3.X9	Balance b/d	13,500

The annual depreciation charge is $\frac{(£16,000 - 2,500)}{3 \text{ years}} = £4,500$ pa

At the end of three years, the asset is fully depreciated down to its residual value. If it continues to be used by Brian Box, it will not be depreciated any further.

P & L ACCOUNT (EXTRACT)

	Date		£
(a)	28 Feb 20X7	Depreciation	4,500
(b)	28 Feb 20X8	Depreciation	4,500
(c)	28 Feb 20X9	Depreciation	4,500

BALANCE SHEET (EXTRACT) AS AT 28 FEBRUARY

	20X7	*20X8*	*20X9*
	£	£	£
Computer equipment at cost	16,000	16,000	16,000
Less accumulated depreciation	(4,500)	(9,000)	(13,500)
Net book value	11,500	7,000	2,500

6 DISPOSAL OF FIXED ASSETS

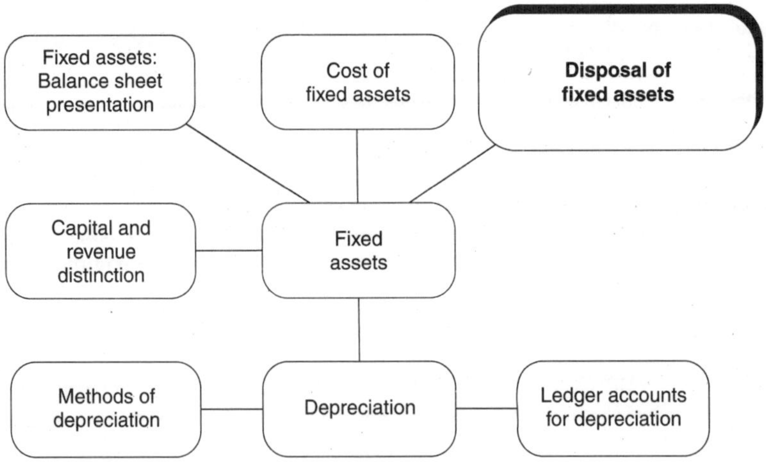

6.1 The disposal of fixed assets

A business may sell off a fixed asset long before its useful life has ended, eg to get more a more up to date model.

Whenever a business sells something, it makes a profit or a loss. So when fixed assets are disposed of, there is a profit or loss on disposal. This is a **capital gain** (income) or a **capital loss** (expense).

These gains or losses are reported in the profit and loss account of the business. They are commonly referred to as '**profit on disposal of fixed assets**' or '**loss on disposal**'.

6.2 The principles behind calculating the profit or loss on disposal

The profit or loss on the disposal of a fixed asset is the difference between:

(a) The net book value of the asset at the time of its disposal.
(b) Its net sale price, which is the price received less any costs of making the sale.

A profit is made when the net sale price exceeds the net book value, and a loss is made when the net sale price is less than the net book value.

EXAMPLE: DISPOSAL OF A FIXED ASSET

A business purchased a fixed asset on 1 January 20X1 for £25,000. It had an estimated life of six years and an estimated residual value of £7,000. The asset was eventually sold after three years on 1 January 20X4 to another trader who paid £17,500 for it.

What was the profit or loss on disposal, assuming that the business uses the straight line method for depreciation?

Solution

$$\text{Annual depreciation} = \frac{£(25{,}000 - 7{,}000)}{6 \text{ years}}$$

$$= £3{,}000 \text{ per annum}$$

	£
Cost of asset	25,000
Less accumulated depreciation (3 × £3,000)	(9,000)
Net book value at date of disposal	16,000
Sale price	17,500
Profit on disposal	1,500

This profit will be shown in the profit and loss account of the business, where it will be an item of other income added to the gross profit as shown below.

	£
Gross profit	30,000
Profit on disposal of fixed assets	1,500
	31,500
Expenses (say)	(21,500)
Net profit	10,000

Activity 3 **(15 minutes)**

A business purchased a machine on 1 July 20X1 for £39,000. The machine had an estimated residual value of £3,000 and a life of eight years. The machine was sold for £18,600 on 31 December 20X4. To make the sale, the business had to incur dismantling costs and costs of transporting the machine to the buyer's premises of £1,200.

The business uses the straight line method of depreciation. What was the profit or loss on disposal of the machine?

6.3 The disposal of fixed assets: ledger accounting entries

A profit on disposal is an item of 'other income' in the P & L account, and a loss on disposal is an item of expense in the P & L account.

It is customary in ledger accounting to record the disposal of fixed assets in a **disposal of fixed assets** account.

(a) The profit or loss on disposal is the difference between:

- (i) The net sale price of the asset (if any) and
- (ii) The net book value of the asset at the time of disposal.

(b) The relevant items which must appear in the disposal of fixed assets account are therefore:

- (i) The cost of the asset.
- (ii) The accumulated depreciation up to the date of sale.
- (iii) The net sale price of the asset.

(c) The ledger accounting entries are:

(i) DEBIT Disposal of fixed asset account
CREDIT Fixed asset cost account

With the cost of the asset disposed of.

(ii) DEBIT Accumulated depreciation account
CREDIT Disposal of fixed asset account

With the accumulated depreciation on the asset as at the date of sale.

(iii) DEBIT Debtor account or cash book
CREDIT Disposal of fixed asset account

With the net sale price of the asset. The sale is therefore not recorded in a sales account, but in the disposal of fixed asset account itself.

(iv) The balance on the disposal account is the profit or loss on disposal and the corresponding double entry is recorded in the P & L account itself.

EXAMPLE: DISPOSAL OF ASSETS: LEDGER ACCOUNTING ENTRIES

A business has machinery that cost £110,000. Its policy is to charge depreciation at 20% per annum straight line. Accumulated depreciation stands at £70,000. The business now sells for £19,000 a machine which it purchased exactly two years ago for £30,000.

Show the relevant ledger entries.

Solution

PLANT AND MACHINERY COST ACCOUNT

	£		£
Balance b/d	110,000	Plant disposals account	30,000
		Balance c/d	80,000
	110,000		110,000
Balance b/d	80,000		

PLANT AND MACHINERY ACCUMULATED DEPRECIATION

	£		£
Plant disposals (20% of £30,000 for 2 years)	12,000	Balance b/d	70,000
Balance c/d	58,000		
	70,000		70,000
		Balance b/d	58,000

PLANT DISPOSALS

	£		£
Plant and machinery cost account	30,000	Accumulated depreciation	12,000
		Cash	19,000
Profit and loss a/c (profit on disposal)	1,000		
	31,000		31,000

Check:

	£
Asset at cost	30,000
Accumulated depreciation at time of disposal	12,000
Net book value at time of disposal	18,000
Sale price	19,000
Profit on sale	1,000

7 FIXED ASSETS: BALANCE SHEET PRESENTATION

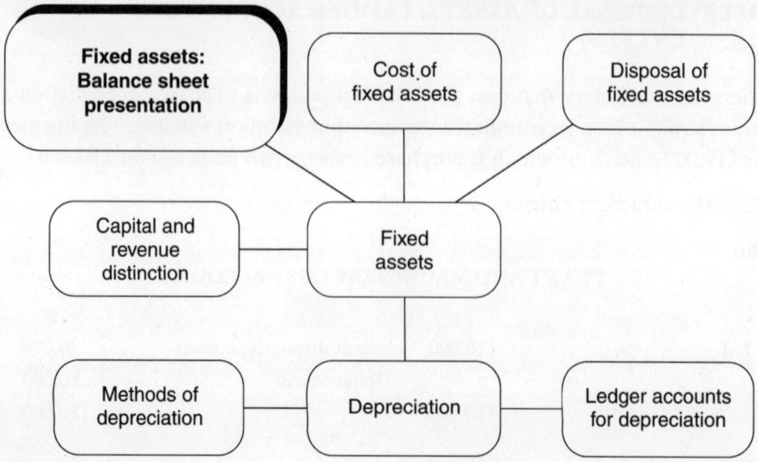

7.1 The fixed assets note

Notes to the financial statements must show, for each class of fixed assets, an analysis of the movements of both cost and accumulated depreciation. The following format (notional figures) is commonly used to disclose fixed assets movements.

	Total	*Land and buildings*	*Plant and machinery*
	£	£	£
Cost			
At 1 January 20X4	62,000	52,000	10,000
Additions in year	4,000	–	4,000
Disposals in year	(1,000)	–	(1,000)
At 31 December 20X4	65,000	52,000	13,000
Accumulated depreciation			
At 1 January 20X4	16,000	10,000	6,000
Charge for year	4,000	1,000	3,000
Eliminated on disposals	(500)	–	(500)
At 31 December 20X4	19,500	11,000	8,500
Net book value			
At 31 December 20X4	45,500	41,000	4,500
At 1 January 20X4	46,000	42,000	4,000

On the face of the balance sheet, the presentation is as follows.

BALANCE SHEET (EXTRACT) AS AT 31 DECEMBER

	Note	*20X4*	*20X3*
		£	£
Fixed assets	1	45,500	46,000

Activity 4 **(1 hour)**

Annette Book is the financial controller of a medium-sized publishing company. The managing director, Eddie Torial, is a man of sound literary judgement and marketing instinct, but has no accountancy training. Annette has received from him the following note.

'I understand that we have to provide "depreciation" on all our fixed assets except land. This is going to come out of our profit, so there has to be a reason for it. Could you answer the following questions?'

(a) Why do we provide depreciation?

(b) What exactly is net book value? (I think I know roughly what it is.)

(c) Why do we sometimes use the reducing balance method and not the straight line method?

Required

Write Annette's reply to Eddie, addressing each of the above queries.

Chapter roundup

- **Capital expenditure** is expenditure which results in the acquisition of fixed assets.

  Revenue expenditure is expenditure incurred for the purpose of the trade or to maintain fixed assets.

- **Depreciation** is charged in the profit and loss account each year in respect of each fixed asset, so as to match the cost of the asset with the profit it generates over several accounting periods.

- Each year's depreciation charge is collected together as **accumulated depreciation**, a credit balance which is set off against the fixed asset's cost in each year's balance sheet.

- When a fixed asset is **sold**, there is likely to be a **profit or loss on disposal**. This is the difference between the net sale price of the asset and its net book value at the time of disposal.

Quick quiz

1 Which of the following statements regarding depreciation is correct?

A All fixed assets must be depreciated.
B Straight line depreciation is the most appropriate method of depreciation.
C The amount of deprecation charged each year decreases over time.
D Depreciation charges must be based upon the depreciable amount.

2 What is an asset's net book value?

A Its cost less annual depreciation
B Its cost less accumulated depreciation
C Its net realisable value
D Its replacement value

3 Give two common depreciation methods.

4 A fixed asset (cost £10,000, depreciation £7,500) is scrapped for £3,500. The profit and loss account will include

A A loss on disposal £1,000
B A profit on disposal £1,000
C A loss on disposal of £3,500
D A profit on disposal £3,500

Answers to quick quiz

1 D Correct.

A Incorrect, some fixed assets are not depreciated eg land.

B Incorrect, management should choose the most appropriate method.

C Incorrect, as this only applies to the reducing balance method; with straight line depreciation, the amount is constant in each year.

2 B Its cost less accumulated depreciation.

3 Straight-line and reducing balance.

4 B

	£
Net book value at disposal	2,500
Net sale price	3,500
Profit	1,000

Answers to activities

1 (a) Capital expenditure.

(b) Depreciation of a fixed asset is revenue expenditure.

(c) The legal fees associated with the purchase of a property may be added to the purchase price and classified as capital expenditure. The cost of the leasehold premises in the balance sheet of the business will then include the legal fees.

(d) Capital expenditure (enhancing an existing fixed asset).

(e) Revenue expenditure.

(f) Capital income (net of the costs of disposal).

(g) Revenue income.

(h) Capital expenditure.

(i) If customs duties are borne by the purchaser of the fixed asset, they may be added to the cost of the machinery and classified as capital expenditure.

(j) Similarly, if carriage costs are paid for by the purchaser of the fixed asset, they may be included in the cost of the fixed asset and classified as capital expenditure.

(k) Installation costs of a fixed asset are also added to the fixed asset's cost and classified as capital expenditure.

(l) Revenue expenditure.

2 (a) Under the straight line method, depreciation for each of the five years is:

$$\frac{£17,000 - £2,000}{5} = £3,000 \text{ pa } (5 \times £3,000 = £15,000).$$

(b) Under the reducing balance method, depreciation for each of the five years is:

Year	*Depreciation*		£
1	35% × £17,000	=	5,950
2	35% × (£17,000 – £5,950) = 35% × £11,050	=	3,868
3	35% × (£11,050 – £3,868) = 35% × £7,182	=	2,514
4	35% × (£7,182 – £2,514) = 35% × £4,668	=	1,634
5	Balance to bring book value down to £2,000 = £4,668 – £1,634 – £2,000	=	1,034
			15,000

3 Depreciation expense $\frac{£(39,000 - 3,000)}{8}$ = £4,500 per annum

In 20X1 only six months depreciation was charged, because the asset was purchased six months into the year.

	£	£
Fixed asset at cost		39,000
Depreciation in 20X1 (6/12 × £4,500)	2,250	
20X2, 20X3 and 20X4 (3 × £4,500)	13,500	
Accumulated depreciation		(15,750)
Net book value at date of disposal		23,250
Sale proceeds	18,600	
Costs incurred in making the sale	(1,200)	
Net sale proceeds		(17,400)
Loss on disposal		(5,850)

This loss will be shown as an expense in the business's profit and loss account. It is a capital expense, not a trading loss, and therefore should not be part of the calculation of gross profit.

4 To: Eddie Torial, Managing Director
From: Annette Book
Date: 5 March 20X9
Subject: Depreciation

(a) The accounts of a business try to recognise that the cost of a fixed asset is gradually consumed as the asset wears out. This is done by gradually writing off the asset's cost in the profit and loss account over several accounting periods. This process is known as depreciation, and is an example of the accruals concept. FRS 15 *Tangible Fixed Assets* requires that depreciation should be allocated to charge against income a fair proportion of cost or valuation of the asset to each accounting period expected to benefit from its use.

With regard to the accruals concept, it is fair that the profits should be reduced by the depreciation charge; this is not an arbitrary exercise. Depreciation is not, as is sometime supposed, an attempt to set aside funds to purchase new fixed assets when required. Depreciation is not generally provided on freehold land because it does not 'wear out' (unless it is held for mining etc).

(b) In simple terms the net book value of an asset is the cost of the asset less its 'accumulated depreciation', that is all depreciation charged so far. It should be emphasised that the main purpose of charging depreciation is to ensure that profits are fairly reported. Thus depreciation is concerned with the profit and loss account rather than the balance sheet. In consequence the net book value figure in the balance sheet can be quite arbitrary. In particular, it does not necessarily bear any relation to the market value of an asset and is of little use for planning and decision making.

An obvious example of the disparity between net book value and market value is found in the case of buildings, which may be worth more than ten times as much as their net book value.

(c) The reducing balance method of depreciation is used instead of the straight line method when it is considered fair to allocate a greater proportion of the total depreciable amount to the earlier years and a lower proportion to the later years, on the assumption that the benefits obtained by the business from using the asset decline over time.

In favour of this method it may be argued that it links the depreciation charge to the costs of maintaining and running the asset. In the early years these costs are low and the depreciation charge is high, while in later years this situation is reversed.

Chapter 6:
STOCK

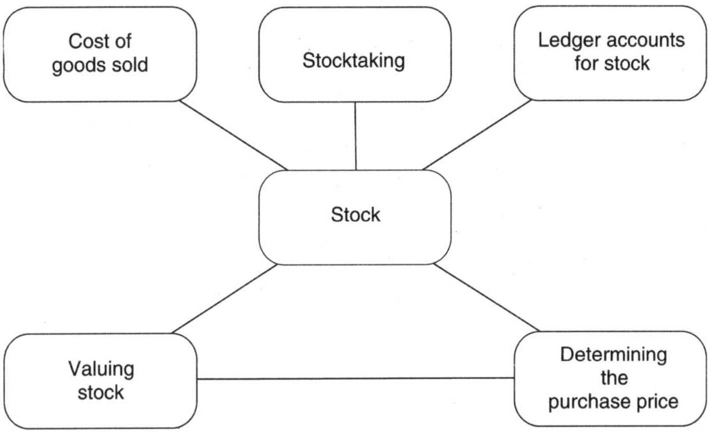

Introduction

Stock is one of the most important assets in a company's balance sheet, and it also appears in the profit and loss account.

So far you have come across stock just as the first current asset in a simple balance sheet. Here we will look at the calculation of the cost of goods sold in the profit and loss account. This is an important figure which is deducted from sales to give the gross profit. The cost of goods sold includes items purchased in the year, plus stock held at the start of the year, **but stock held at the year-end must be excluded.**

This chapter also explores the **difficulties of valuing stock.**

Your objectives

After completing this chapter you should be able to:

1. Calculate the cost of goods sold, and hence the business's gross profit.
2. Identify the key issues regarding stocktaking
3. Understand that stock should be valued at the lower of cost and net realisable value
4. Determine the cost of stock using FIFO and AVCO
5. Account for opening and closing stocks

1 COST OF GOODS SOLD

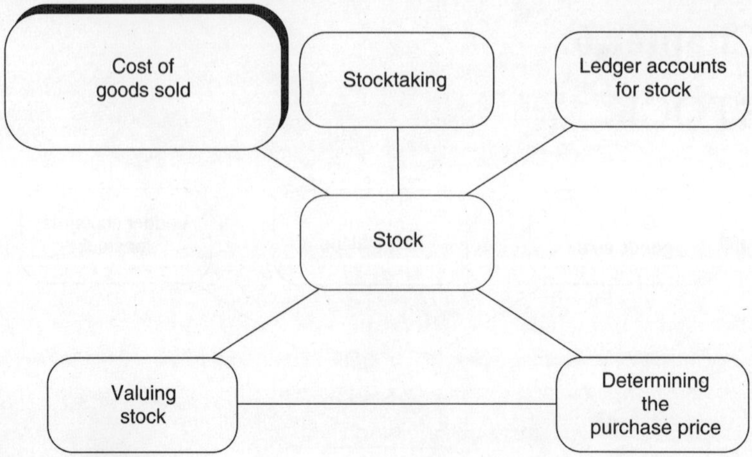

Definition

Cost of goods sold: Opening stock + purchases – closing stock.

1.1 Unsold goods in stock at the end of an accounting period

Goods might be unsold at the end of an accounting period and so still be **held in stock** at the end of the period. The purchase cost of these goods **should not be included in the cost of goods sold** in the period, which is the figure deducted from sales to arrive at gross profit.

EXAMPLE: CLOSING STOCK

Perry P Louis, trading as the Umbrella Shop, ends his financial year on 30 September each year. On 1 October 20X4 he had no goods in stock. During the year to 30 September 20X5, he purchased 30,000 umbrellas costing £60,000 from umbrella wholesalers and suppliers. He resold the umbrellas for £5 each, and sales for the year amounted to £100,000 (20,000 umbrellas). At 30 September there were 10,000 unsold umbrellas left in stock, valued at £2 each.

What was Perry P Louis's gross profit for the year?

Solution

Perry P Louis purchased 30,000 umbrellas, but only sold 20,000. Purchase costs of £60,000 and sales of £100,000 do not relate to the same quantity of goods.

The gross profit for the year should be calculated by 'matching' the sales value of the 20,000 umbrellas sold with the cost of those 20,000 umbrellas. The cost of sales in this example is therefore the cost of purchases minus the cost of goods in stock at the year end.

	£	£
Sales (20,000 units)		100,000
Purchases (30,000 units)	60,000	
Less closing stock (10,000 units @ £2)	(20,000)	
Cost of sales (20,000 units)		(40,000)
Gross profit		60,000

EXAMPLE: OPENING AND CLOSING STOCK

The Umbrella Shop's next accounting year runs from 1 October 20X5 to 30 September 20X6. During the course of this year, Perry P Louis purchased 40,000 umbrellas at a total cost of £95,000. During the year he sold 45,000 umbrellas for £230,000. At 30 September 20X6 he had 5,000 umbrellas left in stock, which had cost £12,000.

What was his gross profit for the year?

Solution

In this accounting year, Perry purchased 40,000 umbrellas for £100,000 to add to the 10,000 he already had in stock at the start of the year. He sold the opening stock, plus a further 35,000, for £5.50 each, leaving 5,000 umbrellas in stock at the year end. Once again, gross profit should be calculated by matching the value of 45,000 units of sales with the cost of those 45,000 units.

The cost of sales is the value of the 10,000 umbrellas in stock at the beginning of the year, plus the cost of the 40,000 umbrellas purchased, less the value of the 5,000 umbrellas in stock at the year end.

We can calculate the gross profit using a trading account.

THE UMBRELLA SHOP
TRADING ACCOUNT FOR YEAR ENDED 30 SEPTEMBER 20X6

	£	£
Sales (45,000 units @ £5.50)		247,500
Opening stock (10,000 units @ £2*)	20,000	
Add purchases (40,000 units @ £2.50)	120,000	
	120,000	
Less closing stock (5,000 units @ £2.50)	(12,500)	
Cost of sales (45,000 units)		(107,500)
Gross profit		140,000

*Taken from the closing stock value of the previous accounting year.

1.2 The cost of goods sold

The cost of goods sold is found by applying the following formula.

	£
Opening stock value	X
Add cost of purchases (or, in the case of a manufacturing company, the cost of production)	X
	X
Less closing stock value	(X)
Equals cost of goods sold	X

In other words, to match 'sales' and the 'cost of goods sold', it is necessary to adjust the cost of goods manufactured or purchased to allow for increases or reduction in stock levels during the period.

Hopefully you will agree that the 'formula' above is logical. You should learn it, because it is fundamental among the principles of accounting.

Test your knowledge of the formula with the following activity.

Activity 1 **(15 minutes)**

On 1 January 20X6, the Grand Union Food Stores had goods in stock valued at £6,000. During 20X6 its proprietor, who ran the shop, purchased supplies costing £50,000. Sales for the year to 31 December 20X6 amounted to £80,000. The cost of goods in stock at 31 December 20X6 was £12,500.

Calculate the gross profit for the year by producing a trading account.

1.3 The cost of carriage inwards and outwards

'Carriage' refers to the **cost of transporting purchased goods** from the supplier to the premises of the business which has bought them. Someone has to pay for these delivery costs: sometimes the supplier pays, and sometimes the purchaser pays. When the purchaser pays, the cost to the purchaser is carriage inwards (**into** the business). When the supplier pays, there is no cost to the purchaser. The cost to the supplier is known as carriage outwards (**out of** the business).

The **cost of carriage inwards** is usually added to the **cost of purchases,** and is therefore included in the **trading account**.

(The **cost of carriage outwards** incurred by a business delivering goods to a customer is a **selling and distribution expense** in the **profit and loss account**.)

EXAMPLE: CARRIAGE INWARDS AND CARRIAGE OUTWARDS

Gwyn Tring, trading as Clickety Clocks, imports and resells cuckoo clocks and grandfather clocks. He must pay for the costs of delivering the clocks from his supplier in Switzerland to his shop in Wales.

He resells the clocks to other traders throughout the country, paying the costs of carriage for the consignments from his business premises to his customers.

On 1 July 20X5, he had clocks in stock valued at £17,000. During the year to 30 June 20X6 he purchased more clocks at a cost of £75,000. Carriage inwards amounted to £2,000. Sales for the year were £162,100. Other expenses of the business amounted to £56,000, excluding carriage outwards which was £2,500. Gwyn Tring took drawings of £20,000 from the business during the course of the year. The value of the goods in stock at the year end was £15,400.

Required

Prepare the full profit and loss account of Clickety Clocks for the year ended 30 June 20X6, clearly showing the business's gross and net profit.

SOLUTION

CLICKETY CLOCKS
PROFIT AND LOSS ACCOUNT FOR THE YEAR ENDED 30 JUNE 20X6

	£	£
Sales		162,100
Opening stock	17,000	
Purchases	75,000	
Carriage inwards	2,000	
	94,000	
Less closing stock	(15,400)	
Cost of goods sold		(78,600)
Gross profit		83,500
Carriage outwards	2,500	
Other expenses	56,000	
		(58,500)
Net profit		25,000

1.4 Goods written off or written down

A trader might be unable to sell all the goods that he purchases, because a number of things might happen to the goods before they can be sold. For example:

(a) Goods might be lost or stolen.

(b) Goods might be damaged, and so become worthless. Such damaged goods might be thrown away.

(c) Goods might become obsolete or out of fashion. These might have to be thrown away, or possibly sold off at a very low price in a clearance sale.

When goods are **lost, stolen or thrown away** as worthless, the business will make a loss on those goods because their **'sales value' will be nil.**

Similarly, when goods lose value because they have become **obsolete** or out of fashion, the business will **make a loss** if their clearance sales value is less than their cost. For example, if goods which originally cost £500 are now obsolete and could only be sold for £150, the business would suffer a loss of £350 on the sale.

If, at the end of an accounting period, a business still has goods in stock which are either worthless or worth less than their original cost, the value of the stocks should be **written down** to:

(a) Nothing, if they are worthless.
(b) Or their net realisable value, if this is less than their original cost.

This means that the loss will be reported as soon as the loss is foreseen, even if the goods have not yet been thrown away or sold off at a cheap price. This is an application of the prudence concept which we looked at in Chapter 1.

The costs of stock written off or written down do not cause any problems in calculating the gross profit of a business, because the cost of goods sold includes the cost of stocks written off or written down, as the following example shows.

EXAMPLE: STOCKS WRITTEN OFF AND WRITTEN DOWN

Lucas Wagg, trading as Fairlock Fashions, ends his financial year on 31 March. At 1 April 20X5 he had goods in stock valued at £8,800. During the year to 31 March 20X6, he purchased goods costing £48,000. Fashion goods which cost £2,100 were still held in stock at 31 March 20X6, and Lucas Wagg believes that these can only now be sold at a sale price of £400. The goods still held in stock at 31 March 20X6 (including the fashion goods) had an original purchase cost of £7,600. Sales for the year were £81,400.

Required

Calculate the gross profit of Fairlock Fashions for the year ended 31 March 20X6.

SOLUTION

Initial calculation of closing stock values:

	At cost	*Realisable value*	*Amount written down*
	£	£	£
Fashion goods	2,100	400	1,700
Other goods (balancing figure)	5,500	5,500	
	7,600	5,900	1,700

FAIRLOCK FASHIONS
TRADING ACCOUNT FOR THE YEAR ENDED 31 MARCH 20X6

	£	£
Sales		81,400
Value of opening stock	8,800	
Purchases	48,000	
	56,800	
Less closing stock (including fashion goods written down)	(5,900)	
Cost of goods sold		(50,900)
Gross profit		30,500

Activity 2 **(5 minutes)**

Gross profit for 20X7 can be calculated from:

A Purchases in 20X7, plus stock at 31 December 20X7, less stock at 1 January 20X7

B Purchases in 20X7, less stock at 31 December 20X7, plus stock at 1 January 20X7

C Cost of goods sold during 20X7, plus sales during 20X7

D Net profit for 20X7, plus expenses for 20X7

2 STOCKTAKING

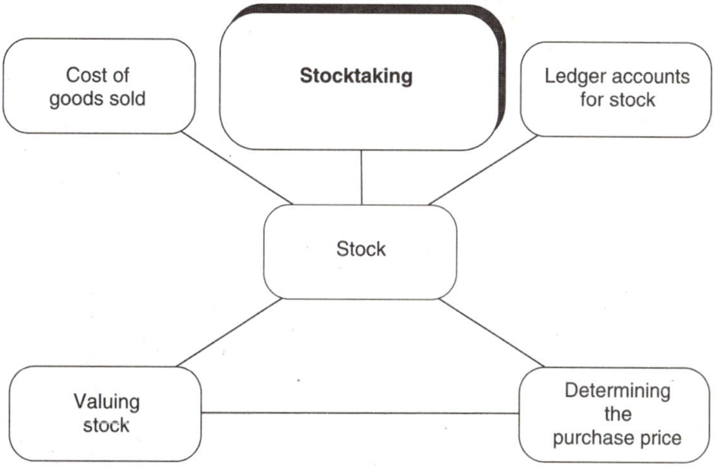

Definition

A **stocktake** is a means of physically counting the stock still held.

Business trading is a continuous activity, but financial statements must be drawn up at a particular date. In preparing a balance sheet it is necessary to '**freeze**' the activity of a business so as to determine its assets and liabilities at a given moment. This includes establishing the quantities of stocks on hand, which can create problems.

A business buys stocks continually during its trading operations and either sells the goods onwards to customers or incorporates them as raw materials in manufactured products. This constant movement of stocks makes it difficult to establish what exactly is held at any precise moment.

In simple cases, when a business holds easily counted and relatively small amounts of stock, quantities of stocks on hand at the balance sheet date can be determined by physically counting them in a **stocktake**.

The continuous nature of trading activity may cause a problem in that stock movements will not necessarily cease during the time that the physical stocktake is in progress. Two possible solutions are:

(a) To **close down** the business while the count takes place; or

(b) To keep **detailed records** of stock movements during the course of the stocktake.

Closing down the business for a short period for a stocktake (eg over a weekend or at Christmas) is considerably **easier** than trying to keep detailed records of stock movements during a stocktake. So most businesses prefer that method unless they happen to keep detailed records of stock movements anyway (for example, because they wish to keep strict control on stock movements).

In more complicated cases, where a business holds considerable quantities of varied stock, an alternative approach to establishing stock quantities is to maintain **continuous stock records**. This means that a file is kept for every item of stock, showing receipts and issues from stores, and a running total. A few stock items are counted each day to make sure their files are correct – this is called a 'continuous' stocktake because it is spread out over the year rather than completed in one stocktake at a designated time.

One obstacle is overcome once a business has established how much stock is on hand. But another problem immediately raises its head. What **value** should the business place on those stocks?

3 VALUING STOCK

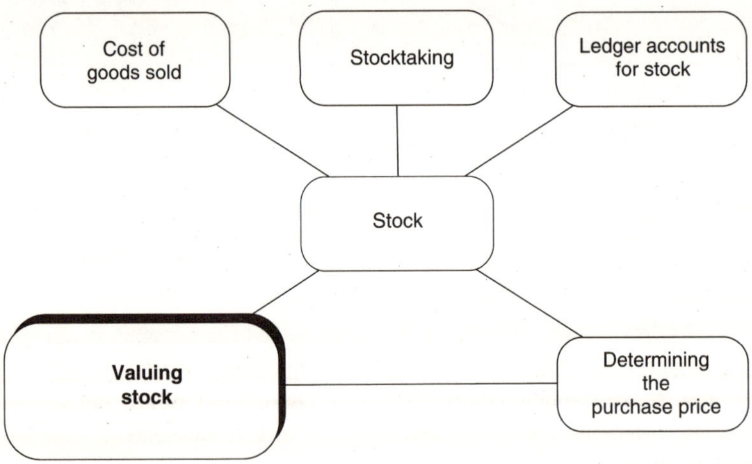

There are **several methods** which, in theory, might be used for the valuation of stock items.

(a) Stocks might be valued at their **historical cost** (ie the cost at which they were originally bought).

(b) Stocks might be valued at their **expected selling price**.

(c) Stocks might be valued at their expected selling price, less any costs still to be incurred in getting them ready for sale and then selling them. This amount is referred to as the **net realisable value** (NRV) of the stocks.

The use of selling prices in stock valuation is **ruled out** because this would create a profit for the business before the stock has been sold.

EXAMPLE: VALUING STOCK AT SELLING PRICE

Suppose that a trader buys two items of stock, each costing £100. He can sell them for £140 each, but in the accounting period we shall consider, he has only sold one of them. The other is closing stock in hand.

Since only one item has been sold, you might think it is common sense that profit ought to be £40. But if closing stock is valued at selling price, profit would be £80 – ie profit would be taken on the closing stock as well.

	£	£
Sales		140
Opening stock		
Purchases (2 × 100)	200	
	200	
Less closing stock (at selling price)	140	
Cost of sale		60
Profit		80

This would contradict the accounting concept of prudence – to claim a profit before the item has actually been sold.

The same objection **usually** applies to the use of NRV in stock valuation. Say that the item purchased for £100 requires £5 of further expenditure in getting it ready for sale and then selling it (eg £5 of processing costs and distribution costs). If its expected selling price is £140, its NRV is £(140-5) = £135. To value it at £135 in the balance sheet would still be to anticipate a £35 profit.

We are left with **historical cost** as the normal basis of stock valuation. **The only time when historical cost is not used is where the prudence concept requires a lower value to be used.**

EXAMPLE CONTINUED: VALUING STOCK AT NRV

Staying with the above example, suppose that the market in this kind of product suddenly slumps and the item's expected selling price is only £90. The item's NRV is then £(90 – 5) = £85 and the business has in effect made a loss of £15 (£100 – £85). The prudence concept requires that losses should be recognised as soon as they are foreseen. This can be achieved by valuing the stock item in the balance sheet at its NRV of £85.

3.1 The basic rule: valuing stock at the lower of cost and NRV

The argument developed above suggests that the rule to follow is that stocks should be valued at cost or, if lower, net realisable value. The accounting treatment of stock is governed by an accounting standard, SSAP 9 *Stocks and Long-term Contracts*, developed to remove subjectivity and to enhance comparability of financial statements. SSAP 9 states that **stock should be valued at the lower of cost and net realisable value**. This is an important rule and one which you should learn by heart.

3.2 Applying the basic valuation rule

If a business has many stock items on hand the comparison of cost and NRV should theoretically be carried out for each item separately. It is not sufficient to compare the total cost of all stock items with their total NRV. An example will show why.

EXAMPLE: SEPARATE VALUATION OF STOCK LINES

Suppose a business has four items of stock on hand at the end of its accounting period. Their cost and NRVs are as follows.

Stock item	*Cost*	*NRV*	*Valuation: lower of cost/NRV*
	£	£	£
1	27	32	27
2	14	8	8
3	43	55	43
4	29	40	29
	113	135	107

It would be incorrect to compare total cost (£113) with total NRV (£135) and to state stocks at £113 in the balance sheet. The company can foresee a loss of £6 on item 2 and this should be recognised. If the four items are taken together in total the loss on item 2 is masked by the anticipated profits on the other items. By performing the cost/NRV comparison for each item separately the prudent valuation of £107 can be derived. This is the value which should appear in the balance sheet.

Activity 3 **(10 minutes)**

From the following figures, calculate the figure for stock valuation item by item.

Stock at 31 December 20X7		
Item	**Cost**	**Net realisable value**
1	560	660
2	880	740
3	780	960
4	340	500
5	420	620
6	800	700
7	1,720	1,200
8	1,140	1,320
9	1,540	1,980

So have we now solved the problem of how a business should value its stocks? It seems that all the business has to do is to choose the lower of cost and net realisable value. This is true as far as it goes, but there is one further problem, perhaps not so easy to foresee: for a given item of stock, **what was** the **cost**?

4 DETERMINING THE PURCHASE PRICE

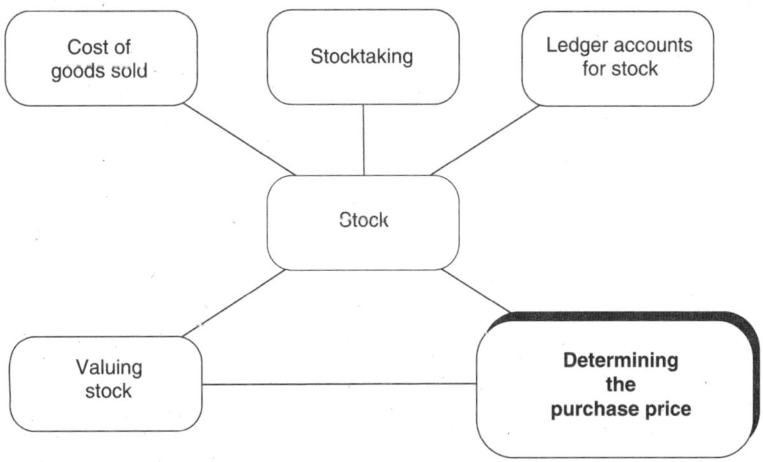

Stock may be **raw materials** or **components** or **goods for resale** bought from suppliers, **finished goods** which have been made by the business but not yet sold, or work in the process of production, but only part-completed (this type of stock is called **work in progress** or WIP). It will simplify matters, however, if we just think about the historical cost of items bought from suppliers, which ought to be their purchase price.

A business may be continually purchasing consignments of a particular item. As each consignment is received from suppliers they are stored on the appropriate shelf, where they will be mingled with previous consignments. When the storekeeper issues items to production or despatch he will simply pull out from the shelf the nearest items to hand, which may have arrived in the latest consignment, or in an earlier consignment, or in several different consignments. Our concern is to devise a costing technique, a rule of thumb which we can use to attribute a cost to each of the items issued from stores.

There are two main techniques, known as FIFO and AVCO.

Definitions

(a) **FIFO (first in, first out)**. Using this technique, we assume that items are used in the order in which they are received from suppliers. The items issued are deemed to have formed part of the oldest consignment still unused and are costed accordingly.

(b) **Average cost (AVCO)**. As purchase prices change with each new consignment, the average price of items in the bin is constantly changed. Each item in the bin at any one moment is assumed to have been purchased at the average price of all items in the bin at that time.

FIFO or AVCO are used for the balance sheet valuation of stock, but the terms refer to **costing techniques** only. The actual items can be used in any order.

To illustrate the two costing methods, the following transactions will be used in each case:

TRANSACTIONS DURING MAY 20X3

	Quantity	*Unit cost*	*Total cost*
	Units	£	£
Opening balance 1 May	100	2.00	200
Receipts 3 May	400	2.10	840
Issues 4 May	200		
Receipts 9 May	300	2.12	636
Issues 11 May	400		
Receipts 18 May	100	2.40	240
Issues 20 May	100		
Closing balance 31 May	200		
			1,916

'Receipts' mean items are received into store and 'issues' mean the issue of goods from store.

The problem is to put a valuation on two things:

(a) The issues of items
(b) The closing stock

How would issues and closing stock be valued using:

(a) FIFO?
(b) AVCO?

4.1 FIFO (first in, first out)

FIFO assumes that items are **issued out of stock in the order in which they were delivered into stock**, ie issues are costed at the cost of the earliest delivery remaining in stock.

EXAMPLE: FIFO COSTING

The cost of issues and closing stock value, using FIFO would be as follows (note that o/s stands for opening stock).

Date of issue	*Quantity*	*Value issued*	*Cost of issues*	
	Units	£	£	£
4 May	200	100 o/s at £2	200	
		100 at £2.10	210	
				410
11 May	400	300 at £2.10	630	
		100 at £2.12	212	
				842
20 May	100	100 at £2.12		212
				1,464
Closing stock value	200	100 at £2.12	212	
		100 at £2.40	240	
				452
				1,916

Note that the cost of items issued plus the value of closing stock equals the cost of purchases plus the value of opening stock (£1,916).

4.2 AVCO (Average cost)

There are various ways in which average costs may be used in costing stock issues. The most common (cumulative weighted average pricing) is illustrated below.

The **cumulative weighted average pricing method** calculates a weighted average price for all units in stock. Issues are costed at this average cost, and the balance of stock remaining has the same unit valuation.

A new weighted average price is calculated whenever a new delivery of items into store is received. This is the key feature of cumulative weighted average pricing.

EXAMPLE: AVCO COSTS

Issue costs and closing stock values would be as follows.

Date	*Received*	*Issued*	*Balance*	*Total stock value*	*Unit cost*	*Price of issue*
	Units	Units	Units	£	£	£
Opening stock			100	200	2.00	
3 May	400			840	2.10	
			500	1,040	2.08 *	
4 May		200		(416)	2.08 **	416
			300	624	2.08	
9 May	300			636	2.12	
			600	1,260	2.10 *	
11 May		400		(840)	2.10 **	840
			200	420	2.10	
18 May	100			240	2.40	
			300	660	2.20 *	
20 May		100		(220)	2.20 **	220
						1,476
Closing stock value			200	440	2.20	440
						1,916

* A new unit cost of stock is calculated whenever a new receipt of items occurs.

** Whenever stocks are issued, the unit value of the items issued is the current weighted average cost per unit at the time of the issue.

For this method too, the cost of materials issued plus the value of closing stock equals the cost of purchases plus the value of opening stock (£1,916).

4.3 FIFO, AVCO and profit

In the previous descriptions of FIFO and AVCO, each method of valuation produced different costs both of closing stocks and of issues. Since such costs affect the cost of sales, it follows that the different methods – FIFO and AVCO – will provide different profit figures. An example may help to illustrate this point.

EXAMPLE: FIFO, AVCO AND PROFIT

On 1 November 20X2 a business held 300 units of goods for resale item No 9639 in stock. These were valued at £12 each. During November 20X2 three batches of goods for resale were received into store from the supplier as follows:

Date	*Units received*	*Cost per unit*
10 November	400	£12.50
20 November	400	£14
25 November	400	£15

Goods sold out of stock during November were as follows.

Date	*Units sold*	*Sale price per unit*
14 November	500	£20
21 November	500	£20
28 November	100	£20

What was the profit from selling stock item 9639 in November 20X2, applying the following principles of stock valuation:

(a) FIFO
(b) AVCO?

SOLUTION

(a) FIFO

		Issue cost Total	*Closing stock*
		£	£
Date	Issue costs		
14 November	300 units × £12 plus		
	200 units × £12.50	6,100	
21 November	200 units × £12.50 plus		
	300 units × £14	6,700	
28 November	100 units × £14	1,400	
Closing stock	400 units × £15		6,000
		14,200	6,000

(b) AVCO

			Unit cost	*Balance in stock*	*Total cost of issues*	*Closing stock*
			£	£	£	£
1 November	Opening stock	300	12.000	3,600		
10 November		400	12.500	5,000		
		700	12.286	8,600		
14 November		500	12.286	6,143	6,143	
		200	12.286	2,457		
20 November		400	14.000	5,600		
		600	13.428	8,057		
21 November		500	13.428	6,714	6,714	
		100	13.428	1,343		
25 November		400	15.000	6,000		
		500	14.686	7,343		
28 November		100	14.686	1,469	1,469	
30 November		400	14.686	5,874	14,326	5,874

Summary: profit

	FIFO	*AVCO*
	£	£
Opening stock	3,600	3,600
Purchases	16,600	16,600
	20,200	20,200
Closing stock	(6,000)	(5,874)
Cost of sales	14,200	14,326
Sales (1,100 × £20)	22,000	22,000
Profit	7,800	7,674

Different stock valuations have produced different cost of sales figures, and therefore different profits. In our example opening stock values are the same, therefore the difference in the amount of profit under each method is the same as the difference in the valuations of closing stock.

These profit differences are only temporary. In our example, the opening stock in December 20X2 will be £6,000 or £5,874, depending on the stock valuation used. Different opening stock values will affect the cost of sales and profits in December, so that in the long run inequalities in stock levels each month will even themselves out.

Activity 4 **(1 hour)**

A business has the following transactions for its product R.

Year 1

Opening stock: nil
Buys 10 units at £300 per unit
Buys 12 units at £250 per unit
Sells 8 units at £400 per unit
Buys 6 units at £200 per unit
Sells 12 units at £400 per unit

Year 2

Buys 10 units at £200 per unit
Sells 5 units at £400 per unit
Buys 12 units at £150 per unit
Sells 25 units at £400 per unit

Required

Using FIFO, calculate the following on an item by item basis for both year 1 and year 2.

(i) The closing stock
(ii) The sales
(iii) The cost of sales
(iv) The gross profit

5 LEDGER ACCOUNTS FOR STOCK

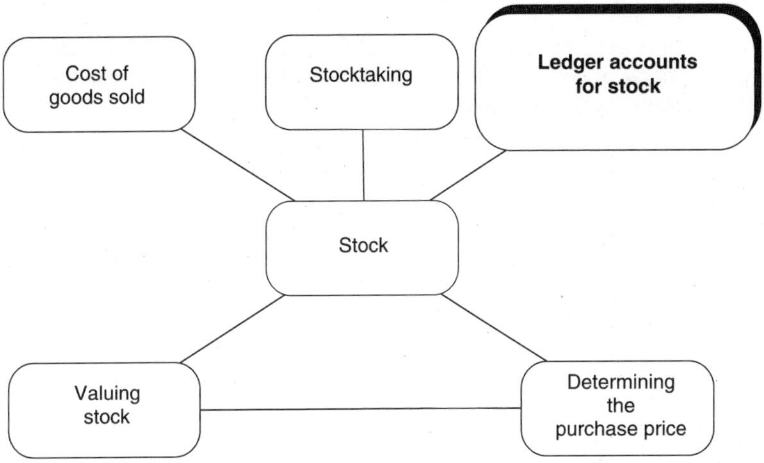

The double entry for stocks is very simple.

At its first the year end the business transfers the purchases account balance to the P & L account, as we have seen:

DR P & L account
CR Purchases

It then removes the amount of closing stock that it holds on that date from the P & L account, and includes it in a stock account, where the debit balance is a balance sheet current asset.

DR Stock account (closing stock value)
CR P & L account (closing stock value)

In its second year the amount on the stock account is brought down as an asset (a debit balance, being the opening stock in the new year). No further entries are made in the stock account until the end of the second year. During the year, all purchases of stock are accounted for via the purchases account, and the balance on this account at the year end is transferred to the P & L account as above. In addition, the opening stock balance is transferred to the P & L account, and then the closing stock adjustment is made as before:

DR P & L account
CR Purchases

DR P & L account (opening stock value)
CR Stock account (opening stock value)

DR Stock account (closing stock value)
CR P & L account (closing stock value)

Activity 5 **(1 hour)**

A business is established with capital of £2,000 and this amount is paid into a business bank account by the proprietor. During the first year's trading, the following transactions occurred.

	£
Purchases of goods for resale, on credit	4,300
Payments to creditors	3,600
Sales, all on credit	4,000
Receipts from debtors	3,200
Fixed assets purchased for cash	1,500
Other expenses, all paid in cash	900

The bank has provided an overdraft facility of up to £3,000.

Closing stocks of goods are valued at £1,800. (Because this is the first year of the business, there are no opening stocks.)

Ignore depreciation and drawings.

Required

Prepare the ledger accounts including a profit and loss ledger account for the year, and a balance sheet as at the end of the year.

Chapter roundup

- You must learn the formula for cost of goods sold: Opening stock + purchases – closing stock.
- A stocktake is a means of physically counting the stock still held.
- The **value** of stock is calculated at the lower of **cost** and **net realisable value** for each separate item or group of items. **Cost** can be arrived at by using **FIFO** or **AVCO**.
- Stock should be valued at the lower of cost and net realisable value.
- Opening stocks brought forward in the stock account are transferred to the P & L account, and so at the end of the accounting year the balance on the stock account ceases to be the opening stock value b/d and becomes instead the closing stock value c/d.
- The value of closing stock is accounted for in the nominal ledger by debiting a stock account and crediting the P & L account at the end of an accounting period. Stock will therefore have a debit balance at the end of a period, and this balance will be shown in the balance sheet as a current asset.

Quick quiz

1 What is 'continuous' stocktaking?

2 An item of stock was purchased for £10. However, due to a fall in demand, its selling price will be only £8. In addition further costs will be incurred prior to sale of £1. What is the net realisable value?

A £7
B £8
C £10
D £11

3 Why is stock not valued at expected selling price?

4 What are the most likely situations when the NRV of stock fall below cost?

Answers to quick quiz

1 A card is kept for every item of stock. It shows receipts and issues, with a running total. A few inventory items are counted each day to test that the cards are correct.

2 ANet realisable value is selling price (£8) less further costs to sale (£1), ie £7.

3 Mainly because this would result in the business taking a profit before the goods have been sold.

4
- Increase in costs or a fall in selling price
- Physical deterioration of stock
- Obsolescence
- Marketing strategy
- Errors in production or purchasing

Answers to activities

1 GRAND UNION FOOD STORES
TRADING ACCOUNT FOR THE YEAR ENDED 31 DECEMBER 20X6

	£	£
Sales		80,000
Opening stock	6,000	
Add purchases	50,000	
	56,000	
Less closing stock	(12,500)	
Cost of goods sold		(43,500)
Gross profit		36,500

2 The correct answer is D. Gross profit less expenses = net profit. Therefore net profit plus expenses = gross profit.

3 Item by item: 560 + 740 + 780 + 340 + 420 + 700 + 1,200 + 1,140 + 1,540 = £7,420

4 *Year 1*

Purchases (units)	*Sales* (units)	*Balance* (units)	*Stock value*	*Unit cost*	*Cost of sales*	*Sales*
			£	£	£	£
10		10	3,000	300		
12			3,000	250		
		22	6,000			
	8		(2,400)		2,400	3,200
		14	3,600			
6			1,200	200		
		20	4,800			
	12		(3,100)*		3,100	4,800
		8	1,700		5,500	8,000

* 2 @ £300 + 10 @ £250 = £3,100

Year 2

Purchases (units)	*Sales (units)*	*Balance (units)*	*Stock value*	*Unit cost*	*Cost of sales*	*Sales*
			£	£	£	£
B/f		8	1,700			
10			2,000	200		
		18	3,700			
	5		(1,100)*		1,100	2,000
		13	2,600			
12		25	1,800	150		
			4,400			
25			(4,400)**		4,400	10,000
		0	0		5,500	12,000

* 2 @ £250 + 3 @ £200 = £1,100
** 13 @ £200 + 12 @ £150 = £4,400

Trading account

Year 1	£	£
Sales		8,000
Opening stock	0	
Purchases	7,200	
	7,200	
Closing stock	1,700	
Cost of sales		5,500
Gross profit		2,500

Year 2	£	£
Sales		12,000
Opening stock	1,700	
Purchases	3,800	
	5,500	
Closing stock	0	
Cost of sales		5,500
Gross profit		6,500

5

CASH

	£		£
Capital	2,000	Creditors	3,600
Debtors	3,200	Fixed assets	1,500
Balance c/d	800	Other expenses	900
	6,000		6,000
		Balance b/d	800

CAPITAL

	£		£
Balance c/d	2,600	Cash	2,000
		P & L a/c	600
	2,600		2,600
		Balance b/d	2,600

CREDITORS

	£		£
Cash	3,600	Purchases	4,300
Balance c/d	700		
	4,300		4,300
		Balance b/d	700

PURCHASES ACCOUNT

	£		£
Creditors	4,300	P & L a/c	4,300

FIXED ASSETS

	£		£
Cash	1,500	Balance c/d	1,500
Balance b/d	1,500		

SALES

	£		£
P&L a/c	4,000	Debtors	4,000

DEBTORS

	£		£
Sales	4,000	Cash	3,200
		Balance c/d	800
	4,000		4,000
Balance b/d	800		

OTHER EXPENSES

	£		£
Cash	900	P & L a/c	900

PROFIT AND LOSS ACCOUNT

	£		£
Purchases account	4,300	Sales	4,000
Gross profit c/d	1,500	Closing stock (stock a/c)	1,800
	5,800		5,800
Other expenses	900	Gross profit b/d	1,500
Net profit (transferred to capital account)	600		
	1,500		1,500

STOCK ACCOUNT

	£		£
P&L account (closing stock)	1,800	Balance c/d (balance sheet)	1,800

BALANCE SHEET AS AT THE END OF THE YEAR

	£	£
Fixed assets		1,500
Current assets		
Stock	1,800	
Debtors	800	
	2,600	
Current liabilities		
Bank overdraft	800	
Creditors	700	
	1,500	
Net current assets		1,100
		2,600
Capital		£
At start of period		2,000
Profit for period		600
		2,600

Chapter 7:
DEBTORS

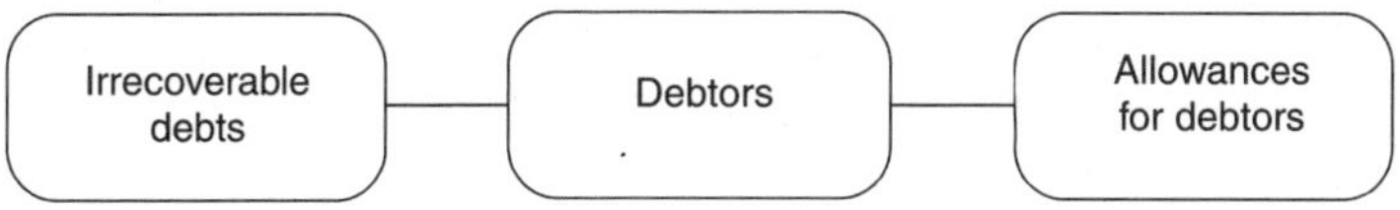

Introduction

We have now covered the first two items that we encounter on a balance sheet: fixed assets and stock. In doing so we have also covered accumulated depreciation, the depreciation charge, and cost of goods sold. Therefore, you should be well aware that balance sheet items and profit and loss account items are inextricably linked. This is also an important issue when it comes to the next asset on the balance sheet: **debtors**.

Debtors – amounts owed by customers – are a major asset on the balance sheets of most businesses. They arise when a credit sale is made to a customer, and most of them are settled by the receipt of cash from the customer. Sadly, however, this is not always the case; sometimes customers never pay, in which case the business has suffered an **irrecoverable debt,** and has to write off the debt entirely.

In other cases the customer may eventually pay but may do so very slowly, so there is a great deal of uncertainty surrounding the matter. It should not surprise you therefore that the prudence concept comes into play: where there is uncertainty we have to make sure that assets are not overstated, so we keep the debtor on the balance sheet but charge the profit and loss account with an **allowance for debtors**, which is set off against the debtor on the face of the balance sheet.

Your objectives

When you have completed this chapter you should be able to:

1. Explain the difference between writing off irrecoverable debts and making an allowance for debtors
2. Account for writing off debts and making an allowance

1 IRRECOVERABLE DEBTS

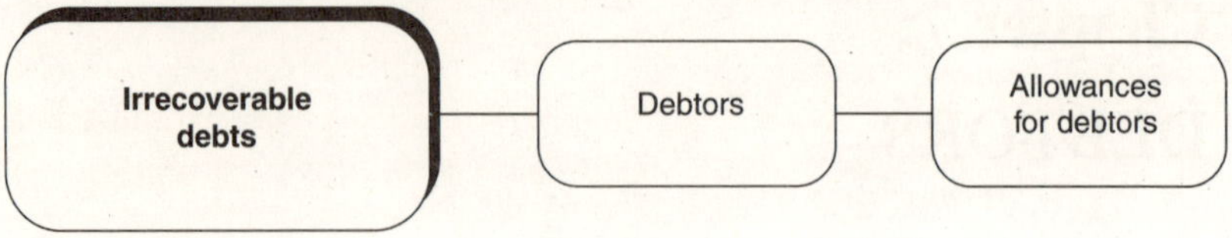

Very few businesses expect to be paid immediately in cash, unless they are retail businesses on the high street. Most businesses buy and sell to one another on credit terms. This has the **benefit** of allowing businesses to keep trading without having to provide cash 'up front'. So a business will allow credit terms to customers and receive credit terms from its suppliers. Ideally a business wants to receive money from its customers as quickly as possible, but delay paying its suppliers for as long as possible. This can lead to problems.

Most businesses aim to control such problems by means of **credit control**. A customer will be given a **credit limit**, which cannot be exceeded (compare an overdraft limit or a credit card limit). If an order would take the account over its credit limit, it will not be filled until a payment is received.

Another tool in **credit control** is the **aged debtors analysis**. This shows how long invoices have been outstanding and may indicate that a customer is unable to pay. Most credit controllers will have a system for chasing up payment of late outstanding invoices.

Customers who buy goods on credit might fail to pay for them, perhaps out of dishonesty or perhaps because they have gone bankrupt and cannot pay. Customers in another country might be prevented from paying by the unexpected introduction of foreign exchange control restrictions by their country's government during the credit period. Therefore the **costs** of offering credit facilities to customers can include:

(a) Interest costs of an overdraft, if customers do not pay promptly
(b) Costs of trying to obtain payment
(c) Court costs

For one reason or another, a business might decide to give up expecting payment and to write the debt off.

Definition

> An **irrecoverable debt** is a debt which is not expected to be repaid.

1.2 Writing off irrecoverable debts

When a business decides that a particular debt is unlikely ever to be repaid, the amount of the debt should be '**written off**' as an expense in the profit and loss account.

		£	£
Debit	Irrecoverable debts expense (profit and loss account)	X	
Credit	Debtors account (balance sheet)		X

EXAMPLE: WRITING OFF AN IRRECOVERABLE DEBT

If Alfred's Mini-Cab Service sends an invoice for £300 to a customer who subsequently does a 'moonlight flit' from his office premises, never to be seen or heard of again, the debt of £300 must be written off. It might seem sensible to record the business transaction as:

Sales £(300 – 300) = £0.

However, irrecoverable debts written off are accounted for as follows.

(a) **Sales** are shown at their invoice value in the **profit and loss account**. The sale has been made, and gross profit should be earned.

(b) The subsequent failure to collect the debt is a separate matter, which is reported as an expense in the P & L account.

For Alfred's Mini-Cab Service:

	£
Sales	300
Irrecoverable debt written off (expense)	(300)
Net profit on this transaction	0

Obviously, when a debt is written off, the value of the debtor as a current asset falls to zero. If the debt is expected to be uncollectable, its '**net realisable value**' is nil, and so it has a zero balance sheet value.

1.3 Irrecoverable debts written off and subsequently paid

An irrecoverable debt which has been written off might occasionally be unexpectedly paid. The amount recovered should be recorded as a **negative expense** in the profit and loss account (irrecoverable debts expense).

		£	£
DEBIT	Cash or bank	X	
CREDIT	Irrecoverable debts expense		X

No entry is made in the debtors account.

At the end of the period, the balance on the irrecoverable debts expense account is transferred to the P & L ledger account:

		£	£
DEBIT	Irrecoverable debts expense	X	
CREDIT	P & L account		X

Activity 1 **(30 minutes)**

Prepare a full profit and loss account for the Blacksmith's Forge for the year to 31 December 20X5 from the following information.

	£
Stocks of goods in hand, 1 January 20X5	6,000
Purchases of goods	122,000
Stocks of goods in hand, 31 December 20X5	8,000
Cash sales	100,000
Credit sales	70,000
Irrecoverable debts written off	9,000
Debts paid in 20X5 which were previously written off as irrecoverable in 20X4 (ie irrecoverable debts received)	2,000
Other expenses	31,800

2 ALLOWANCES FOR DEBTORS

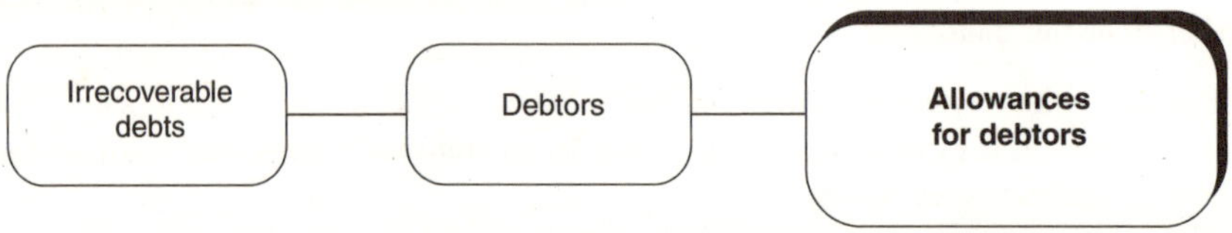

2.1 General allowance for debtors

When irrecoverable debts are written off, specific debts owed to the business are identified as unlikely ever to be collected.

However, because of the risks involved in selling goods on credit, it might be accepted that a certain percentage of outstanding debts at any time are unlikely to be collected. But although it might be estimated that, say, 5% of debts will turn out bad, the business will not know until later which specific debts are bad.

EXAMPLE: GENERAL ALLOWANCE FOR DEBTORS

A business commences operations on 1 July 20X4, and in the twelve months to 30 June 20X5 makes sales of £300,000 (all on credit) and writes off irrecoverable debts of £6,000. Cash received from customers during the year is £244,000, so that at 30 June 20X5 the business has outstanding debtors of £50,000.

	£
Credit sales during the year	300,000
Add debtors at 1 July 20X4	0
Total debts owed to the business	300,000
Less cash received from credit customers	(244,000)
	56,000
Less irrecoverable debts written off	(6,000)
Debtors outstanding at 30 June 20X5	50,000

Now, some of these outstanding debts might turn out to be irrecoverable. The business does not know on 30 June 20X5 which specific debts in the total £50,000 owed will be irrecoverable, but it might guess (from experience perhaps) that 5% of debts will eventually be found to be so.

When a business expects irrecoverable debts amongst its current debtors, but does not yet know which specific debts will be bad, it can make a **general allowance for debtors**.

Definition

A **general allowance for debtors** is an estimate of the percentage of debts which are not expected to be paid, based on prior experience.

An allowance for debtors provides for **future irrecoverable debts**, as a prudent precaution by the business. The business will be more likely to avoid claiming profits which subsequently fail to materialise because some debts turn out to be irrecoverable.

(a) When an allowance is first made, the amount of this initial allowance is charged as an expense in the profit and loss account of the business, for the period in which the allowance is created.

(b) When an allowance already exists, but is subsequently increased in size, the amount of the **increase** in allowance is charged as an **expense** in the profit and loss account, for the period in which the increased allowance is made.

(c) When an allowance already exists, but is subsequently reduced in size, the amount of the **decrease** in allowance is recorded as a **negative expense** in the profit and loss account, for the period in which the reduction in allowance is made.

The balance sheet, as well as the profit and loss account of a business, must be adjusted to show an allowance for debtors: The value of debtors in the balance sheet must be shown **after deducting the allowance for debtors**.

This is because the net realisable value of all the debtors of the business is estimated to be less than their 'sales value'. After all, this is the reason for making the allowance in the first place. The net realisable value of debtors is the total value of debtors minus the allowance for debtors. Such an allowance is an example of the **prudence concept**, discussed in detail in Chapter 1.

EXAMPLE CONTINUED: GENERAL ALLOWANCE FOR DEBTORS

The newly created allowance for debtors at 30 June 20X5 will be 5% of £50,000 = £2,500. This means that although total debtors are £50,000, eventual payment of only £47,500 is prudently expected.

(a) In the P & L account, the newly created allowance of £2,500 will be shown as an expense, added to the expenses in the irrecoverable debts ledger account.

(b) In the balance sheet, debtors will be shown as follows.

	£
Total debtors at 30 June 20X5	50,000
Less allowance for debtors	(2,500)
	47,500

		£	£
DEBIT	Irrecoverable debts expenses	2,500	
CREDIT	Allowance for debtors (balance sheet)		2,500

2.2 Specific allowances for debtors

A business may face a 'halfway house' situation, where its doubts about the recoverability of a specific debt are not so great that it wants to write the debt off completely, but are still great enough that an allowance is required. In such a case the business could choose to make a **specific allowance** for that debtor. The debtor's balance remains in the ledger account and on the balance sheet, but it is set off against a specific allowance in relation to it. The double entry for creating this allowance and charging it to the profit and loss account is the same as for a general allowance.

If the allowance is not needed at the end of the next year, because the debtor has paid, then it is written back to the irrecoverable debts expense account:

DEBIT Specific allowance (balance sheet)
CREDIT Irrecoverable debts expense

Where a business has made a specific allowance, it is usual to deduct the amount of that debt from the total of debtors before calculating the general allowance.

EXAMPLE: SPECIFIC AND GENERAL ALLOWANCES FOR DEBTORS

At 1 January 20X5 Hebden had a specific allowance of £5,300 against the debt of Ismail, and a general allowance for debtors of £2,200. Hebden has a balance on his debtors account of £120,400 as at 31 December 20X5, having written off a debt from Patrick for £3,700 during the year. Ismail has settled his debt but now Hebden is concerned about a debt of £1,000 from George. He decides that he needs a specific allowance against this debt, plus a 3% allowance against all other outstanding debts at the year end.

We need to calculate Hebden's net figure for debtors in his balance sheet at 31 December 20X5, plus the total irrecoverable debts expense for the year then ended.

SOLUTION

	£	£
Debtors at 31 December 20X5		120,400
Specific allowance needed	1,000	
General allowance needed £(120,400 – 1,000) × 3%	3,582	
Total allowance for debtors		(4,582)
Net figure for debtors at 31 December 20X5		115,818

Irrecoverable debts expense:

	£
Patrick's debt written off in year	3,700
Ismail's specific allowance written back	(5,300)
George's specific debt allowed for	1,000
Increase in general allowance (3,582 – 2,200)	1,382
Total irrecoverable debts expense	782

Activity 2 **(30 minutes)**

Corin Flakes owns and runs the Aerobic Health Foods Shop in Dundee. He commenced trading on 1 January 20X1, selling health foods to customers, most of whom make use of a credit facility that Corin offers. (Customers are allowed to purchase up to £200 of goods on credit but must repay a certain proportion of their outstanding debt every month.)

This credit system gives rise to a large number of bad debts, and Corin Flake's results for his first three years of operations are as follows.

Year to 31 December 20X1

Gross profit	£27,000
Irrecoverable debts written off	£8,000
Debts owed by customers as at 31 December 20X1	£40,000
General allowance for debtors	2½% of outstanding debtors
Other expenses	£20,000

Year to 31 December 20X2

Gross profit	£45,000
Irrecoverable debts written off	£10,000
Debts owed by customers as at 31 December 20X2	£50,000
General allowance for debtors	2½% of outstanding debtors
Other expenses	£28,750

Year to 31 December 20X3

Gross profit	£60,000
Irrecoverable debts written off	£11,000
Debts owed by customers as at 31 December 20X3	£30,000
Specific allowance for debtors	£2,000
General allowance for debtors	3% of other outstanding debtors
Other expenses	£32,850

Required

For each of these three years, prepare the profit and loss account of the business, and state the value of debtors appearing in the balance sheet as at 31 December.

Activity 3 **(1 hour)**

Horace Goodrunning fears that his business will suffer an increase in defaulting debtors in the future and so he decides to make an allowance for debtors of 2% of outstanding debtors at balance sheet dates from 28 February 20X6. On 28 February 20X8, Horace decides that the allowance has been over-estimated and he reduces it to 1% of outstanding debtors. Outstanding debtors balances at the various balance sheet dates are as follows.

	£
28.2.20X6	15,200
28.2.20X7	17,100
28.2.20X8	21,400

You are required to show extracts from the following ledger accounts for each of the three years above.

(a) Debtors
(b) Allowance for debtors
(c) Irrecoverable debts expense

Show how debtors would appear in the balance sheet at the end of each year.

Chapter roundup

- Irrecoverable debts are specific debts owed to a business which it decides are never going to be paid. They are written off as an expense in the profit and loss account.
- Allowances for debtors may be specific (an allowance against a particular debtor) or general: a percentage allowance based on past experience of irrecoverable debts. An increase in the allowance for debtors is a debit to the irrecoverable debts expense account; a decrease is a credit.
- Debtors in the balance sheet are shown net of any debtors allowance.

Quick quiz

1 An irrecoverable debt arises in which of the following situations?

A A customer pays part of the account
B An invoice is in dispute
C The customer goes bankrupt
D The invoice is not yet due for payment

2 Irrecoverable debts are £5,000. Debtors at the year end are £120,000. If an allowance for debtors of 5% is required, what is the entry for irrecoverable debts expense in the profit and loss account?

A £5,000
B £11,000
C £6,000
D £10,750

3 An allowance for debtors of 2% is required. Debtors at the period end are £200,000 and the allowable for debtors brought forward from the previous period is £2,000. What movement on the allowance is required this year?

A Increase by £4,000
B Decrease by £4,000
C Increase by £2,000
D Decrease by £2,000

4 If a debtors allowance is increased, what is the effect on the profit and loss account?

A Reduction in expenses
B Increase in expenses

5 What is the double entry to record an irrecoverable debt written off?

A Debit: expenses Credit: debtors
B Debit: debtors Credit: expenses

Answers to quick quiz

1 C

2 B £5,000 + (5% × £120,000)

3 C 2% of £200,000 = £4,000. Therefore the allowable needs to be increased by £2,000.

4 B The increase in the allowance is debited to the irrecoverable debts expense account and therefore to the P & L account.

5 A DEBIT Irrecoverable debts expense
CREDIT Debtors

Answers to activities

1 BLACKSMITH'S FORGE
TRADING, PROFIT AND LOSS ACCOUNT FOR THE YEAR ENDED 31.12.20X5

	£	£
Sales		170,000
Opening stock	6,000	
Purchases	122,000	
	128,000	
Less closing stock	(8,000)	
Cost of goods sold		(120,000)
Gross profit		50,000
Expenses		
Irrecoverable debts written off (9,000 – 2,000)	7,000	
Other expenses	31,800	
		38,800
Net profit		11,200

2 AEROBIC HEALTH FOOD SHOP

PROFIT AND LOSS ACCOUNTS FOR THE YEARS ENDED 31 DECEMBER

	20X1		*20X2*		*20X3*	
	£	£	£	£	£	£
Gross profit		27,000		45,000		60,000
Expenses:						
Irrecoverable debts written off	8,000		10,000		11,000	
Increase in allowances for debtors*	1,000		250		1,590	
Other expenses	20,000		28,750		32,850	
		(29,000)		(39,000)		(45,440)
Net(loss)/profit		(2,000)		6,000		14,560

*At 1 January 20X1 when Corin began trading the allowance for debtors was nil.

At 31 December 20X1 the allowance required was 2½% of £40,000 = £1,000.

The increase in the allowance is therefore £1,000. At 31 December 20X2 the allowance required was 2½% of £50,000 = £1,250. The 20X1 allowance must therefore be increased by £250. At 31 December 20X3 the allowances required are £2,000 plus 3% × (30,000 – 2,000) = £2,840. The 20X2 allowance is therefore increased by £1,590.

VALUE OF DEBTORS IN THE BALANCE SHEET

	As at 31.12.20X1	*As at 31.12.20X2*	*As at 31.12.20X3*
	£	£	£
Total value of debtors	40,000	50,000	30,000
Less allowance for debtors	(1,000)	(1,250)	(2,840)
Balance sheet value	39,000	48,750	27,160

3 The entries for the three years are denoted by (a), (b) and (c) in each account.

DEBTORS (EXTRACT)

			£
(a)	28.2.20X6	Balance	15,200
(b)	28.2.20X7	Balance	17,100
(c)	28.2.20X8	Balance	21,400

ALLOWANCE FOR DEBTORS

			£			£
(a)	28.2.20X6	Bal c/d (2% of 15,200)	304	28.2.20X6	Irrecoverable debts	304
			304			304
(b)	28.2.20X7	Bal c/d (2% of 17,100)	342	1.3.20X6	Balance b/d	304
				28.2.20X7	Irrecoverable debts (note (i))	38
			342			342
(c)	28.2.20X8	Irrecoverable debts (note (ii))	128	1.3.20X7	Balance b/d	342
	28.2.20X8	Bal c/d (1% of 21,400)	214			
			342			342
				1.3.20X8	Balance b/d	214

IRRECOVERABLE DEBTS EXPENSE

		£			£
28.2.20X6	Allowance for debtors	304			
28.2.20X7	Allowance for debtors	38			
			28.2.20X8	Allowance for debtors	128

Notes

(i) The increase in the allowance is £(342 – 304) = £38
(ii) The decrease in the allowance is £(342 – 214) = £128

We calculate the net debtors figure for inclusion in the balance sheet as:

	20X6	*20X7*	*20X8*
	£	£	£
Current assets			
Debtors	15,200	17,100	21,400
Less allowance for debtors	304	342	214
Balance sheet debtors	14,896	16,758	21,186

Chapter 8:
ACCRUALS AND PREPAYMENTS

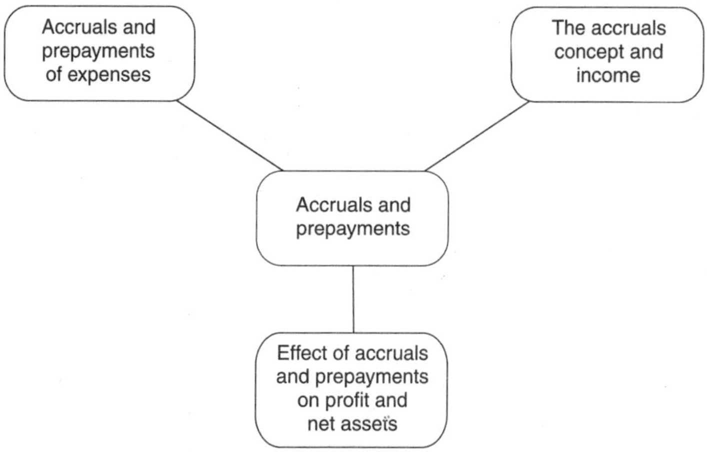

Introduction

In Chapter 6, we looked at the adjustments which may need to be made to the **cost of goods sold** with regard to stock, so as to arrive at gross profit. This chapter deals with the adjustments which may need to be made to **expenses** to arrive at net profit.

Your objectives

After completing this chapter you should be able to:

1. Explain the concept behind accruals and prepayments
2. Account for accruals and prepayments of expenses
3. Apply the accruals concept to income

1 ACCRUALS AND PREPAYMENTS OF EXPENSES

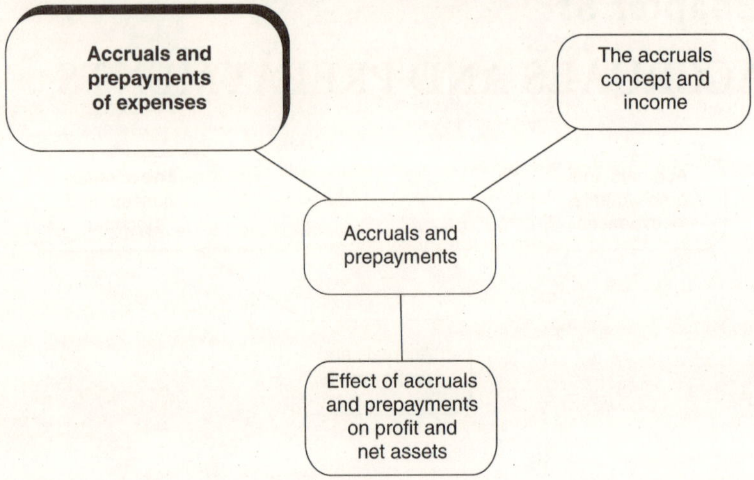

We have already seen that the gross profit for a period should be calculated by **matching** sales and the cost of goods sold, applying the **accruals concept**. In the same way, the net profit for a period should be calculated by charging the expenses which relate to that period. For example, in preparing the profit and loss account of a business for a period of, say, six months, it would be appropriate to charge six months' expenses for rent and rates, insurance costs and telephone costs etc.

The problem is that expenses might not be paid for during the period to which they relate. For example, if a business rents a shop for £20,000 per annum, it might pay the full annual rent on, say, 1 April each year. Now if we were to calculate the profit of the business for the first six months of the year 20X7, the correct charge for rent in the profit and loss account would be £10,000 even though the rent payment would be £20,000 in that period. Similarly, the rent charge in a profit and loss account for the business in the second six months of the year would be £10,000, even though no rent payment would be made in that six-month period.

Definitions

Accruals (or accrued expenses) are expenses which are charged against the profit for a particular period, even though they have not yet been paid for.

Prepayments (or prepaid expenses) are payments which have been made in one accounting period, but which should not be charged against profit until a later period, because they relate to that later period.

The following examples will help to clarify the principle involved: that expenses should be matched against the period to which they relate.

EXAMPLE: ACCRUALS

Horace Goodrunning, trading as Goodrunning Motor Spares, ends his financial year on 28 February each year. His telephone was installed on 1 April 20X6 and he receives his telephone account quarterly at the end of each quarter. He pays it promptly as soon as he receives it. On the basis of the following data, you are required to calculate the telephone expense to be charged to the business's profit and loss account for the year ended 28 February 20X7.

Goodrunning Motor Spares – telephone expense paid for the three months ended:

	£
30.6.20X6	23.50
30.9.20X6	27.20
31.12.20X6	33.40
31.3.20X7	36.00

SOLUTION

The telephone expenses for the year ended 28 February 20X7 are:

	£
1 March – 31 March 20X6 (no telephone)	0.00
1 April – 30 June 20X6	23.50
1 July – 30 September 20X6	27.20
1 October – 31 December 20X6	33.40
1 January – 28 February 20X7 (two months £36.00 × 2/3)	24.00
	108.10

The charge for the period 1 January – 28 February 20X7 is two-thirds of the quarterly charge received on 31 March. As at 28 February 20X7, no telephone bill has been received for the quarter, because it is not due for another month. However, it would be inappropriate to ignore the telephone expenses for January and February, and so an accrued charge of £24 should be made, being two-thirds of the quarter's bill of £36.

The accrued charge will also appear in the balance sheet of the business as at 28 February 20X7, as a **current liability**.

Activity 1 **(1 hour)**

Ratsnuffer is a business dealing in pest control. Its owner, Roy Dent, employs a full-time team of eight who were paid £12,000 per annum each in the year to 31 December 20X5. At the start of 20X6 he raised full-time salaries by 10% to £13,200 per annum each.

On 1 July 20X6, he hired a part-time worker at £8,400 per annum.

Roy pays his work force on the first working day of every month, one month in arrears, so that his employees receive their salary for January on the first working day in February, etc.

Required

(a) Calculate the cost of salaries which would be charged in the profit and loss account of Ratsnuffer for the year ended 31 December 20X6.

(b) Calculate the amount actually paid in salaries during the year (ie the amount of cash received by the work force).

(c) State the amount of accrued charges for salaries which would appear in the balance sheet of Ratsnuffer as at 31 December 20X6.

EXAMPLE: PREPAYMENTS

The Square Wheels Garage pays fire insurance annually in advance on 1 June each year. The firm's financial year end is 28 February. From the following record of insurance payments you are required to calculate the charge to profit and loss for the financial year to 28 February 20X8.

Insurance paid

	£
1.6.20X6	600
1.6.20X7	700

Insurance cost for:

		£
(a)	The 3 months 1 March – 31 May 20X7 (3/12 × £600)	150
(b)	The 9 months 1 June 20X7 – 28 February 20X8 (9/12 × £700)	525
Insurance cost for the year, charged to the P & L account		675

At 28 February 20X8 there is a prepayment for fire insurance, covering the period 1 March – 31 May 20X8. This insurance premium was paid on 1 June 20X7, but only nine months worth of the full annual cost is chargeable to the accounting period ended 28 February 20X8. The prepayment of (3/12 × £700) £175 as at 28 February 20X8 will appear as a current asset in the balance sheet of the Square Wheels Garage as at that date.

In the same way, there was a prepayment of (3/12 × £600) £150 in the balance sheet one year earlier as at 28 February 20X7.

Summary	£
Prepaid insurance premiums as at 28 February 20X7	150
Add insurance premiums paid 1 June 20X7	700
	850
Less insurance costs charged to the P & L account for the year ended 28 February 20X8	(675)
Equals prepaid insurance premiums as at 28 February 20X8	175

Activity 2 **(1 hour)**

The Batley Print Shop rents a photocopying machine from a supplier for which it makes a quarterly payment as follows:

(a) three months rental in advance;
(b) a further charge of 2 pence per copy made during the quarter just ended.

The rental agreement began on 1 August 20X4 and the first six quarterly bills were as follows.

Bills dated and received	*Rental*	*Costs of copies taken*	*Total*
	£	£	£
1 August 20X4	2,100	0	2,100
1 November 20X4	2,100	1,500	3,600
1 February 20X5	2,100	1,400	3,500
1 May 20X5	2,100	1,800	3,900
1 August 20X5	2,700	1,650	4,350
1 November 20X5	2,700	1,950	4,650

The bills are paid promptly, as soon as they are received.

(a) Calculate the charge for photocopying expenses for the year to 31 August 20X4 and the amount of prepayments and/or accrued charges as at that date.

(b) Calculate the charge for photocopying expenses for the following year to 31 August 20X5, and the amount of prepayments and/or accrued charges as at that date.

1.1 Double entry for accruals and prepayments

To set up an accrual at the year end we need to open a new account, called an accruals account, in which we can collect all the accruals that apply at the year end:

DEBIT	Relevant expense (profit and loss account)	£X	
CREDIT	Accruals account (balance sheet liability)		£X

To set up a prepayment at the year end we also need to open a new account, called a prepayments account, in which we can collect all the prepayments that apply at the year end:

DEBIT	Prepayments account (balance sheet asset)	£X	
CREDIT	Relevant expense (profit and loss account)		£X

In the next period these entries need to be reversed.

2 THE ACCRUALS CONCEPT AND INCOME

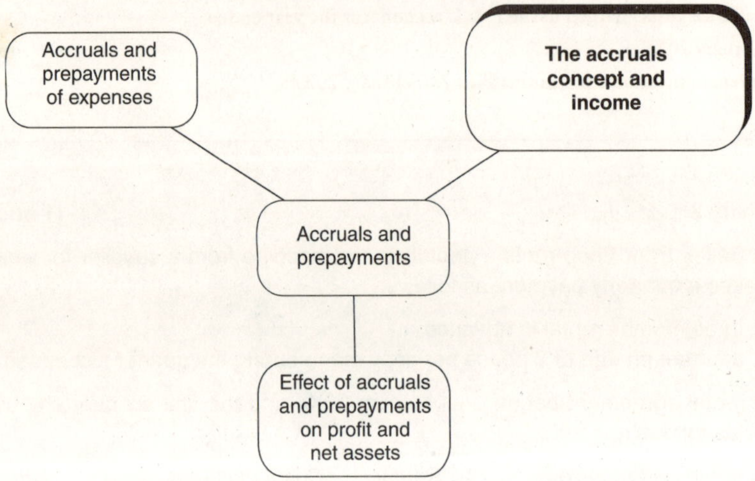

So far we have concentrated on accrued and prepaid expenses arising from the need to match expenses with the income to which they relate. It is also necessary sometimes to treat income in line with the accruals concept.

- Cash may be received in one period although the actual sale to which it relates occurs in the subsequent period. An example is a deposit (or advance payment, or payment on account) received from a customer on an item which will be delivered in the future. The deposit is banked but until the actual sale is recognised the cash should be treated as still being owing to the customer, not as income. This is known as deferred income, a current liability in the balance sheet
- Cash may be received in one period in relation to an event which arose in a previous period. An example is where a supplier makes a refund in relation to a purchase in a previous period. This is known as accrued income, a current asset on the balance sheet.

The treatment is similar to accruals and prepayments of expenses:

- Calculate the amount of the deferred or accrued income
- At the end of the accounting period, write up a journal which updates the relevant profit and loss ledger accounts, and which sets up the relevant asset and liability accounts
- At the beginning of the next accounting period, reverse the double entry

Most frequently this situation is seen in relation to subscriptions to clubs or associations, which generally just use a cash book and do not account day to day for credit transactions. Some members pay an annual subscription earlier than they need to (in advance), and others pay late (in arrears). At the year end there are bound to be amounts in arrears and amounts paid in advance, but the club will nevertheless need to make sure that the income figure it shows relates only to the actual period.

3 EFFECT OF ACCRUALS AND PREPAYMENTS ON PROFIT AND NET ASSETS

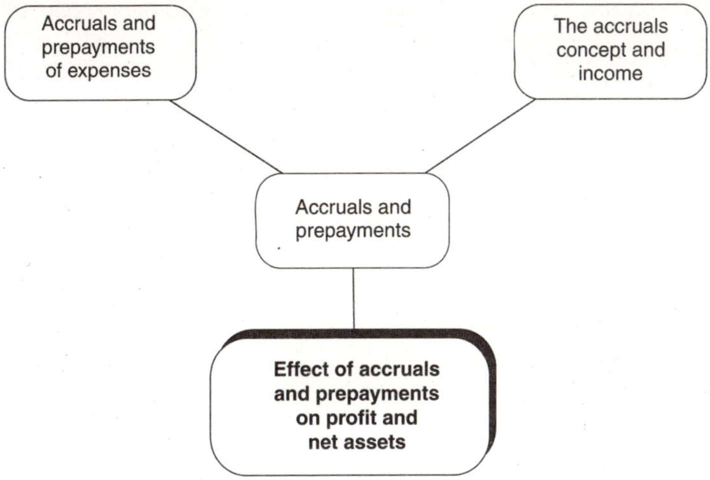

You may find the following table a useful summary of the effects of accruals and prepayments.

	Effect on income/expenses	**Effect on profits in current year**	**Effect on assets/liabilities**
Accruals	Increases expenses	Reduces profit	Increases liabilities
Prepayments	Reduces expenses	Increases profit	Increases assets
Deferred income	Reduces income	Reduces profit	Increases liabilities
Accrued income	Increases income	Increases profit	Increases assets

Activity 3 **(1 hour)**

The Umbrella Shop has the following trial balance as at 30 September 20X8.

	£	£
Sales		156,000
Purchases	65,000	
Land & buildings – net book value at 30.9.X8	125,000	
Plant & machinery – net book value at 30.9.X8	75,000	
Stock at 1.10.X7	10,000	
Cash at bank	12,000	
Debtors	54,000	
Creditors		40,000
Selling expenses	10,000	
Cash in hand	2,000	
Administration expenses	15,000	
Finance expenses	5,000	
Carriage inwards	1,000	
Carriage outwards	2,000	
Capital account at 1.10.X7		180,000
	376,000	376,000

The following information is available:

(a) Closing stock at 30.9.X8 is £13,000, after writing off damaged goods of £2,000.

(b) Included in administration expenses is machinery rental of £6,000 covering the year to 31 December 20X8.

(c) A late invoice for £12,000 covering rent for the year ended 30 June 20X9 has not been included in the trial balance.

Prepare a full profit and loss account and balance sheet for the year ended 30 September 20X8.

Chapter roundup

- **Accrued expenses** (**accruals**) are expenses which relate to an accounting period but have not been paid for. They are shown in the balance sheet as a liability.
- **Prepaid expenses** (**prepayments**) are expenses which have already been paid but relate to a future accounting period. They are shown in the balance sheet as an asset.
- **Accrued income** is income which is due but which has not yet been received in the accounting period. It is shown on the balance sheet as an asset.
- **Deferred income** is cash that has been received in advanced of when it was due. It is shown on the balance sheet as a liability, as it is still owed to the person who paid it.

Quick quiz

1 How is the cost of goods sold calculated?

A Opening stock + purchases + closing stock
B Opening stock + closing stock – purchases
C Opening stock + purchases – closing stock
D Closing stock + purchases – closing stock

2 Electricity paid during the year is £14,000. There was an opening accrual b/d of £500. A bill for the quarter ended 31 January 20X7 was £900. What is the electricity charge in the profit and loss for the year ended 31 December 20X6?

A £14,000
B £14,100
C £13,900
D £14,400

3 If a business has paid rent of £1,000 for the year to 31 March 20X9, what is the prepayment in the accounts for the year to 31 December 20X8?

A £250
B £750

4 What is the correct double entry for an electricity prepayment of £500?

A	Debit:	prepayment	£500	
	Credit:	expense		£500
B	Debit:	expense	£500	
	Credit:	prepayment		£500

5 An accrual is an expense charged against profit for a period, even though it has not yet been paid or invoiced.

A True
B False

Answers to quick quiz

1 C

2 B

ELECTRICITY

	£		£
Cash	14,000	Accrual b/d	500
Accrual c/f (2/3 × 900)	600	Profit and loss account	14,100
	14,600		14,600

3 A $^{3}/_{12} \times £1,000 = £250$

4 A A prepayment needs to reduce the expense and is set up as an asset in the balance sheet.

5 A True.

Answers to activities

1 (a) *Salaries cost in the profit and loss account*

	£
Cost of eight employees for a full year at £13,200 each	105,600
Cost of part-time worker for a half year	4,200
	109,800

(b) *Salaries actually paid in 20X6*

	£
December 20X5 salaries paid in January (8 employees × £1,000 per month)	8,000
Salaries of eight full-time workers for January – November 20X6 paid in February – December (8 × £1,100 per month × 11 months)	96,800
Salary of part-time worker (for July – November paid in August – December 20X6: 5 months × £700 per month)	3,500
Salaries actually paid	108,300

(c) *Accrued salaries costs as at 31 December 20X6*
(ie costs charged in the P & L account, but not yet paid)

	£
8 full-time workers x 1 month x £1,100 per month	8,800
1 part-time worker x 1 month x £700 per month	700
	9,500

(d) *Summary*

	£
Accrued wages costs as at 31 December 20X5	8,000
Add salaries cost for 20X6 (P & L account)	109,800
	117,800
Less salaries paid	(108,300)
Equals accrued wages costs as at 31 December 20X6	9,500

2 (a) *Year to 31 August 20X4*

	£
One months' rental (1/3 × £2,100) *	700
Accrued copying charges (1/3 × £1,500) **	500
Photocopying expense (P & L account)	1,200

* From the quarterly bill dated 1 August 20X4

** From the quarterly bill dated 1 November 20X4

There is a prepayment for 2 months' rental (£1,400) as at 31 August 20X4.

(b) *Year to 31 August 20X5*

	£	£
Rental from 1 September 20X4 – 31 July 20X5 (11 months at £2,100 per quarter or £700 per month)		7,700
Rental from 1 August – 31 August 20X5 (1/3 × £2,700)		900
Rental charge for the year		8,600
Copying charges:		
1 September – 31 October 20X4 (2/3 × £1,500)	1,000	
1 November 20X4 – 31 January 20X5	1,400	
1 February – 30 April 20X5	1,800	
1 May – 31 July 20X5	1,650	
Accrued charges for August 20X5 (1/3 × £1,950)	650	
		6,500
Total photocopying expenses (P & L account)		15,100

There is a prepayment for 2 months' rental (£1,800) as at 31 August 20X5.

Summary of year 1 September 20X4 – 31 August 20X5

	Rental charges £	*Copying costs* £
Prepayments as at 31.8.20X4	1,400	
Accrued charges as at 31.8.20X4		(500)
Bills received during the year		
1 November 20X4	2,100	1,500
1 February 20X5	2,100	1,400
1 May 20X5	2,100	1,800
1 August 20X5	2,700	1,650
Prepayment as at 31.8.20X5	(1,800)	
Accrued charges as at 31.8.20X5		650
Charge to the P & L account for the year	8,600	6,500
Balance sheet items as at 31 August 20X5		
Prepaid rental (current asset)	1,800	
Accrued copying charges (current liability)		650

3 THE UMBRELLA SHOP
TRADING AND PROFIT AND LOSS ACCOUNT FOR THE YEAR END 30 SEPTEMBER 20X8

	£	£
Sales		156,000
Opening stock	10,000	
Purchases	65,000	
Carriage inwards	1,000	
	76,000	
Closing stock (W1)	(13,000)	
Cost of goods sold		(63,000)
Gross profit		93,000
Selling expenses	10,000	
Carriage outwards	2,000	
Administration expenses (W2)	16,500	
Finance expenses	5,000	
		(33,500)
Net profit (transferred to the balance sheet)		59,500

THE UMBRELLA SHOP
BALANCE SHEET AS AT 30 SEPTEMBER 20X8

	£	£
Fixed assets		
Land & buildings		125,000
Plant & machinery		75,000
		200,000
Current assets		
Stock (W1)	13,000	
Debtors	54,000	
Prepayments (W4)	1,500	
Cash at bank and in hand	14,000	
	82,500	
Current liabilities	40,000	
Creditors	3,000	
Accruals (W3)	43,000	
Net current assets		39,500
		239,500
Capital		
Proprietor's capital		
Balance brought forward		180,000
Profit for the period		59,500
Balance carried forward		239,500

Workings

1 *Closing stock*

As the figure of £13,000 is **after** writing off damaged goods, no further adjustments are necessary. Remember that you are effectively crediting closing stock to the profit and loss account and the corresponding debit is to the balance sheet.

2 *Administration expenses*

	£
Per trial balance	15,000
Add: accrual (W3)	3,000
	18,000
Less: prepayment (W4)	(1,500)
	16,500

3 *Accrual*

	£
Rent for year to 30 June 20X9	12,000
Accrual for period to 30 September 20X8 ($^3/_{12} \times$ £12,000)	3,000

4 *Prepayment*

	£
Machinery rental for the year to 31 December 20X8	6,000
Prepayment for period 1 October to 31 December 20X8 ($^3/_{12} \times$ £6,000)	1,500

Part C

Company Accounts and Interpretation

Chapter 9:

COMPANY ACCOUNTS

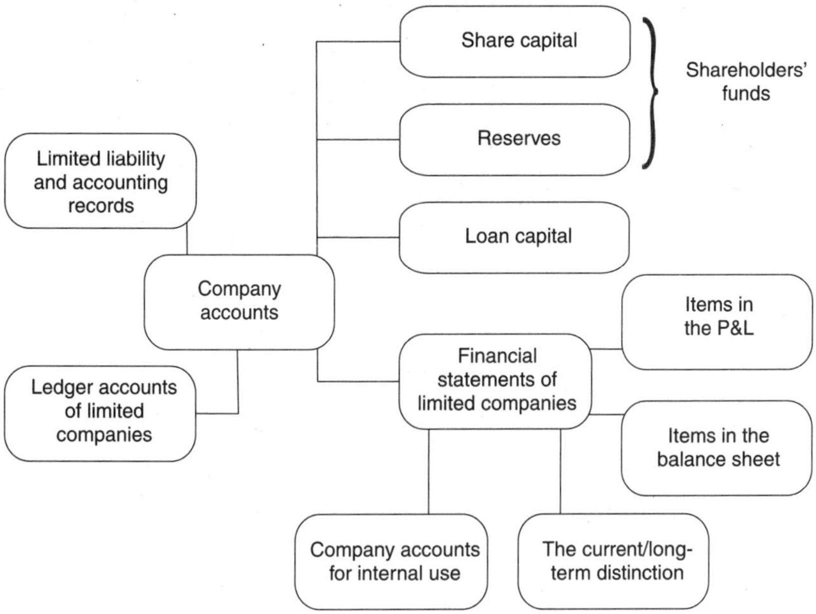

Introduction

So far we have concentrated on the financial statement of sole traders. For the remainder of this Course Book we shall concentrate on those of limited companies, the legal form adopted by most businesses of any significant size.

We begin this chapter by considering the **status of limited** companies and the type of accounting records they maintain in order to prepare financial statements.

Then we will look at those accounting entries unique to limited companies: share capital, reserves, and bonus and rights issues.

We shall then move on to prepare company financial statements.

Your objectives

After completing this chapter you should be able to:

1. Describe what is meant by a company's share capital and reserves, and loan capital
2. Identify the differences and the similarities between company and sole trader financial statements
3. Prepare a basic set of financial statements for companies

1 LIMITED LIABILITY AND ACCOUNTING RECORDS

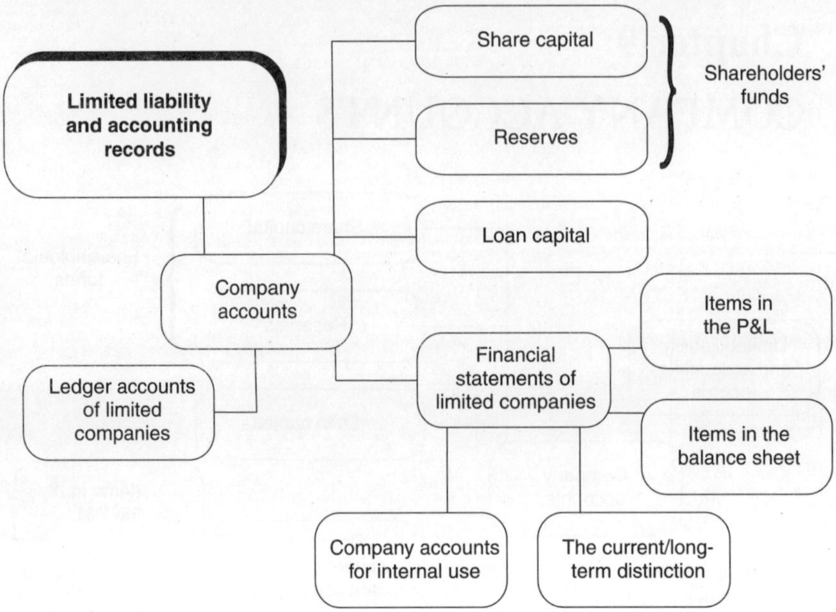

So far, we have dealt mainly with the accounts of businesses in general. In this chapter we shall turn our attention to the accounts of limited companies. As we should expect, the accounting rules and conventions for recording the business transactions of limited companies and then preparing their final financial statements are much the same as for sole traders.

For example, companies will have a cash book, sales day book, purchase day book, journal and nominal ledger. They will also prepare a profit and loss account annually and a balance sheet at the end of the accounting year.

There are, however, some **differences** in the accounts of limited companies, of which the following are perhaps the most significant.

(a) The **legislation** governing the activities of limited companies is very extensive, and includes the Companies Act 2006 and associated secondary legislation. Amongst other things, the Companies Act defines certain minimum accounting records which must be maintained by companies.
   (i) The **annual accounts** of a company must be filed with the Registrar of Companies and so be available for public inspection
   (ii) There are detailed requirements on the **minimum information** which must be disclosed in a company's financial statements. Businesses which are not limited companies (non-incorporated businesses) enjoy comparative freedom from statutory regulation.

(b) The owners of a company (its **members** or **shareholders**) may be very numerous. Their capital is shown differently from that of a sole trader; and instead of drawings they take **dividends,** meaning 'a share of profits'.

(c) Because it is a legal entity separate from its owners, a company is liable for tax in its own right, affecting both the profit and loss account and the balance sheet.

1.1 Limited liability

Definition

> **Unlimited liability** means that if the business runs up debts that it is unable to pay, the proprietors will become personally liable for the unpaid debts, and would be required, if necessary, to sell their private possessions in order to repay them.

Limited companies offer limited liability to their owners.

Definition

> **Limited liability** means that in the event that the company becomes insolvent and cannot pay off its debts, the maximum amount an owner stands to lose is his share of the capital in the business.

Thus limited liability is a major advantage of turning a business into a limited company. However, in practice, banks will normally seek personal guarantees from shareholders of a small owner-managed company before making loans or granting an overdraft facility, and so the advantage of limited liability is often lost.

There are other disadvantages too. In comparison with sole trader businesses, there is a significantly increased administrative and financial burden. This arises from:

(a) Compliance with the Companies Act, notably in having to prepare annual accounts and have them audited, in keeping statutory registers and having to publish accounts

(b) Having to comply with all SSAPs and FRSs

(c) Formation and annual registration costs

As a business grows, it needs more capital to finance its operations, often significantly more than the people currently managing the business can provide themselves. One way of obtaining more capital is to invite **investors from outside** the business to invest in the ownership or equity of the business. These new co-owners would not usually be expected to help with managing the business. To such investors, **limited liability is very attractive.**

Investments are always risky undertakings, but with limited liability the investor knows the maximum amount that he stands to lose when he puts some capital into a company.

1.2 Public and private companies

There are two classes of limited company.

(a) **Private companies.** These have the word 'limited' at the end of their name. Being private, they cannot invite members of the public to invest in their capital (ownership).

(b) **Public companies.** These are much fewer in number than private companies, but are generally much larger in size. They have the words 'public limited company' – shortened to PLC or plc (or the Welsh language equivalent) at the end of their name. Public limited companies can invite members of the general public to invest in their equity, and the 'shares' of these companies may be traded on The Stock Exchange.

Activity 1 **(10 minutes)**

Limited liability means that the directors do not have to account for their mistakes. True or false? Justify your answer.

1.3 The accounting records of limited companies

The company's accounting records should:

(a) Disclose the company's current financial position at any time.

(b) Contain:

(i) Day-to-day entries of money received and spent.

(ii) A record of the company's assets and liabilities.

(iii) Where the company deals in goods:

- A statement of stocks held at the year end, and supporting stocktaking sheets.
- With the exception of retail sales, statements of goods bought and sold which identify the sellers and buyers of those goods.

(c) Enable the directors of the company to ensure that its final accounts give a true and fair view of the company's profit or loss and balance sheet position.

2 SHARE CAPITAL

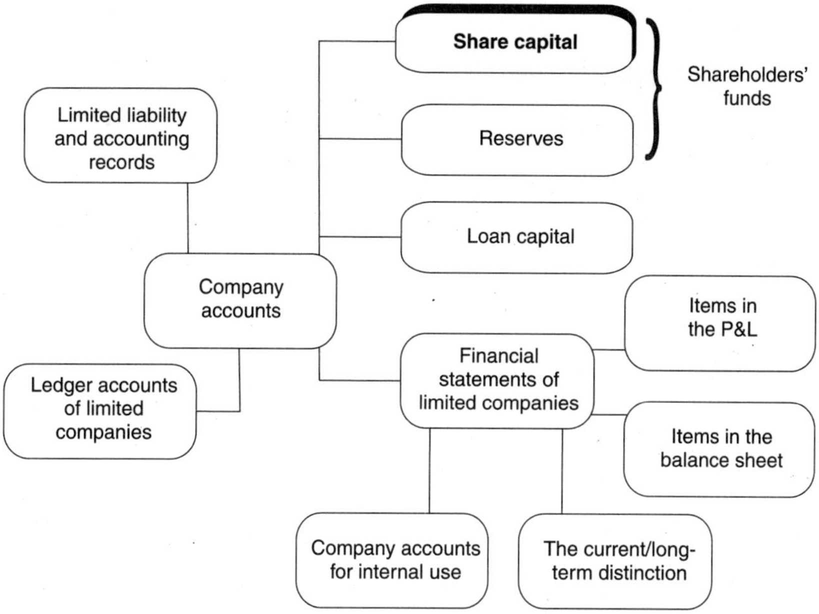

The key differences between company and sole trader financial statements are seen in the bottom half of the balance sheet.

EXAMPLE: SOLE TRADER AND COMPANY OWNERSHIP INTEREST

Two businesses have net assets (assets less liabilities) of £80,000 at 31 December 20X3, the end of their first year of trading. Both businesses started with £50,000 capital. The sole trader's ownership interest would be shown as follows.

	£
Capital introduced 1 January 20X3	50,000
Profit for the year	150,000
Drawings	(120,000)
Capital at 31 December 20X3	80,000

The company's ownership interest – or equity – could be more complicated, as follows:

	£	£
Share capital		
Issued share capital of 50,000 50p shares		25,000
Reserves		
Share premium account		25,000
Retained profits reserve		
Profit for the year after tax	150,000	
Dividends at £2.40 per share	(120,000)	
Transfer to general reserve	(15,000)	
		15,000
General reserve		15,000
Total shareholders' funds		80,000

As we go through this chapter we shall address each of the points that arise in the company balance sheet.

2.1 The capital of limited companies

When a company is set up for the first time, it issues shares. These are paid for by investors who are initially called subscribers, who then become shareholders of the company. Shares are denominated in units of 25 pence, 50 pence, £1 or whatever seems appropriate. This 'face value' of the shares is called their **nominal value** (or par value).

For example, when a company is set up with a share capital of, say, £100,000, it may decide to issue:

(a) 100,000 shares of £1 each nominal value
(b) 200,000 shares of 50p each
(c) 400,000 shares of 25p each
(d) 250,000 shares of 40p each etc

The amount at which the shares are issued may exceed their nominal value. For example, a company might issue 100,000 £1 shares at a price of £1.20 each. Subscribers will then pay a total of £120,000. The issued share capital of the company would be shown in its balance sheet at nominal value, £100,000; the excess of £20,000 is described not as share capital, but **as share premium** (see Section 3.2).

We shall come back to how the balance sheet presents the ownership interest in the company shortly.

2.2 Issued, called-up and paid-up share capital

A distinction must be made between , issued, called-up and paid-up share capital.

(a) **Issued capital** is the nominal amount of share capital that has actually been issued to shareholders.

When share capital is issued, shares are allotted to shareholders. The term 'allotted' share capital means the same thing as issued share capital.

(b) **Called-up capital**. When shares are issued, a company does not always expect to be paid the full amount for the shares at once. It might instead 'call up' only a part of the issue price, and wait until a later time before it calls up the remainder.

For example, if a company allots 400,000 ordinary shares of £1, it might call up only, say, 75 pence per share. The issued share capital would be £400,000, but the called-up share capital would only be £300,000. The shareholders still owe the company 25p per share, or £100,000.

(c) **Paid-up capital**. Like everyone else, investors are not always prompt or reliable payers. When share capital is called up, some shareholders might delay their payment (or even default on payment). Paid-up capital is the amount of called-up capital that has been paid.

For example, if a company issues 400,000 ordinary shares of £1 each, calls up 75 pence per share, and receives payments of £290,000, we would have:

	£
Issued capital	400,000
Called-up capital	300,000
Paid-up capital	290,000
Called-up capital not paid	10,000

The balance sheet of the company would then include called-up capital not paid on the assets side, as a debtor:

	£
Called-up capital not paid	10,000
Cash at bank	290,000
	300,000
Called-up share capital	
400,000 ordinary shares of £1, with 75p per share called-up.	300,000

You may also hear the term 'authorised share capital'. Under the old Companies Act 1985, companies were required to identify the maximum amount of share capital that they were empowered to issue, this amount known as authorised capital. This is not, however, a requirement of the Companies Act 2006.

Activity 2 **(10 minutes)**

Distinguish between issued and called-up share capital.

2.3 Preference shares

Definition

Preference shares are shares which confer certain preferential rights on their holder.

Preference shares carry the right to a dividend (a share of the profits) which is expressed as a percentage of their nominal value: eg a 6% £1 preference share carries a right to an annual dividend of 6p. Preference dividends have priority over ordinary dividends; in other words, if the directors of a company wish to pay a dividend (which they are not obliged to do) they must pay any preference dividend first. Otherwise, no ordinary dividend may be paid.

Preference shares may be redeemable or irredeemable. Redeemable preference shares have a finite life and at a specified time in the future the issuing company will pay the shareholders an agreed amount and the shares will cease to exist. Such an instrument has the characteristics of debt and listed and some unlisted companies are required to account for redeemable preference shares as a liability and the associated dividend as interest. Irredeemable shares do not have a limited life and therefore are always classified as share capital.

The rights attaching to preference shares are set out in the company's constitution. They may vary from company to company, but typically:

(a) Preference shareholders have a **priority right** over ordinary shareholders to a fixed dividend and to a **return of their capital** if the company goes into liquidation.

(b) Preference shares do **not carry a right to vote.**

(c) If the preference shares are **cumulative**, this means that before a company can pay an ordinary dividend it must not only pay the current year's preference dividend, but must also make good any arrears of preference dividends unpaid in previous years.

2.4 Ordinary shares

Ordinary shares are by far the most common. They carry no right to a fixed dividend, but are entitled to all profits left after payment of any preference dividend. Generally, however, only a part of such remaining profits is distributed, the rest being kept in reserve (see below).

Definition

> **Ordinary shares** are shares which are not preferential with regard to dividend payments. Thus a holder only receives a dividend after fixed dividends have been paid to preference shareholders.

The amount of ordinary dividends fluctuates, although there is a general expectation that it will increase over time. Should the company be wound up, any surplus not distributed to creditors and preference shareholders is shared between the ordinary shareholders. Ordinary shares normally carry voting rights.

Ordinary shareholders are thus the effective owners of a company. They own the 'equity' of the business, and any reserves of the business (described later) belong to them; ordinary shareholders are, therefore, sometimes referred to as equity shareholders. Preference shareholders are in many ways more like creditors (although legally they are members, not creditors).

It should be emphasised that the precise rights attached to preference and ordinary shares vary from company to company; the distinctions noted above are generalisations.

EXAMPLE: DIVIDENDS, ORDINARY SHARES AND PREFERENCE SHARES

Garden Gloves Ltd has issued 50,000 ordinary shares of 50 pence each and 20,000 7% irredeemable preference shares of £1 each. Its profits after taxation for the year to 30 September 20X5 were £8,400. The board of directors has decided to pay an ordinary dividend (ie a dividend on ordinary shares) which is 50% of profits after tax and preference dividend. (This is generally called the company's **earnings**.)

Required

Show the amount in total of dividends and of retained profits (ie profits for the year that are held back in reserve), and calculate the dividend per share on ordinary shares.

SOLUTION

	£
Profit after tax	8,400
Preference dividend (7% of £1 × 20,000)	(1,400)
Profit after tax and preference dividend (earnings)	7,000
Ordinary dividend (50% of earnings)	(3,500)
Retained profit (also 50% of earnings)	3,500

The ordinary dividend is 7 pence per share (£3,500 ÷ 50,000 ordinary shares).

2.5 The market value of shares

The nominal value of shares will be different from their market value, which is the price at which someone is prepared to purchase shares in the company from an existing shareholder. If Mr A owns 1,000 £1 shares in Z Ltd, which he bought for £1.20 each, he may sell them to B for £1.60 each.

This transfer of existing shares does not affect Z Ltd's own financial position in any way and, apart from changing the register of members, Z Ltd does not have to bother about the sale by Mr A to Mr B at all. There are certainly no accounting entries to be made for the share sale.

Shares in private companies do not change hands very often, hence their market value is often hard to estimate. Public companies are usually (not always) listed; a listed company is one whose shares are listed and traded on The Stock Exchange, and the market value of its shares is quoted on that Exchange.

3 RESERVES

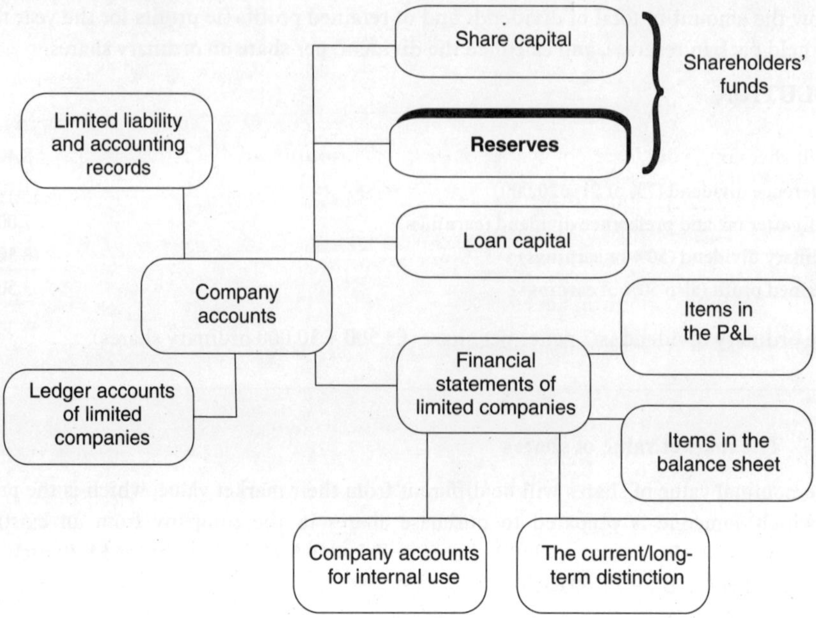

When we looked at sole traders, we saw that their ownership interest consisted of capital plus profit less drawings. There is no need to differentiate between capital introduced and retained profits.

In contrast, shareholders' total ownership interest must be carefully separated between:

(a) Called-up share capital at nominal value.

(b) Reserves, including the share premium account, retained profit and other reserves.

The share capital itself might consist of both ordinary shares and preference shares. All reserves, however, are owned by the ordinary shareholders, who own the 'equity' in the company. Remember that loan capital is not part of equity; it is a liability.

3.1 Reserves

In the case of a sole trader, the proprietor's ownership interest = net assets of the business. For a company the equation is:

Shareholders' ownership interest, or 'funds' = net assets (assets less liabilities)

Furthermore:

Shareholders' funds = share capital and reserves

A company's share capital will remain fixed from year to year, unless new shares are issued.

Reserves are difficult to define neatly since different reserves arise for different reasons, but it follows from the above that:

Reserves = net assets less share capital

So if the share capital remains fixed, the total amount of reserves in a company varies according to changes in its net assets of the business.

A typical balance sheet may show a number of reserves. A distinction should be made between:

(a) **Statutory reserves,** which are reserves a company is required to set up by law and which are not available for the distribution of dividends.

(b) **Non-statutory reserves,** which are reserves consisting of profits distributable as dividends, if the company so wishes.

3.2 The share premium account

The most important statutory (or **capital**) reserve is the **share premium account**.

Shares may be issued at a **premium** to their nominal value. The premium is the difference between the issue price of the share and its nominal value. When a company is first incorporated (set up) the issue price of its shares will probably be the same as their nominal value and so there would be no share premium. If the company does well the market value of its shares will increase, but not the nominal value, so the price of any new shares issued will be approximately their market value.

The difference between cash received by the company and the nominal value of the new shares issued is transferred to the share premium account.

EXAMPLE: ISSUING SHARES AT A PREMIUM

If X Ltd issues 1,000 £1 ordinary shares at £2.60 each the double entry will be:

		£	£
DEBIT	Cash	2,600	
CREDIT	Ordinary share capital		1,000
	Share premium account		1,600

The **share premium account** only comes into being when a company issues shares at a price in excess of their nominal value. The market price of the shares, once they have been issued, has no bearing at all on the company's accounts, and so if their market price goes up or down, the share premium account would remain unaltered.

Definition

> A **share premium account** is an account into which sums received as payment for shares in excess of their nominal value must be placed. The share premium account cannot be distributed as dividend under any circumstances.

Once established, the share premium account is capital of the company which **cannot be paid out in dividends.**

The reason for creating statutory reserves is to **maintain the capital** of the company. This capital 'base' provides some **security for the company's creditors,** bearing in mind that the liability of shareholders is limited in the event that the company cannot repay its debts. It would be most unjust – and illegal – for a company to pay its shareholders a dividend out of its capital base when it is not even able to pay back its debts.

Activity 3 **(10 minutes)**

What are the ledger entries needed to record the issue of 200,000 £1 ordinary shares at a premium of 30p and paid for in full by cheque?

Activity 4 **(15 minutes)**

AB Ltd issues 5,000 50p shares for £6,000. At how much will share capital and share premium be shown in the balance sheet?

	Share capital	*Share premium*
A	£5,000	£1,000
B	£1,000	£5,000
C	£3,500	£3,500
D	£2,500	£3,500

3.3 Other reserves including the general reserve

Other non-statutory reserves may be set up. These may have a specific purpose (eg plant and machinery replacement reserve) or not (eg general reserve). The creation of these reserves usually indicates a general intention **not to distribute the profits** contained in them at any future date, although legally any such reserves, being non-statutory, remain available for the payment of dividends.

Profits are transferred to these reserves as follows.

	£	£
Profit after taxation		100,000
Appropriations of profit		
Dividend	60,000	
Transfer to general reserve	10,000	
		(70,000)
Retained profits for the year		30,000

3.4 Retained profit (profit and loss reserve)

3.4.1 Dividends

Definition

Dividends are appropriations of profit after tax for shareholders.

Preference shareholders are entitled to a share of the profits made by the company; ordinary shareholders may also be paid at dividend.

Many companies pay dividends in two stages during the course of their accounting year.

(a) In mid-year, after the half-year financial results are known, the company might pay an **interim dividend.**

(b) At the end of the year, the company might propose a further **final dividend.**

The total dividend for the year is the sum of the interim and the final dividend. (Not all companies by any means pay an interim dividend. Interim dividends are, however, commonly paid out by larger limited companies.)

At the end of an accounting year, a company's managers may have proposed a final dividend payment, but this will not yet have been paid. The final dividend **does not appear in the accounts.**

The terminology of dividend payments can be confusing, since they may be expressed either in the form, as 'x pence per share' or as 'y%'. In the latter case, the meaning is always 'y% of the *nominal value* of the shares in issue'.

EXAMPLE: RATE OF DIVIDEND

A company's issued share capital consists of 100,000 50p ordinary shares which were issued at a premium of 10p per share. The company's balance sheet would include the following.

		£
Ordinary shares:	100,000 50p ordinary shares	50,000
Share premium account	(100,000 × 10p)	10,000

If the directors wish to pay a dividend of £5,000, they may propose either:

(a) a dividend of 5p per share (100,000 × 5p = £5,000); or
(b) a dividend of 10% (10% × £50,000 = £5,000).

Not all profits are distributed as dividends; some will be retained in the business to finance future projects. And the company may signify its intention **never** to distribute some profits as dividends by transferring them to the general reserve, as we saw above.

Activity 5 **(10 minutes)**

A company has authorised share capital of 1,000,000 50p ordinary shares and an issued share capital of 800,000 50p ordinary shares. If an ordinary dividend of 5% is declared, what is the amount payable to shareholders?

A £50,000
B £20,000
C £40,000
D £25,000

3.4.2 Profit and loss reserve (retained profits)

This most significant **non-statutory reserve** is variously described as:

(a) Revenue reserve
(b) Retained profits
(c) Retained earnings
(d) Undistributed profits
(e) Profit and loss account
(f) Unappropriated profits

These are the company's accumulated profits after tax which have not been **appropriated** by dividends or transferred to general reserve.

Provided that a company is earning profits, this reserve generally increases from year to year, as most companies do not distribute all their profits as dividends. Dividends can be paid from it even if a loss is made in one particular year; a dividend can still be paid from previous years' retained profits.

EXAMPLE: PAYMENT OF DIVIDENDS

If a company makes a loss of £100,000 in one year, yet has retained profits from previous years totalling £250,000, it can pay a dividend not exceeding £150,000. One reason for retaining some profit each year is to enable the company to pay dividends even when profits are low (or non-existent). Another reason is usually shortage of cash.

3.5 Statement of movements in reserves

In the published financial statements, the profit and loss account stops at profit after tax, and the balance sheet includes only the final retained profit figure. To reconcile the two, and detail transactions recognised directly in reserves, a company has to provide a statement of movements on reserves.

STATEMENT OF MOVEMENTS IN RESERVES

	Share premium	*General*	*Retained profit*
	£	£	£
At 1 January 20X8	5,000	750	250
Profit for the period after tax	–	–	100
Dividends	–	–	(60)
Transfer to general reserve	–	10	(10)
Share issue	500	–	–
At 31 December 20X8	5,500	760	280

4 LOAN CAPITAL

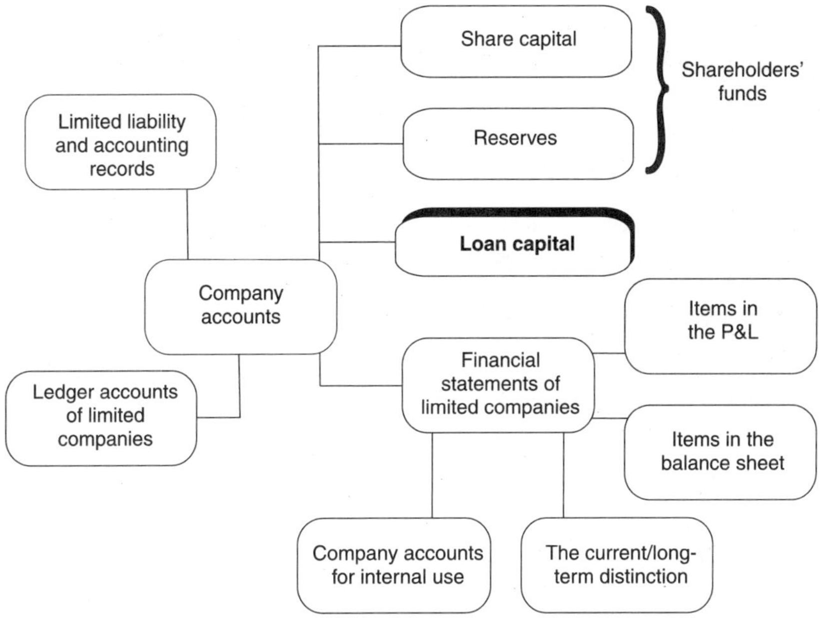

Definition

> **Loan capital** is formed by the company taking on long-term loans to fund its operations. Such loans nearly always take the form of debentures, which are written acknowledgement of the company's debt, also including security taken over the company's assets. Debenture – or loan stock – can be bought and sold.

Loans are different from share capital in the following ways.

(a) **Shareholders** are **members** of a company, while **providers of loan capital** are **creditors**.

(b) **Shareholders** receive **dividends** whereas the holders of loan capital are entitled to a **fixed rate of interest** (an expense charged against profits).

(c) Loan capital holders can take legal action against a company if their interest is not paid when due, whereas **ordinary shareholders cannot enforce the payment of dividends**.

(d) **Debentures** are often **secured on company assets**, whereas shares are not.

The holder of loan capital is generally in a less risky position than the shareholder. He has greater security, although his income is fixed and cannot grow, unlike ordinary dividends. Preference shares are, in practice, very similar to loan capital, not least because the preference dividend is normally fixed, and as we have seen, the shares may be redeemable.

Interest is calculated on the nominal value of loan capital, regardless of its market value. If a company has £700,000 (nominal value) 12% debentures in issue, interest of £84,000 will be charged in the profit and loss account per year. Interest is usually paid half-yearly.

You may often hear of long-term company liabilities referred to as **loan capital**.

EXAMPLE: INTEREST ON LOAN CAPITAL

A company has £700,000 12% debentures in issue and pays interest on 30 June and 31 December each year. It ends its accounting year on 30 September. There would be an accrual of three months' unpaid interest (3/12 × £84,000) = £21,000 at the end of each accounting year that the debentures are still in issue.

Advantages of raising loan capital

(a) Debenture-holders are creditors, not shareholders, and so do not affect the **control** of the company.

(b) The interest rate is fixed and so is a known cost.

(c) The interest is usually allowable as a deduction from taxable profit, ie the profit on which tax is levied

(d) If a debenture is secured on assets the interest rate will normally be lower than, say, an overdraft.

Disadvantages of raising loan capital

(a) Debenture interest **must** be paid, whereas directors do not need to pay ordinary shareholders a dividend.

(b) Debenture-holders can force the sale of any assets used as security, if the company does not comply with terms of their loan.

5 LEDGER ACCOUNTS OF LIMITED COMPANIES

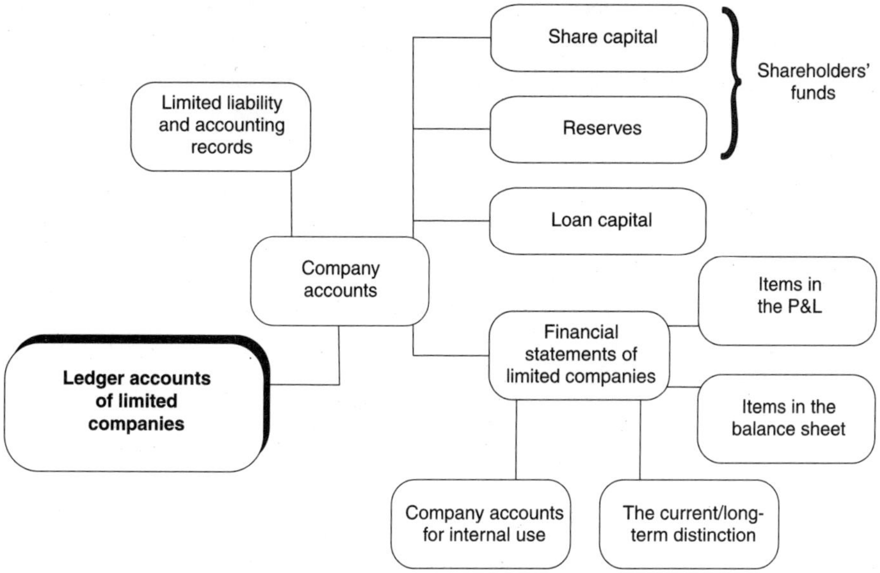

Limited companies keep ledger accounts, and the only difference between the ledger accounts of companies and sole traders is the nature of some of the transactions, assets and liabilities for which accounts need to be kept.

For example, there will be an account for each of the following items:

(a) *Taxation*

(i) Tax charged against profits will be accounted for as follows:

DEBIT P&L account
CREDIT Taxation account (balance sheet)

(ii) The outstanding balance on the taxation account will be a liability in the balance sheet, until eventually paid, when the accounting entry would be:

DEBIT Taxation account
CREDIT Cash

(b) **Dividends**

A separate account will be kept for the dividends for each different class of shares (eg preference, ordinary).

(i) Dividends declared out of profits will be disclosed in the notes if they are unpaid at the year end.

(ii) When dividends are paid, we have:

DEBIT Dividends paid account
CREDIT Cash

(c) *Loan capital*

Loan capital, being a long-term liability, will be shown as a credit balance in a loan capital account.

Interest payable on such loans is not credited to the loan capital account, but is credited to a separate liability account for interest until it is eventually paid: ie

DEBIT	Interest account (an expense, chargeable against profits)
CREDIT	Interest payable (a current liability until eventually paid)

(d) *Share capital and reserves*

There will be a separate account with a credit balance b/d for:

(i) each different class of share capital.

(ii) each different type of reserve.

6 FINANCIAL STATEMENTS OF LIMITED COMPANIES

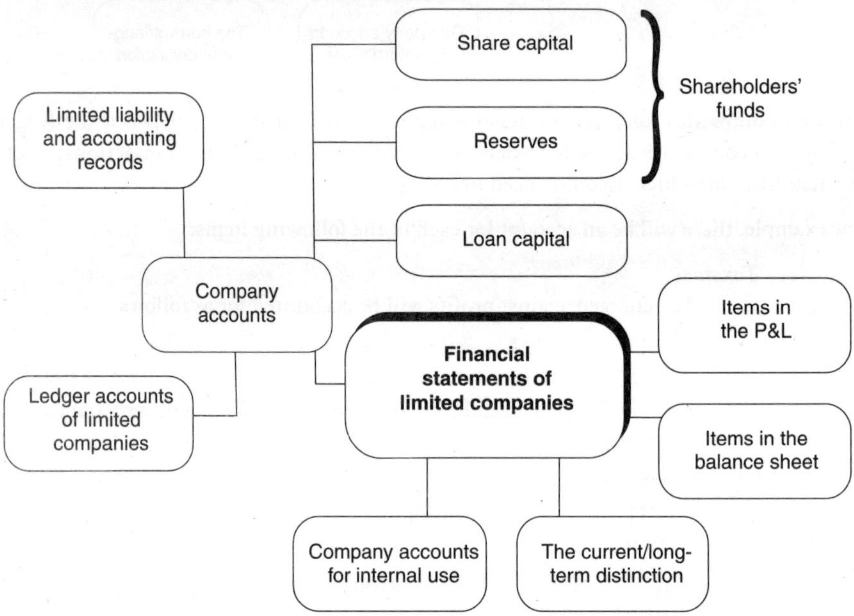

At this stage we are concerned with the preparation of limited company financial statements for **internal use**. The general format of the balance sheet and profit and loss account of a limited company is shown below, with some simplifications.

TYPICAL COMPANY LIMITED BALANCE SHEET AS AT....

		£	£	£
Fixed assets				X
Current assets	Stocks		X	
	Debtors and prepayments		X	
	Cash at bank and in hand		X	
			X	
Creditors: amounts falling due within one year (ie current liabilities)				
	Bank overdraft and loans	X		
	Creditors	X		
	Taxation	X		
	Accruals	X		
			(X)	
Net current assets (ie working capital)				X
Total assets less current liabilities				X
Creditors: amounts falling due after more than one year (ie long term liabilities or loan capital)				
	Debentures			(X)
				X
Shareholders' funds				
Share capital	Called-up share capital			
	Ordinary shares		X	
	Irredeemable preference shares		X	
				X
Reserves	Share premium account		X	
	(from the statement of movements on reserves)			
	Other reserves		X	
	Retained profits		X	
				X
				X

The profit and loss account of a company might have a format roughly similar to the one below.

TYPICAL COMPANY LIMITED
PROFIT AND LOSS ACCOUNT FOR THE YEAR ENDED...

	£	£
Turnover (sales)		X
Cost of sales		(X)
Gross profit		X
Distribution costs	X	
Administrative expenses	X	
		(X)
		X
Other income		X
		X
		X
Interest payable		(X)
Profit before taxation (ie net profit)		X
Tax		(X)
Profit after tax (including in statement of movement on reserves)		X

We will now consider some of the components in more detail in the following sections.

7 ITEMS IN THE PROFIT AND LOSS ACCOUNT

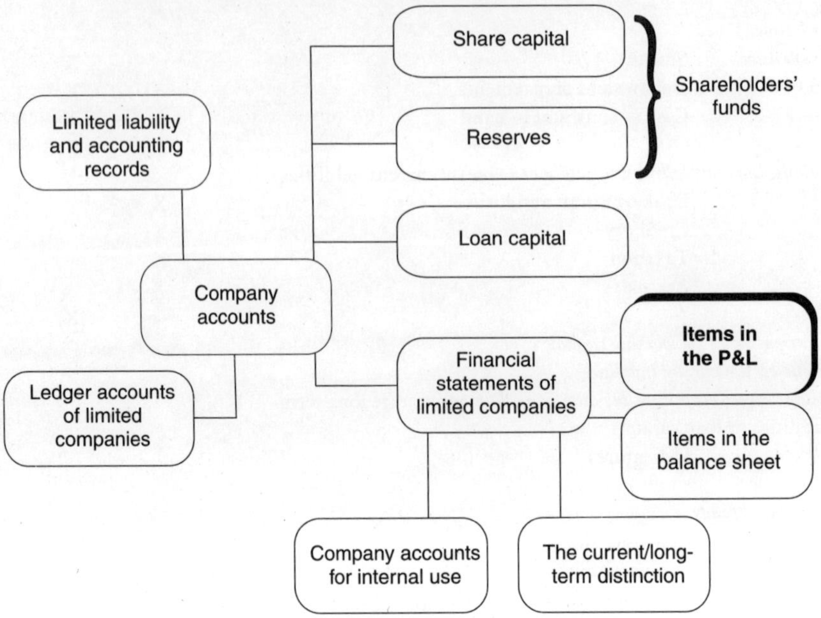

7.1 Managers' salaries

The 'salary' of a sole trader is not a charge to the profit and loss account but is an appropriation of profit, ie drawings. The **salary of a manager or member of management board of a limited liability company**, however, is an **expense in the profit and loss account**, even when the manager is a shareholder in the company. Management salaries are included in **administrative expenses.**

7.2 Taxation

Taxation affects both the balance sheet and the profit and loss account.

All companies pay some kind of corporation tax on the profits they earn. The rate of corporation tax will vary for different types or size of company.

As noted earlier, because a company has a **separate legal personality, its tax is included in its accounts**. An unincorporated business would not show tax in its accounts, as it would not be a business expense but the personal affair of the proprietors.

For a company:

(a) The **charge for tax on profits for the year** is shown as a **deduction from net profit**.

(b) In the balance sheet, **tax payable** is a **current liability** as it is usually due within 12 months of the year end.

(c) For various reasons, the tax on profits in the profit and loss account and the tax payable in the balance sheet are not normally the same amount.

EXAMPLE: TAXATION

A company has a tax liability for tax on its previous year's profit brought forward of £15,000. The liability is finally agreed at £17,500 and this is paid during the year. The company estimates that the tax liability on the current year's profit will be £20,000. Prepare the tax liability account for the year.

SOLUTION

TAX LIABILITY ACCOUNT

	£		£
Cash paid	17,500	Balance b/d	15,000
		Profit and loss a/c	22,500
Balance c/d	20,000		
	37,500		37,500

Notice that the profit and loss account charge consists of the following:

	£
Extra tax payable for previous year (17,500 – 15,000)	2,500
Estimated tax liability for current year	20,000
	22,500

Notice also that the balance carried down consists solely of the estimated tax liability for the current year.

7.3 Cost of sales

This represents the summary of the detailed workings we have used in a sole trader's financial statements.

7.4 Expenses

Notice that expenses are gathered under a number of headings. Any detail needed will be given in the notes to the financial statements.

7.5 Interest payable

This is interest **payable** during the period. Remember that this may include accruals for interest payable on debentures.

7.6 Accounting concepts

You will notice from the above that the accounting concepts apply to revenue and expenses. In particular, the accruals concept applies and so expect to have to adjust for accruals and prepayments.

7.7 Interrelationship of profit and loss account and balance sheet

When we were dealing with the financial statements of sole traders, we transferred the net profit to the capital account. In the case of limited companies, the net profit is transferred to retained profits in the statement of movements in reserves. The closing balance of the reserves are then transferred to the balance sheet.

8 ITEMS IN THE BALANCE SHEET

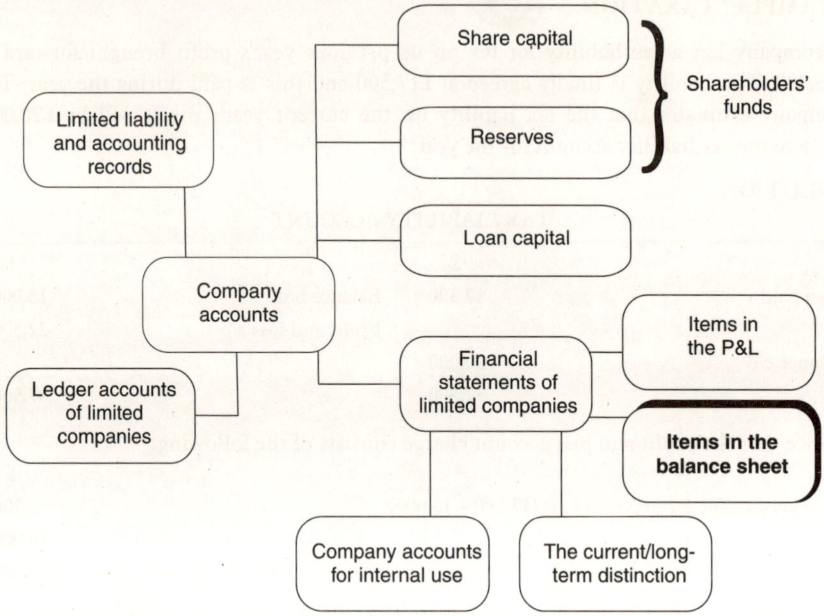

8.1 Fixed assets

As with any other type of business, fixed assets are shown in the balance sheet at their net book value (ie at cost less accumulated depreciation).

8.2 Other assets

Other assets are exactly the same as those found in a sole trader's accounts.

8.3 Liabilities

These are split between current and long-term liabilities, including what we have called loan capital (see Section 4).

8.4 Accounting equation

The balance sheet relies on the accounting equation that:

Assets – liabilities = capital

You will not be surprised to learn that the accounting equation is also called the **balance sheet equation**.

9 THE CURRENT/LONG-TERM DISTINCTION

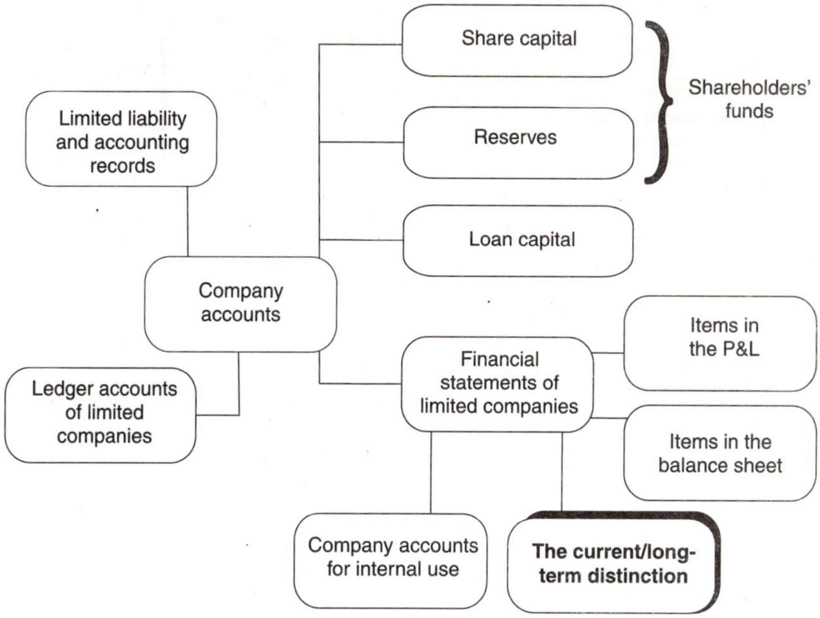

The term '**creditors: amounts falling due within one year**' is used in the Companies Act as an alternative phrase meaning 'current liabilities'. You will therefore come across this term increasingly often as you progress through your accountancy studies. Similarly, the term '**creditors: amounts falling due after more than one year**' is the Companies Act 2006 term for long-term liabilities. The sub-headings in Section 1 show the main types of liabilities.

10 COMPANY ACCOUNTS FOR INTERNAL PURPOSES

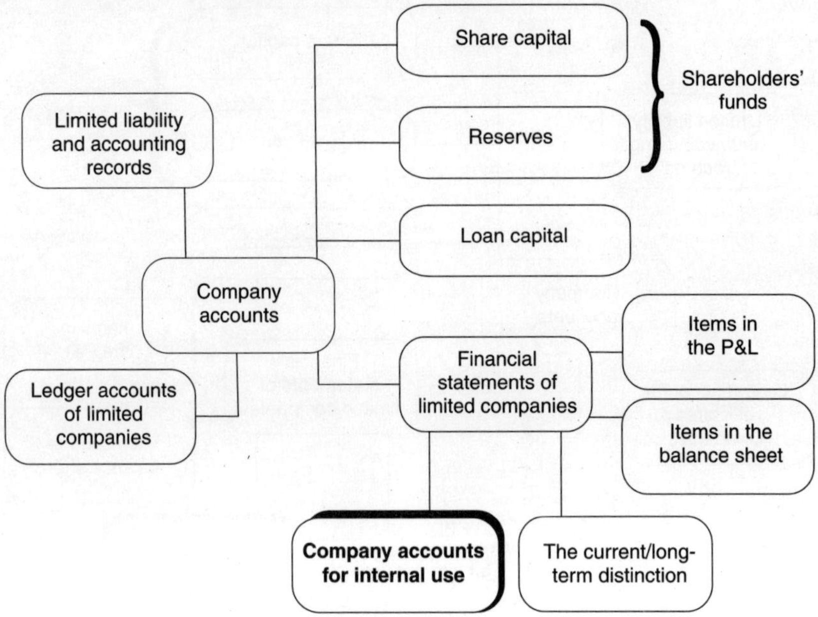

We can now try to draw together several of the items described in this chapter into an illustrative example. Study it carefully.

EXAMPLE: WISLON LTD

The accountant of Wislon Ltd has prepared the following trial balance as at 31 December 20X7.

	DR	*CR*
	£'000	£'000
50p ordinary shares (fully paid)		400
Share premium account		70
7% £1 irredeemable preference shares (fully paid)		100
10% debentures (secured)		200
Retained profit 1.1.X7		242
General reserve 1.1.X7		171
Freehold land and buildings 1.1.X7 (cost)	430	
Plant and machinery 1.1.X7 (cost)	830	
Accumulated depreciation:		
Freehold buildings 1.1.X7		20
Plant and machinery 1.1.X7		222
Stock 1.1.X7	190	
Sales		2,695
Purchases	2,152	
Preference dividend	7	
Ordinary dividend (interim)	8	
Debenture interest	10	
Wages and salaries	254	
Light and heat	31	
Sundry expenses	113	
Disposals		300
Debtors	464	
Creditors		195
Cash	126	
	4,615	4,615

Notes

(a) Sundry expenses include £9,000 paid in respect of insurance for the year ending 1 September 20X8. Light and heat does not include an invoice of £3,000 for electricity for the three months ending 2 January 20X8, which was paid in February 20X8. Light and heat also includes £20,000 relating to salesmen's commission.

(b) Proceeds from the sale of plant of £300,000 were debited to cash, and credited to disposals.

(c) The freehold property was acquired some years ago. The buildings element of the cost was estimated at £100,000 and the estimated useful life of the assets was fifty years at the time of purchase.

(d) The plant which was sold had cost £350,000 and had a net book value of £274,000 as on 1.1.X7. £36,000 depreciation is to be charged on plant and machinery for 20X7.

(e) The debentures have been in issue for some years. The 50p ordinary shares all rank for dividends at the end of the year.

(f) The directors wish to provide for:
(i) Debenture interest due
(ii) A transfer to general reserve of £16,000
(iii) Audit fees of £4,000

(g) Stock as at 31 December 20X7 was valued at £220,000 (cost).

(h) Taxation is to be ignored.

Required

Prepare the final accounts of Wislon Ltd in a form suitable for internal purposes.

Approach and suggested solution

(a) Normal adjustments are needed for accruals and prepayments (insurance, light and heat, debenture interest and audit fees). The debenture interest accrued is calculated as follows:

	£'000
Charge needed in P & L account (10% × £200,000)	20
Amount paid so far, as shown in trial balance	10
Accrual – six months' interest now payable	10

The accrued expenses shown in the balance sheet comprise:

	£'000
Debenture interest	10
Light and heat	3
Audit fee	4
	17

(b) The misposting of £20,000 to light and heat is also adjusted, by reducing the light and heat expense, but charging £20,000 to salesmen's commission.

(c) Depreciation on the freehold building is calculated as $\frac{£100{,}000}{50} = £2{,}000$.

The NBV of the freehold property is then £430,000 – £20,000 – £2,000 = £408,000 at the end of the year.

(d) The profit on disposal of plant is calculated as proceeds £300,000 less NBV £274,000, ie £26,000. The cost of the remaining plant is calculated at £830,000 – £350,000 = £480,000. The accumulated depreciation at the year end is:

	£'000
Balance 1.1.X7	222
Charge for 20X7	36
Less depreciation on disposals (350 – 274)	(76)
	182

(e) The transfer to general reserve increases that reserve to £171,000 + £16,000 = £187,000.

WISLON LIMITED
TRADING AND PROFIT AND LOSS ACCOUNT FOR THE YEAR ENDED 31 DECEMBER 20X7

		£'000	£'000	£'000
Sales				2,695
Less cost of sales				
Opening stock			190	
Purchases			2,152	
			2,342	
Less closing stock			(220)	
				(2,122)
Gross profit				573
Profit on disposal of plant				26
				599
Less expenses				
Wages, salaries and commission			274	
Sundry expenses			107	
Light and heat			14	
Depreciation:	freehold buildings		2	
	plant		36	
Audit fees			4	
Debenture interest			20	
				(457)
Net profit				142
Movement on retained profits				
Profit for the period				142
Transfer to general reserve				(16)
Dividends:	preference (paid)	7		
ordinary:	interim (paid)	8		
				(15)
Retained profit for the year				111
Retained profit brought forward				242
Retained profit carried forward				353

WISLON LIMITED
BALANCE SHEET AS AT 31 DECEMBER 20X7

	Cost/val'n	*Dep'n*	
Fixed assets	£'000	£'000	£'000
Tangible assets			
Freehold property	408	–	408
Plant and machinery	480	182	298
	888	182	
			706
Current assets			
Stock		220	
Debtors		464	
Prepayment		6	
Cash		126	
		816	
Creditors: amounts falling due within one year			
Creditors	195		
Accrued expenses	17		
		212	
Net current assets			604
Total assets less current liabilities			1,310
Creditors: amounts falling due after more than one year			
10% debentures (secured)			(200)
			1,110
Capital and reserves			
Called up share capital			
50p ordinary shares		400	
7% £1 irredeemable preference shares		100	
			500
Reserves			
Share premium		70	
General reserve		187	
Retained profits reserve		353	
			610
			1,110

Chapter roundup

- As we should expect, the accounting rules and conventions for recording the business transactions of limited companies and then preparing their final financial statements are much the same as for sole traders. However there are some important differences as well.
- There is a legal requirement for companies in the UK to keep **accounting records** which are sufficient to show and explain the company's transactions.
- In preparing a balance sheet you must be able to deal with:
  - ordinary and preference share capital
  - reserves
  - loan capital
- Share capital may take the form of **preference shares** or **ordinary shares**.
- Limited companies may issue **debentures** as loan capital. These are **long-term liabilities**.
- The fixed assets of a company, plus the working capital (ie current assets minus current liabilities) minus the long-term liabilities, are its net assets 'financed' by the shareholders' funds.
- The preparation and publication of the final accounts of limited companies in the UK are governed by the Companies Act, and related secondary legislation.

Quick quiz

1 What is the meaning of limited liability?

A Shareholders are responsible for the company's debts.
B Shareholders are responsible only for the amount unpaid on their shares.

2 What is the difference between issued capital and called-up capital?

3 What are the differences between ordinary shares and preference shares?

4 What are the differences between debentures and share capital?

5 A company issues 50,000 £1 shares at a price of £1.25 per share. How much should be credited to the share premium account?

A £50,000
B £12,500
C £62,500
D £60,000

6 According to the Companies Act 2006, private limited companies have to produce their accounts within what period?

A Within six months of the balance sheet date
B Within nine months of the balance sheet date

7 Managers' salaries are appropriations of profit.

A True
B False

8 Which of the following items are fixed assets?

(i) Land
(ii) Machinery
(iii) Bank loan
(iv) Stock

A (i) only
B (i) and (ii)
C (i), (ii) and (iii)
D (ii), (iii) and (iv)

9 How is a bank overdraft classified in the balance sheet?

A Fixed asset
B Current asset
C Current liability
D Long-term liability

10 In the published accounts of XYZ Co, the profit for the period is £3,500,000. The balance of retained profits at the beginning of the year is £500,000. If dividends of £2,500,000 were paid, what is the closing balance of retained profit?

A £4,000,000
B £1,500,000
C £500,000
D £1,000,000

Answers to quick quiz

1 B The maximum amount that a shareholder has to pay is the amount unpaid on his shares.

2 Issued share capital is the nominal value of shares issued to shareholders. Called-up share capital is the amount payable to date by the shareholders.

3 Ordinary shareholders can be paid any or no dividend. The dividend attaching to preference shares is set from the start. Preference shares may be redeemable.

4 Debentures are long-term loans, and so debenture holders are long-term creditors. Equity shareholders own the company.

5 B (50,000 × 25p)

6 B

7 B False. Managers' salaries are an expense charged to the income statement.

8 B Item (iii) is a liability and item (iv) is a current asset.

9 C A bank overdraft is strictly payable on demand and so it is a current liability.

10 B

	£'000
Retained profits	
Opening balance	500
Profit for the period	3,500
	4,000
Dividends paid	(2,500)
Closing balance	1,500

Answers to activities

1 False. But what *does* it mean? Look back to Section 1.1.

2 Look back to paragraph 2.2 (a) and (b).

3

		£	£
DEBIT	Bank	260,000	
CREDIT	Share capital		200,000
CREDIT	Share premium		60,000

4 Did you notice that the shares are 50p each, not £1? The shares were issued for £1.20 each (£6,000/5,000 shares). Of this, 50p is share capital and 70p is share premium. Therefore option D is the correct answer.

5 B 800,000 × 50p × 5% = £20,000.

Chapter 10:
CASH FLOW STATEMENTS

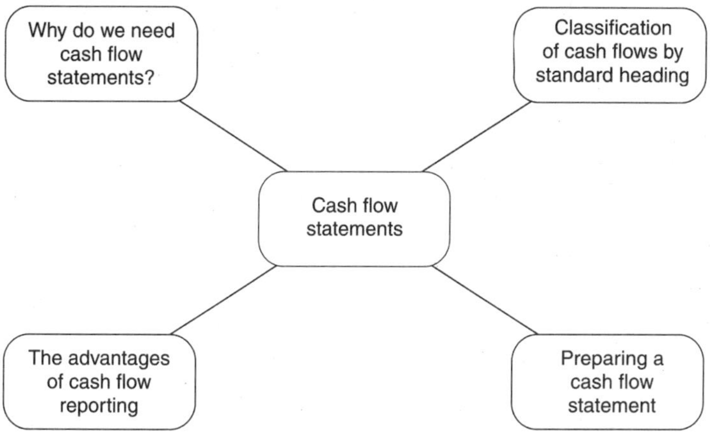

Introduction

In the short run, the making of a profit will not necessarily result in an increased cash balance. The observation leads us to two questions:

- What is the difference between cash and profit?
- How useful are the profit and loss account and balance sheet in demonstrating whether a company has sufficient cash to finance its operations?

The importance of the distinction between cash and profit and the scant attention paid to this by the profit and loss account has resulted in the development of cash flow statements.

Your objectives

After completing this chapter you should be able to:

1. Appreciate the difference between profit and cash flow
2. Describe the main elements of cash flow
3. Prepare a basic cash flow statement and note adjusting operating profit to net cash flows from operating activities
4. Describe the advantages of cash flow accounting

1 WHY DO WE NEED CASH FLOW STATEMENTS?

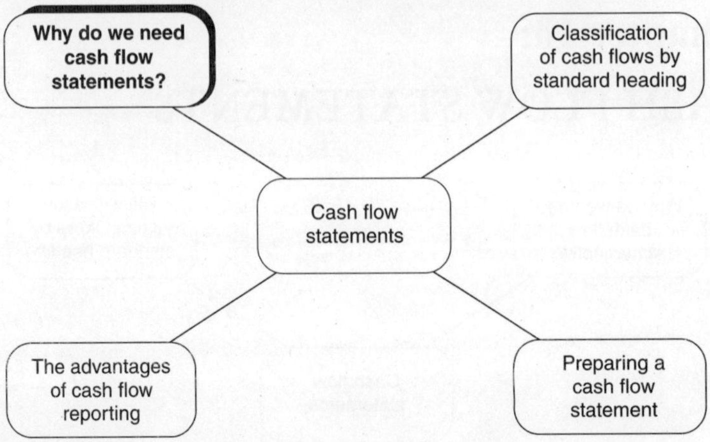

It has been argued that 'profit' does not always give a useful or meaningful picture of a company's operations. Readers of a company's financial statements might even be **misled by a reported profit figure.**

(a) Shareholders might believe that if a company makes a profit after tax, of say, £100,000 then this is the amount which it could afford to pay as a dividend. Unless the company has sufficient cash available to stay in business and also to pay a dividend, the shareholders' expectations would be wrong.

(b) Employees might believe that if a company makes profits, it can afford to pay higher wages next year. This opinion may not be correct: the ability to pay wages depends on the availability of cash.

(c) Cash is the lifeblood of the business. Survival of a business entity depends not so much on profits as on its ability to pay its debts when they fall due. Such payments might include 'profit and loss' items such as material purchases, wages, interest and taxation etc, but also capital payments for new fixed assets and the repayment of loan capital when this falls due (for example, on the redemption of debentures).

From these examples, you should be able to see that a company's performance and prospects depend not so much on the 'profits' earned in a period, but more realistically on liquidity or **cash flows**.

The great advantages of a cash flow statement are that:

- it is unambiguous
- it provides information which is additional to that provided in the profit and loss account and balance sheet, and it describes the cash flows of an organisation by activity and not by balance sheet classification.

1.1 Basic cash flow statement

A very basic cash flow statement is as follows.

	£
Net cash flow from operating activities (see sections 1.2 and 2.1)	X/(X)
Cash flows from:	
Returns on investment and servicing of finance (see sections 1.3 and 2.2)	X
Taxation (see section 2.3)	(X)
Capital expenditure (see sections 1.3 and 2.4)	(X)
Equity dividends paid (see sections 1.4 and 2.5)	(X)
Financing activities (see sections 1.4 and 2.6)	X/(X)
Increase/(decrease) in cash	X/(X)

Definition

'Cash' in this context includes *cash in hand* and *at bank* less *overdrafts* repayable to the bank on demand.

1.2 Net cash flow from operating activities

To arrive at net cash flow from operating activities we start with operating profit (from the profit and loss account) and adjust for non-cash items, such as depreciation, changes in debtors etc. A proforma calculation is given below.

It is important to understand why certain items are added and others subtracted.

(a) Depreciation is not a cash expense, but is deducted in arriving at the profit figure in the profit and loss account. To eliminate it we add it back.

(b) By the same logic, a loss on disposal of a fixed asset (arising through under-charging depreciation) needs to be added back. A profit on disposal should be deducted.

(c) An increase in stocks means less cash – you have spent cash on buying stock.

(d) An increase in debtors means debtors have not paid as much, therefore less cash.

(e) If we pay off creditors, causing the creditors figure to decrease, again we have less cash.

Activity 1 **(15 minutes)**

Quest Ltd has operating profit for the year to 31 December 20X6 of £850, after charging £650 for depreciation and making a profit on disposal of a car of £120.

The balance sheets for the years shows the following entries.

	20X6	*20X5*
Stock	586	763
Trade debtors	1,021	589
Trade creditors	443	1,431

Required

Calculate the net cash flow from operating activities for the year ended 31 December 20X6.

1.3 Cash flows from returns on investment and servicing of finance

Cash flows from returns on investment and servicing of finance are calculated separately in the cash flow statement.

The proforma is as follows.

	£
Interest paid	(X)
Interest received	X
Dividends received	X
Cash flows from return on investment and servicing of finance	X

EXAMPLE: INVESTMENT CASH FLOWS AND CAPITAL EXPENDITURE

Pearl Ltd acquired a new factory in the year to 30 June 20X6 at a cost of £805,000. It sold its old factory for £425,000. It also received interest on surplus funds of £350,000. Calculate cash flows arising from returns on investment and servicing of finance.

SOLUTION

	£
Interest received	350,000
Cash flows from returns on investment and financing activities	350,000

The movement in fixed assets will be part of the **capital expenditure** cash flow shown separately in the cash flow statement.

1.4 Cash flows from financing activities

The proforma to learn for this part of the cash flow statement is:

	£
Proceeds from issue of share capital	X
Proceeds from long-term borrowing	X
Cash flows from financing activities	X

EXAMPLE: FINANCING ACTIVITIES

Spear Ltd issued 87,500 £1 shares at par during the year to 31 December 20X6. Loans taken out increased from £18,000 at the beginning of the year to £30,000 at the end of the year. The company declared a dividend of 10p per share. Calculate the cash flows from financing activities.

	£
Proceeds from issue of shares	87,500
Increase in loans	12,000
Cash flows from financing activities	99,500

Note that only **dividends *paid*** in the period represent cash flows; these are shown separately in the cash flow statement as **equity dividends paid.**

---

2 CLASSIFICATION OF CASH FLOWS BY STANDARD HEADING

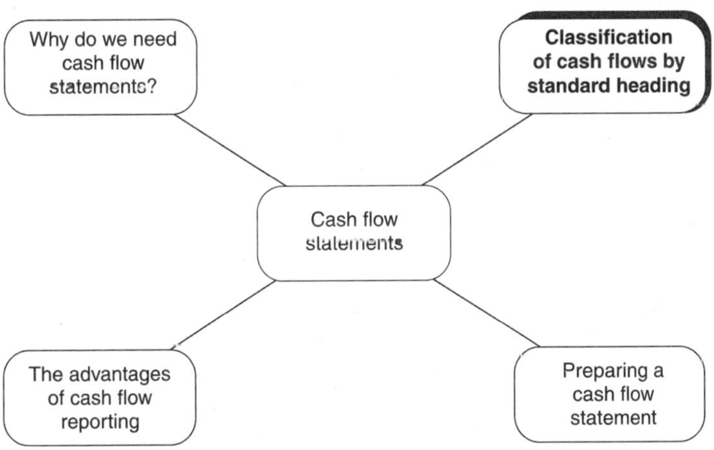

An accounting standard (FRS 1) looks at each of the cash flow categories in the basic statement, shown at Section 1.1, in turn.

2.1 Operating activities

Cash flows from operating activities are in general the cash effects of transactions and other events relating to operating or trading activities, normally shown in the profit and loss account in arriving at operating profit.

The reconciliation between the **operating profit** reported in the profit and loss account and the **net cash flow from operating activities** should be given either adjoining the cash flow statement or as a note. The reconciliation is not part of the cash flow statement: if adjoining the cash flow statement, it should be clearly labelled and kept separate. The reconciliation should disclose separately the movements in stocks, debtors and creditors related to operating activities and other differences between cash flows and profits.

2.2 Returns on investments and servicing of finance

These include:

- receipts resulting from the ownership of an investment, and
- payments to providers of finance and non-equity shareholders (eg the holders of preference shares).

Cash inflows from returns on investments and servicing of finance include:

(a) Interest received
(b) Dividends received

Cash outflows from returns on investments and servicing of finance include:

(a) Interest paid
(b) Issue costs on debt and preference share capital).
(c) The interest element of some lease payments.
(d) Dividends paid on preference shares.

2.3 Taxation

These are cash flows to or from taxation authorities in respect of the company's income and capital profits, excluding VAT and other sales taxes.

(a) Taxation cash inflows include cash receipts from the relevant tax authority of tax rebates, claims or returns of overpayments.

(b) Taxation cash outflows include cash payments to the relevant tax authority of tax.

2.4 Capital expenditure

These cash flows are those related to the acquisition or disposal of any fixed asset.

The cash inflows here include:

(a) Receipts from sales or disposals of property, plant or equipment.
(b) Receipts from the repayment of the company's loans to other entities.

Cash outflows in this category include:

(a) Payments to acquire property, plant or equipment
(b) Loans made by the company

2.5 Equity dividends paid

The cash outflows are dividends paid on the company's ordinary shares.

2.6 Financing

Financing cash flows comprise receipts or repayments from or to external providers of finance.

Financing cash inflows include:

(a) Receipts from issuing ordinary shares

(b) Receipts from issuing debentures, loans and from other long-term and short-term borrowings (other than overdrafts)

Financing cash outflows include:

(a) Repayments of amounts borrowed (other than overdrafts)
(b) The capital element of certain lease payments
(c) Payments to reacquire or redeem the company shares
(d) Payments of expenses or commission on any issue of shares

---

EXAMPLE: CASH FLOW STATEMENT AND NOTE

CAMDEN LIMITED
CASH FLOW STATEMENT FOR THE YEAR ENDED 31 DECEMBER 20X6

Reconciliation of operating profit to net cash inflow from operating activities

	£'000
Operating profit	6,022
Depreciation charges	899
Increase in stocks	(194)
Increase in debtors	(72)
Increase in creditors	234
Net cash inflow from operating activities	6,899

CASH FLOW STATEMENT

	£'000
Net cash inflow from operating activities	6,889
Returns on investments and servicing of finance (note 1)	2,999
Taxation	(2,922)
Capital expenditure (note 1)	(1,525)
	5,441
Equity dividends paid	(2,417)
	3,024
Financing (note 1)	(393)
Increase in cash	2,631

NOTE TO THE CASH FLOW STATEMENT

1 *Gross cash flows*

	£'000
Returns on investments and servicing of finance	
Interest received	3,011
Interest paid	(12)
	2,999

	£'000
Capital expenditure	
Payments to acquire fixed assets	(1,567)
Receipts from sales of fixed assets	42
	(1,525)
Financing	
Issue of ordinary share capital	411
Repurchase of debenture loan	(799)
Expenses paid in connection with share issue	(5)
	(393)

Activity 2 **(10 minutes)**

Close the book for a moment and jot down the format of the cash flow statement.

3 PREPARING A CASH FLOW STATEMENT

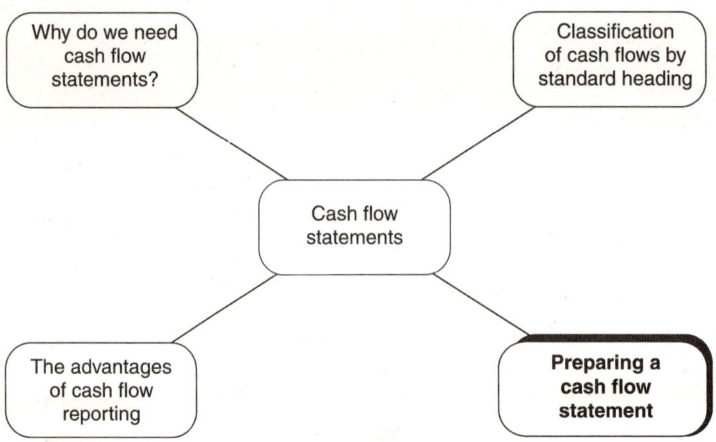

In essence, preparing a cash flow statement is very straightforward. You should therefore simply learn the format and apply the steps noted in the example below.

Note that the following items are treated in a way that might seem confusing, but the treatment is logical if you think in terms of **cash**.

(a) Increase in stock is treated as **negative** (in brackets). This is because it represents a cash **outflow**; cash is being spent on stock.

(b) An increase in debtors is treated as **negative** for the same reasons; more debtors means less cash.

(c) By contrast an increase in creditors is **positive** because cash is being retained and not used to pay off creditors. There is therefore more of it.

EXAMPLE: PREPARATION OF A CASH FLOW STATEMENT

Kane Ltd's profit and loss account for the year ended 31 December 20X2 and balance sheets at 31 December 20X1 and 31 December 20X2 were as follows.

KANE LIMITED
PROFIT AND LOSS ACCOUNT FOR THE YEAR ENDED 31 DECEMBER 20X2

	£'000	£'000
Sales		720
Raw materials consumed	70	
Staff costs	94	
Depreciation charges	118	
Loss on disposal	18	
		(300)
Operating profit		420
Interest payable		(28)
Profit before tax		392
Taxation		(124)
Profit after tax		268

KANE LIMITED
BALANCE SHEETS AS AT 31 DECEMBER

	20X2		*20X1*	
	£'000	£'000	£'000	£'000
Fixed assets				
Cost		1,596		1,560
Depreciation		(318)		(224)
		1,278		1,336
Current assets				
Stock	24		20	
Trade debtors	66		50	
Bank	48		56	
	138		126	
Current liabilities				
Trade creditors	12		6	
Taxation	92		76	
	104		84	
Net current assets		34		42
		1,312		1,378
Long-term liabilities				
Long-term loans		200		500
		1,112		878
Share capital		360		340
Share premium		36		24
Profit and loss		716		514
		1,112		878

Dividends totalling £66,000 were paid during 20X2.

During the year, the company paid £90,000 for a new piece of machinery, and sold fixed assets for £12,000.

Required

Prepare a cash flow statement for Kane Ltd for the year ended 31 December 20X2.

SOLUTION

Step 1 Set out the proforma cash flow statement with all the headings we have covered.

Step 2 Complete the note adjusting operating profit to net cash flow from operating activities.

Step 3 Calculate the figures for tax paid, purchase or sale of fixed assets, issue of shares and repayment of loans. If you are not given the tax charge in the profit and loss account, you will have to assume that the tax paid in the year is last year's year-end balance sheet figure and calculate the charge as the balancing figure.

Step 4 Complete Note 1, the gross cash flows, or put the information straight into the statement.

Step 5 Complete the statement by slotting in the figures given or calculated.

KANE LIMITED
CASH FLOW STATEMENT FOR THE YEAR ENDED 31 DECEMBER 20X2

Reconciliation of operating profit to net cash inflow

	£'000
Operating profit	420
Depreciation charges	118
Loss on sale of tangible fixed assets	18
Increase in stocks (20 – 24)	(4)
Increase in debtors (50 – 66)	(16)
Increase in creditors (12 – 6)	6
Net cash inflow from operating activities	542

CASH FLOW STATEMENT

	£'000	£'000
Net cash flows from operating activities		542
Returns on investment and servicing of finance		
Interest paid		(28)
Taxation		
Tax paid (W1)		(110)
Capital expenditure		
Payments to acquire tangible fixed assets	(90)	
Receipts from sales of tangible fixed assets	12	
Net cash outflow from capital expenditure		(78)
		326
Equity dividends paid		(66)
		260
Financing		
Issues of share capital (360 + 36 – 340 – 24)	32	
Long-term loans repaid (500 – 200)	(300)	
Net cash outflow from financing		(268)
Decrease in cash		(8)

Cash in the balance sheet has gone down by £8,000 (£56,000 – £48,000).

Workings

Tax paid

	£'000
Opening tax payable	78
Charge for year	124
Tax payable at 31.12.X2	(92)
Paid	110

Activity 3 **(1 hour)**

The summarised accounts of Rene plc for the year ended 31 December 20X8 are as follows.

RENE PLC
BALANCE SHEET AS AT 31 DECEMBER 20X8

	20X8		*20X7*	
	£'000	£'000	£'000	£'000
Fixed assets		618		514
Current assets				
Stocks	214		210	
Debtors	168		147	
Cash	7		–	
	389		357	
Creditors: amounts falling due within one year				
Trade creditors	136		121	
Tax payable	39		28	
Overdraft	–		14	
	175		163	
Net current assets		214		194
Total assets less current liabilities		832		708
Creditors: amounts falling due after more than one year				
10% debentures		(80)		(50)
		752		658
Capital and reserves				
Share capital (£1 ords)		250		200
Share premium account		170		160
Profit and loss account		332		298
		752		658

RENE PLC
PROFIT AND LOSS ACCOUNT
FOR THE YEAR ENDED 31 DECEMBER 20X8

	£'000
Sales	600
Cost of sales	(319)
Gross profit	281
Other expenses (including depreciation of £42,000 and interest payable of £8,000)	(194)
Profit before tax	87
Tax	(31)
Profit after tax	56

There have been no disposals of fixed assets during the year. New debentures were issued on 1 January 20X8 and debenture interest has been paid as due. Dividends paid were £22,000.

Required

Produce a cash flow statement using the direct method suitable for inclusion in the financial statements, as per FRS 1 (revised).

4 THE ADVANTAGES OF CASH FLOW REPORTING

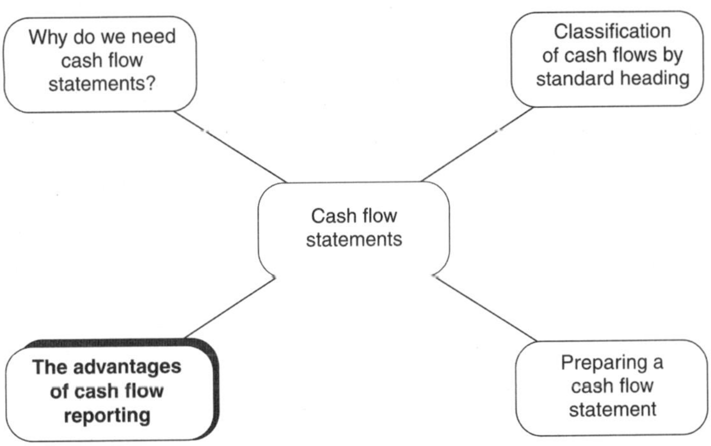

The advantages of cash flow reporting are as follows.

(a) Survival in business depends on the ability to generate cash. Cash flow reporting directs attention towards this critical issue.

(b) Cash flow is more comprehensive than 'profit', which is dependent on accounting conventions and concepts.

(c) Creditors (long and short-term) are more interested in an entity's ability to repay them than in its profitability. Whereas 'profits' might indicate that cash is likely to be available, cash flow reporting is more direct with its message.

(d) Cash flow reporting provides a better means of comparing the results of different companies than traditional profit reporting.

(e) Cash flow reporting satisfies the needs of all users better.

  (i) For management, it provides the sort of information on which decisions should be taken. In management accounting, for instance, 'relevant costs' to a decision are future cash flows; traditional profit accounting does not help with decision-making.

  (ii) As described previously, the information needs of creditors and employees will be better served by cash flow reporting.

(f) Cash flow forecasts are easier to prepare, as well as more useful, than profit forecasts.

(g) The accruals concept is confusing, and cash flows are more easily understood.

(h) Cash flow reporting should be retrospective, but should also include a forecast for the future. This is of great information value to all users of accounting information.

(i) Forecasts can subsequently be monitored by the publication of variance statements which compare actual cash flows against the forecast.

(j) Management needs to control cash flows and the cash flow statement shows exactly which activities are generating, and which are using, cash.

Activity 4 **(15 minutes)**

Can you think of some possible disadvantages of cash flow reporting?

Chapter roundup

- Cash flow is a useful measure of a company's performance.
- You need to be aware of the format laid out for the cash flow statement.

Quick quiz

1 Which of the following headings is **not** a classification of cash flows?

A Operating activities
B Financial investment
C Administration
D Financing

2 A company has the following information about its fixed assets.

	20X7	20X6
	£'000	£'000
Cost	750	600
Accumulated depreciation	250	150
Net book value	500	450

Plant with a net book value of £75,000 (original cost £90,000) was sold for £30,000 during the year.

What is the cash flow from capital expenditure for the year?

A £95,000 inflow
B £210,000 inflow
C £210,000 outflow
D £95,000 outflow

3 A company has the following extract from a balance sheet.

	20X7	20X6
	£'000	£'000
Share capital	2,000	1,000
Share premium	500	–
Debenture	750	1,000

What is the cash flow from financing for the year?

A £1,250 inflow
B £1,750 inflow
C £1,750 outflow
D £1,250 outflow

4 When adjusting profit before tax to arrive at cash generated from operating activities, a decrease in debtors is added to operating profit. Is this statement

A True
B False

Answers to quick quiz

1 C Administration costs are a classification in the profit and loss account, not the cash flow statement.

2 C

FIXED ASSETS

	£'000		£'000
Opening balance	600	Disposals	90
Additions (bal fig)	240	Closing balance	750
	840		840

Purchase of fixed assets	240,000
Proceeds of sale of fixed assets	(30,000)
Net cash outflow	210,000

3 A

	£'000
Issue of share capital (2,000 + 500 – 1,000)	1,500
Repayment of debentures (1,000 – 750)	(250)
Net cash inflow	1,250

4 A True

Answers to activities

1

	£
Operating profit	850
Add depreciation	650
Deduct profit on disposal	(120)
Add decrease in stocks (763 – 586)	177
Deduct increase in debtors (589 – 1,021)	(432)
Deduct decrease in creditors (443 – 1,431)	(988)
Net cash flow from operating activities	137

2 Net cash flows from operating activities:

	£
Operating profit (P & L)	X
Add depreciation	X
Loss (profit) on sale of fixed assets	X/(X)
(Increase)/decrease in stocks	(X)/X
(Increase)/decrease in debtors	(X)/X
Increase/(decrease) in creditors	X/(X)
Net cash flow from operating activities	X

3 RENE PLC
CASH FLOW STATEMENT
FOR THE YEAR ENDED 31 DECEMBER 20X8

	£'000	£'000
Net cash inflow from operating activities (Note 1)		127
Returns on investments and servicing of finance		
Interest paid		(8)
Taxation		
Tax paid (W1)		(20)
Capital expenditure		
Purchase of fixed assets (W2)		(146)
Equity dividends paid		(22)
Financing		
Issue of share capital (250 + 170) – (200 + 160)	60	
Issue of debentures (80 – 50)	30	
Net cash inflow from financing		90
Increase in cash (7 + 14)		21

NOTES TO THE CASHFLOW STATEMENT

1 *Reconciliation of operating profit to net cash inflow from operating activities*

	£'000
Operating profit (87 + 8)	95
Depreciation	42
Increase in stock (210 – 214)	(4)
Increase in debtors (147 – 168)	(21)
Increase in creditors (136 – 121)	15
	127

Workings

1 *Taxation*

TAXATION

	£'000		£'000
∴ Tax paid	20	Balance b/d	28
Balance c/d	39	Charge for year	31
	59		59

2 *Purchase of fixed assets*

	£'000
Opening fixed assets	514
Less depreciation	(42)
	472
Closing fixed assets	618
Difference = additions	146

4 The main disadvantages of cash flow statements are essentially the advantages of accruals accounting (proper matching of related items). There is also the practical problem that few businesses keep historical cash flow information in the form needed to prepare a historical cash flow statement and so extra record keeping is likely to be necessary.

Chapter 11:

INTERPRETING FINANCIAL STATEMENTS

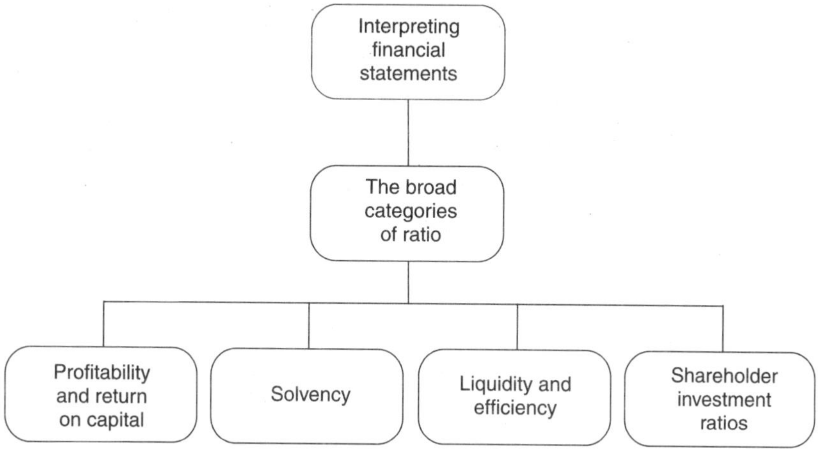

Introduction

So far in this Course Book we have looked at how financial statements are prepared and have described their features and contents.

In this chapter we are concerned with **interpretation of financial statements by means of ratios**. What do they mean?

Your objectives

After completing this chapter you should be able to:

1. Understand the importance of ratios as a means of understanding accounts
2. Calculate, understand and explain profitability and return on capital ratios
3. Calculate, understand and explain the necessary ratios to assess a company's solvency
4. Calculate, understand and explain liquidity and efficiency ratios
5. Calculate, understand and explain the shareholder investment ratios

1 THE BROAD CATEGORIES OF RATIOS

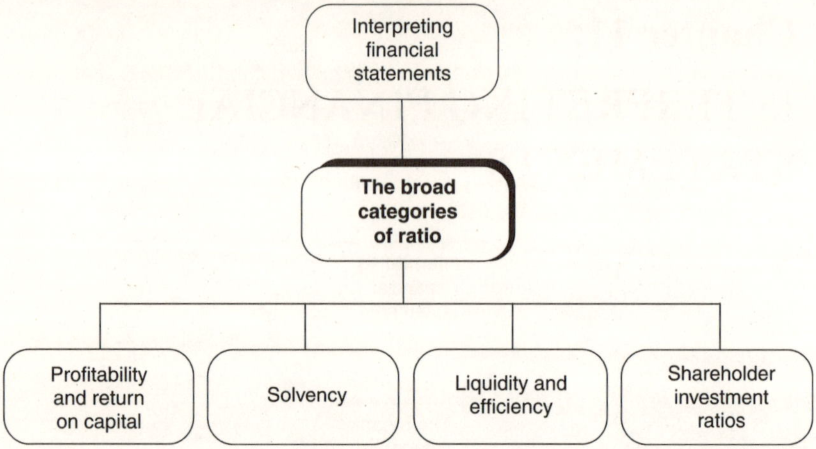

If you were to look at a balance sheet or P & L account, how would you decide whether the company was doing well or badly? Or whether it was financially strong or financially vulnerable? And what would you be looking at in the figures to help you to make your judgement?

A user of financial statements needs to appraise and communicate the position and prospects of a business, based on statements and ratios.

1.1 The broad categories of ratio

Broadly speaking, basic ratios can be grouped into five categories:

(a) Profitability and return
(b) Long-term solvency and stability
(c) Short-term solvency and liquidity
(d) Efficiency (turnover ratios)
(e) Shareholders' investment ratios

Within each heading we will identify a number of standard measures or ratios that are normally calculated and generally accepted as meaningful indicators. Each individual business must be considered separately; a ratio that is meaningful for a manufacturing company may be completely meaningless for a financial institution. Try not to be too mechanical when working out ratios and constantly think about what you are trying to achieve.

The key to obtaining meaningful information from ratio analysis is **comparison**. This may involve:

- Comparing ratios over time **within the same business** to establish whether things are improving or declining, and

- Comparing ratios **between similar businesses** to see whether the company you are analysing is better or worse than average within its specific business sector.

It must be stressed that ratio analysis on its own is not sufficient for interpreting company financial statements, and that there are other items of information which should be looked at, for example:

(a) Comments in the Chairman's report and directors' report

(b) The age and nature of the company's assets

(c) Current and future developments in the company's markets, at home and overseas;

(d) Any other noticeable features of the report and accounts, such as post balance sheet events, contingent liabilities, a qualified auditors' report, the company's taxation position, and so on

In every case, consider also the interest of particular users: a creditor will not be interested in shareholder's investment ratios, for instance.

SCENARIO: CALCULATING RATIOS

To illustrate the calculation of ratios, the following balance sheet and P & L account figures will be used, throughout this chapter.

FURLONG PLC PROFIT AND LOSS ACCOUNT
FOR THE YEAR ENDED 31 DECEMBER 20X8

	Notes	*20X8*	*20X7*
		£	£
Sales turnover	1	3,095,576	1,909,051
Operating profit	1	359,501	244,229
Interest	2	17,371	19,127
Profit on ordinary activities before taxation		342,130	225,102
Taxation on ordinary activities		74,200	31,272
Profit on ordinary activities after taxation		267,930	193,830
Earnings per share		12.8p	9.3p

FURLONG PLC BALANCE SHEET
AS AT 31 DECEMBER 20X8

	Notes	*20X8*	*20X7*
		£	£
Fixed assets		802,180	656,071
Current assets			
Stocks		44,422	76,550
Debtors	3	1,002,701	853,441
Cash at bank and in hand		1,327	68,363
		1,048,450	998,354
Creditors: amounts falling due within one year	4	(881,731)	(912,456)
Net current assets		166,719	85,898
Total assets less current liabilities		968,899	741,969
Creditors: amounts falling due after more than one year			
10% debenture stock 20Y4/20Y9		(100,000)	(100,000)
		868,899	641,969

	Notes	20X8	20X7
		£	£
Capital and reserves			
Called up share capital	5	210,000	210,000
Share premium account		48,178	48,178
Profit and loss account		610,721	383,791
		868,899	641,969

NOTES TO THE ACCOUNTS

			20X8	20X7
1	*Turnover and profit*		£	£
	(i)	Turnover	3,095,576	1,909,051
		Cost of sales	2,402,609	1,441,950
		Gross profit	692,967	467,101
		Administration expenses	333,466	222,872
		Operating profit	359,501	244,229
	(ii)	Operating profit is stated after charging:		
			20X8	20X7
		Depreciation	151,107	120,147
		Auditors' remuneration	6,500	5,000
		Leasing charges	47,636	46,336
		Directors' emoluments	94,945	66,675
2	*Interest*			
	Payable on bank overdrafts and other loans		8,115	11,909
	Payable on debenture stock		10,000	10,000
			18,115	21,909
	Receivable on short-term deposits		744	2,782
	Net payable		17,371	19,127
3	*Debtors*			
	Amounts falling due within one year			
	Trade debtors		884,559	760,252
	Prepayments and accrued income		97,022	45,729
				–
			981,581	805,981
	Amounts falling due after more than one year			
	Trade debtors		21,120	47,460
	Total debtors		1,002,701	853,441
4	*Creditors: amounts falling due within one year*			
	Trade creditors		627,018	545,340
	Accruals and deferred income		81,279	280,464
	Corporation tax		98,000	37,200
	Other taxes and social security costs		75,434	49,452
			881,731	912,456
5	*Called up share capital*			
	Issued and fully paid ordinary shares of 10p each		210,000	210,00

2 PROFITABILITY AND RETURN ON CAPITAL

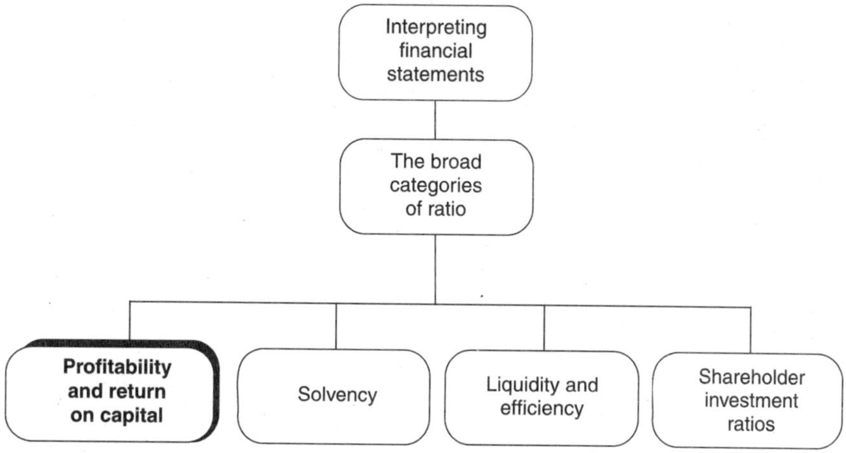

In our example, the company made a profit in both 20X8 and 20X7, and there was an increase in profit on ordinary activities between one year and the next:

(a) of 52% before taxation
(b) of 39% after taxation

Profit on ordinary activities *before* taxation is generally thought to be a better figure to use than profit after taxation, because there might be unusual variations in the tax charge from year to year which would not affect the underlying profitability of the company's operations.

Another profit figure that should be calculated is PBIT, **profit before interest and tax.** This is the amount of profit which the company earned before having to pay interest to the providers of loan capital. By providers of loan capital, we usually mean longer-term loan capital, such as debentures and medium-term bank loans, which will be shown in the balance sheet as 'creditors: amounts falling due after more than one year'.

Profit before interest and tax is therefore:

(a) The profit on ordinary activities before taxation
(b) Plus interest charges on long-term loan capital

Published accounts do not always give sufficient detail on interest payable to determine how much is interest on long-term finance. We will assume in our example that the whole of the interest payable (£18,115, note 2) relates to long-term finance.

PBIT in our example is therefore:

	20X8	*20X7*
	£	£
Profit on ordinary activities before tax	342,130	225,102
Interest payable (Note 2 above)	18,115	21,909
PBIT	360,245	247,011

This shows a 46% growth between 20X7 and 20X8.

2.1 Return on capital employed (ROCE)

It is impossible to assess profits or profit growth properly without relating them to the amount of funds (capital) that were employed in making the profits. The most important profitability ratio is therefore **return on capital employed** (ROCE), which states the PBIT as a percentage of the amount of capital employed.

Definition

$$\text{ROCE} = \frac{\text{Profit on ordinary activities before interest and taxation}}{\text{Capital employed}}$$

Capital employed = Shareholders' funds plus creditors: amounts falling due after more than one year'

The underlying principle is that we must compare like with like, and so if capital means share capital and reserves plus long-term liabilities and debt capital, profit must mean the profit earned by all this capital together. This is PBIT, since interest is the return for loan capital.

EXAMPLE: ROCE

In our example, capital employed = 20X8 868,899 + 100,000 = £968,899
20X7 641,969 + 100,000 = £741,969

These total figures are the total assets less current liabilities figures for 20X8 and 20X7 in the balance sheet.

		20X8	*20X7*
ROCE	=	$\frac{360{,}245}{968{,}899}$	$\frac{247{,}011}{741{,}969}$
	=	37.2%	33.3%

What does a company's ROCE tell us? What should we be looking for? There are three comparisons that can be made.

(a) The change in ROCE from **one year to the next** can be examined. In this example, there has been an increase in ROCE by about 11% or 12% from its 20X7 level.

(b) The ROCE being earned by **other companies**, if this information is available, can be compared with the ROCE of this company. Here the information is not available.

(c) A comparison of the ROCE with **current market borrowing rates** may be made.

(i) What would be the cost of extra borrowing to the company if it needed more loans, and is it earning a ROCE that suggests it could make profits to make such borrowing worthwhile?

(ii) Is the company making a ROCE which suggests that it is getting value for money from its current borrowing?

(iii) Companies are in a risk business and commercial borrowing rates are a good independent yardstick against which company performance can be judged.

In this example, if we suppose that current market interest rates for medium-term borrowing from banks, is around 10%, then the company's actual ROCE of 37% in 20X8 would not seem low. On the contrary, it might seem high.

However, it is easier to spot a low ROCE than a high one, because there is always a chance that the company's fixed assets, especially property, are undervalued in its balance sheet, and so the capital employed figure might be unrealistically low. If the company had earned a ROCE, not of 36%, but of, say, only 6% then its return would have been below current borrowing rates and so disappointingly low.

2.2 Return on shareholders' capital (ROSC)

Another measure of profitability and return is the return on shareholders' capital (ROSC):

Definition

$$\text{ROSC} = \frac{\text{Profit on ordinary activities before tax}}{\text{Share capital and reserves}}$$

ROSC is intended to focus on the return being made by the company for the specific benefit of its shareholders. In our example, the figures are as follows.

20X8	*20X7*
$\frac{342,130}{868,899} = 39.4\%$	$\frac{225,102}{641,969} = 35.1\%$

These figures show an improvement between 20X7 and 20X8, and a return which is clearly in excess of current borrowing rates (assuming these are at 10%).

ROSC is not a widely-used ratio, however, because there are more useful ratios that give an indication of the return to shareholders, such as earnings per share, dividend per share, dividend yield and earnings yield, which are described later.

2.3 Sub-analysis of profitability and return

We often sub-analyse ROCE, to find out more about why the ROCE is high or low, or better or worse than last year. There are two factors that contribute towards ROCE, both related to sales (turnover).

(a) **Profit margin.** A company might make a high or low profit margin on its sales. For example, a company that makes a profit of 25p per £1 of sales is making a bigger return on its sales than another company making a profit of only 10p per £1 of sales.

(b) **Asset turnover**. Asset turnover is a measure of how well the assets of a business are being used to generate sales. For example, if two companies each have capital employed of £100,000 and Company A makes sales of £400,000 per annum whereas Company B makes sales of only £200,000 per annum, Company A is making higher sales from the same amount of assets (twice as much asset turnover as Company B) and this will help A to make a higher return on capital employed than B. Asset turnover is expressed as 'x times' so that assets generate x times their value in annual sales. Here, Company A's asset turnover is 4 times and B's is 2 times.

Profit margin and asset turnover together explain the ROCE. If the ROCE is the primary profitability ratio, these other two are the secondary ratios. The relationship between the three ratios can be shown mathematically.

Definition

Profit margin × Asset turnover = **ROCE**

$$\therefore \frac{\text{PBIT}}{\text{Sales}} \times \frac{\text{Sales}}{\text{Capital employed}} = \frac{\text{PBIT}}{\text{Capital employed}}$$

In our example:

		Profit margin		*Asset turnover*		*ROCE*
(a)	20X8	$\frac{360,245}{3,095,576}$	×	$\frac{3,095,576}{968,899}$	=	$\frac{360,245}{968,899}$
		11.64%	×	3.19 times	=	37.2%
(b)	20X7	$\frac{247,011}{1,909,051}$	×	$\frac{1,909,051}{741,969}$	=	$\frac{247,011}{751,969}$
		12.94%	×	2.57 times	=	33.3%

In this example, the company's improvement in ROCE between 20X7 and 20X8 is attributable to a higher asset turnover. Indeed the profit margin has fallen a little, but the higher asset turnover has more than compensated for this.

It is also worth commenting on the change in sales from one year to the next. You may already have noticed that Furlong plc achieved sales growth of over 60% from £1.9 million to £3.1 million between 20X7 and 20X8. This is very strong growth, and is certainly one of the most significant items in the P & L account and balance sheet.

2.4 Making comments on profit margin and asset turnover

It might be tempting to think that a high profit margin is good, and a low asset turnover means sluggish trading. In broad terms, this is so. But there is a trade-off between profit margin and asset turnover, and you cannot look at one without allowing for the other.

(a) A high profit margin means a high profit per £1 of sales, but if this also means that sales prices are high, there is a strong possibility that sales volume will be depressed, and so asset turnover lower.

(b) A high asset turnover means that the company is generating a lot of sales, but to do this it might have to keep its prices down and so accept a low profit margin per £1 of sales.

Consider the following.

Company A		*Company B*	
Sales	£1,000,000	Sales	£4,000,000
Capital employed	£1,000,000	Capital employed	£1,000,000
PBIT	£200,000	PBIT	£200,000

These figures would give the following ratios.

Company A:

ROCE $= \frac{200{,}000}{1{,}000{,}000} = 20\%$

Profit margin $= \frac{200{,}000}{1{,}000{,}000} = 20\%$

Asset turnover $= \frac{1{,}000{,}000}{1{,}000{,}000} = 1$

Company B:

ROCE $= \frac{200{,}000}{1{,}000{,}000} = 20\%$

Profit margin $= \frac{200{,}000}{4{,}000{,}000} = 5\%$

Asset turnover $= \frac{4{,}000{,}000}{1{,}000{,}000} = 4$

The companies have the same ROCE, but it is arrived at in a very different fashion. Company A operates with a low asset turnover and a comparatively high profit margin whereas company B carries out much more business, but on a lower profit margin. Company A could be operating at the luxury end of the market, while company B is operating at the popular end (Fortnum and Masons v Sainsbury's).

Activity 1 **(15 minutes)**

Which one of the following formulae correctly expresses the relationship between return on capital employed (ROCE), profit margin (PM) and asset turnover (AT)?

A PM $= \frac{AT}{ROCE}$

B ROCE $= \frac{PM}{AT}$

C AT $= PM \times ROCE$

D PM $= \frac{ROCE}{AT}$

2.5 Gross profit margin, net profit margin and profit analysis

Depending on the format of the P & L account, you may be able to calculate the gross profit margin (or trading margin) as well as the net profit margin (or operating margin). Looking at the two together can be quite informative.

For example, suppose that a company has the following summarised profit and loss accounts for two consecutive years.

	Year 1	*Year 2*
	£	£
Sales	70,000	100,000
Cost of sales	42,000	55,000
Gross profit	28,000	45,000
Expenses	21,000	35,000
Net profit	7,000	10,000

Although the net profit margin is the same for both years at 10%, the gross profit margin is not.

In year 1 it is: $\frac{28,000}{70,000} = 40\%$

and in year 2 it is: $\frac{45,000}{100,000} = 45\%$

The improved gross profit margin has not led to an improvement in the net profit margin. This is because expenses as a percentage of sales have risen from 30% in year 1 to 35% in year 2.

3 SOLVENCY

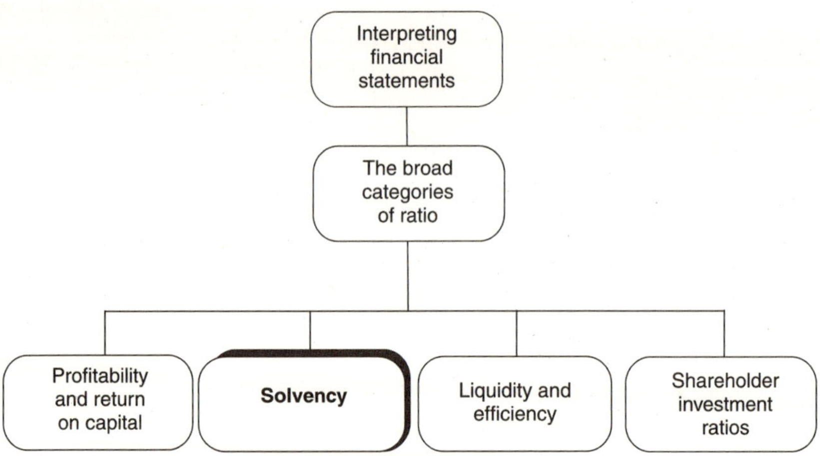

3.1 Long-term solvency: debt and gearing ratios

Debt ratios are concerned with:

- how much the company owes in relation to its size,
- whether it is getting into heavier debt or improving its situation, and
- whether its debt burden seems heavy or light.

Why are debt ratios important?

1 When a company is heavily in debt banks and other potential lenders may be unwilling to advance further funds.

2 When a company is earning only a modest PBIT, and has a heavy debt burden, there will be very little profit left over for shareholders after the interest charges have been paid. And so if interest rates were to go up (on bank overdrafts and so on) or the company were to borrow even more, it might soon be incurring interest charges in excess of PBIT. This might eventually lead to the liquidation of the company.

These are two big reasons why companies should keep their debt burden under control. There are four ratios that are particularly worth looking at: the **debt** ratio, **capital gearing** ratio, **interest cover** and **cash flow** ratio.

3.2 Debt ratio

Definition

$$\textbf{Debt ratio} = \frac{\text{Total debts}}{\text{Total assets}}$$

(a) Assets consist of fixed and current assets.

(b) Debts consist of all creditors, whether amounts falling due within one year or after more than one year.

There is no absolute guide to the maximum safe debt ratio. As a very general guide, you might regard 50% as a safe limit to debt. In practice, many companies operate successfully with a higher debt ratio than this, but 50% is nonetheless a helpful benchmark. In addition, if the debt ratio is over 50% and getting worse, the company's debt position will be worth looking at more carefully.

In the case of Furlong plc the debt ratio is as follows.

	20X8	*20X7*
Total debts / Total assets	$\frac{(881{,}731+100{,}000)}{(802{,}180+1{,}048{,}450)}$	$\frac{(912{,}456+100{,}000)}{(656{,}071+998{,}354)}$
	= 53%	= 61%

In this case, the debt ratio is quite high, mainly because of the large amount of current liabilities. However, the debt ratio has fallen from 61% to 53% between 20X7 and 20X8, and so the company appears to be improving its debt position.

3.3 Capital gearing ratio and debt/equity ratio

Capital gearing is concerned with a company's **long-term capital structure.** We can think of a company as consisting of fixed assets and **net current assets** (ie **working capital,** which is current assets minus current liabilities). These assets must be financed by long-term capital of the company, which is either:

(a) Share capital and reserves (shareholders' funds) divided into:
   (i) Ordinary shares plus reserves
   (ii) And irredeemable preference shares

(b) Long-term loan capital: 'creditors: amounts falling due after more than one year'

Irredeemable preference share capital is not debt. It would certainly not be included as debt in the debt ratio. However, like loan capital, preference share capital has a prior claim over profits before interest and tax, ahead of ordinary shareholders. Preference dividends must be paid out of profits before ordinary shareholders are entitled to an ordinary dividend, and so we refer to preference share capital and loan capital as **prior charge capital**. A company's gearing ratio will rise as it issues more prior charge capital, such as debentures, and decrease as its non-prior charge capital as ordinary shares increases.

The **capital gearing ratio** is a measure of the proportion of a company's capital that is prior charge capital. It is measured as follows:

Definitions

$$\textbf{Capital gearing ratio} = \frac{\text{Prior charge capital}}{\text{Total capital}}$$

(a) **Prior charge capital** is capital carrying a right to a fixed return. It will include preference shares and debentures.

(b) **Total capital** is ordinary share capital and reserves plus prior charge capital. It is easier to identify the figure for total capital as it is the same as total assets less current liabilities, which you will find given to you in the balance sheet.

As with the debt ratio, there is no absolute limit to what a capital gearing ratio ought to be. A company with a capital gearing ratio of more than 50% is said to be high-geared (whereas low gearing means a gearing ratio of less than 50%). Many companies are high-geared, but if a high-geared company is becoming increasingly high-geared, it is likely to have difficulty in the future when it wants to borrow even more, unless it can also boost its ordinary share capital and reserves, either with retained profits or by a new share issue.

A similar ratio to the capital gearing ratio is the **debt/equity ratio**, which is calculated as follows.

Definition

$$\textbf{Debt/equity ratio} = \frac{\text{Prior charge capital}}{\text{Ordinary share capital and reserves}}$$

This gives us the same sort of information as the capital gearing ratio. A ratio of 100% or more would indicate high gearing.

In the example of Furlong plc, we find that the company, although having a high debt ratio because of its current liabilities, has a low capital gearing ratio and low debt/equity ratio. It has no preference share capital and its only long-term debt is the 10% debenture stock.

	20X8	*20X7*
Gearing ratio	$\frac{100,000}{968,899} = 10\%$	$\frac{100,000}{741,969} = 13\%$
Debt/equity ratio	$\frac{100,000}{868,899} = 12\%$	$\frac{100,000}{641,969} = 16\%$

3.4 What do high or low gearing imply?

We mentioned earlier that gearing is, amongst other things, an attempt to quantify the degree of risk involved in holding equity shares in a company. This means risk both in terms of the company's ability to remain in business and in terms of expected ordinary dividends from the company. The problem with a high-geared company is that by definition there is a lot of debt. Debt generally carries a fixed rate of interest (or fixed rate of dividend if in the form of preference shares), hence there is a given (and large) amount to be paid out from profits to holders of debt before arriving at a residue available for distribution to the holders of equity. The riskiness will perhaps become clearer with the aid of an example.

EXAMPLE: RISK AND GEARING

	Company A	*Company B*	*Company C*
	£'000	£'000	£'000
Ordinary share capital	600	400	300
Retained earnings	300	300	300
	900	700	600
6% irredeemable preference shares	–	–	100
10% loan stock	100	300	300
Capital employed	1,000	1,000	1,000
Gearing ratio	10%	30%	40%

Now suppose that each company makes a PBIT of £50,000, and the rate of corporation tax is 30%. Amounts available for distribution to equity shareholders will be as follows.

	Company A	*Company B*	*Company C*
	£'000	£'000	£'000
PBIT	50	50	50
Interest	(10)	(30)	(30)
Profit before tax	40	20	20
Taxation at 30%	(12)	(6)	(6)
Profit after tax	28	14	14
Preference dividend	–	–	(6)
Available for ordinary shareholders	28	14	8

If in the subsequent year PBIT falls to £40,000, the amounts available to ordinary shareholders will be as follows.

	Company A	*Company B*	*Company C*
	£'000	£'000	£'000
PBIT	40	40	40
Interest	(10)	(30)	(30)
Profit before tax	30	10	10
Taxation at 30%	(9)	(3)	(3)
Profit after tax	21	7	7
Preference dividend	–	–	(6)
Available for ordinary shareholders	21	7	1

Note the following for this subsequent year.

Gearing ratio	10%	30%	40%
Change in PBIT	–20%	–20%	–20%
Change in profit available for ordinary shareholders	–25%	–50%	–87.5%

The more highly geared the company, the greater the risk that little (if anything) will be available to distribute by way of dividend to the ordinary shareholders.

(a) The more highly geared companies B and C have a greater percentage change in profit available for ordinary shareholders for any given percentage change in PBIT.

(b) The relationship similarly holds when profits increase. If PBIT had risen by 20% rather than fallen, you would find that once again the largest percentage change in profit available for ordinary shareholders (this means an increase) will be for the highly geared companies.

(c) This means that there will be greater **volatility** of amounts available for ordinary shareholders, and presumably therefore greater volatility in dividends paid to those shareholders, where a company is highly geared. That is the risk: shareholders may do extremely well or extremely badly without a particularly large movement in the PBIT of the company.

The risk of a company's ability to remain in business was referred to earlier. Gearing is relevant to this. A high-geared company has a large amount of interest to pay annually. If those borrowings are 'secured' in any way (and debentures in particular are secured), then the holders of the debt are perfectly entitled to force the company to realise assets to pay their interest if funds are not available from other sources. Clearly the more high-geared a company the more likely this is to occur when and if profits fall. **Higher gearing may mean higher returns, but also higher risk.**

3.5 Interest cover

The interest cover ratio shows whether a company is earning enough PBIT to pay its interest charges comfortably, or whether its interest charges are high in relation to the size of its profits, so that a fall in PBIT would then have a significant effect on profits available for ordinary shareholders.

Definition

> **Interest cover** = $\dfrac{\text{PBIT}}{\text{interest charges}}$

An interest cover of 2 times or less would be low. It should really exceed 3 times before the company's interest charges are to be considered within acceptable limits.

Returning first to the example of Companies A, B and C, the interest cover was as follows.

	Company A	*Company B*	*Company C*
(a) When PBIT was £50,000 =	$\frac{50,000}{10,000}$	$\frac{50,000}{30,000}$	$\frac{50,000}{30,000}$
	5 times	1.67 times	1.67 times
(b) When PBIT was £40,000 =	$\frac{40,000}{10,000}$	$\frac{40,000}{30,000}$	$\frac{40,000}{30,000}$
	4 times	1.33 times	1.33 times

Note. Although preference share capital is included as prior charge capital for the gearing ratio, it is usual to exclude preference dividends from interest charges unless the performance shares are redeemable and classified as the debt in the balance sheet. Interest cover and gearing do not quite look at the same thing.

Both B and C have a low interest cover, which is a warning to ordinary shareholders that their profits are highly vulnerable, in percentage terms, to even small changes in PBIT.

> **Activity 2** **(10 minutes)**
>
> Returning to the example of Furlong plc, what is the company's interest cover? (You should take the interest charge as the gross figure in the notes to the accounts.)

3.6 Cash flow ratio

Definitions

> The **cash flow ratio** is the ratio of a company's net cash inflow from operating activities to its total debts: $\dfrac{\text{Net cash inflow}}{\text{Total debts}}$
>
> (a) **Net cash inflow** is the amount of cash which the company has coming into the business from its operations. A figure for cash inflow from operating activities can be obtained from the cash flow statement.
>
> (b) **Total debts** are short-term and long-term creditors.

Obviously, a company needs to be earning enough cash from operating activities to be able to meet its foreseeable debts and future commitments. The cash flow ratio, and changes in the cash flow ratio from one year to the next, provide useful indicators of a company's cash position.

Activity 3 **(30 minutes)**

Furlong plc made a profit on disposals of fixed assets of £66,500 in 20X8, and of £25,200 in 20X7. At the end of 20X6 it had stocks of £58,149, debtors of £807,527 and creditors due in less than one year of £905,637. Calculate Furlong plc's cash flow ratios for 20X7 and 20X8, and the change in the ratio between the two years.

4 LIQUIDITY AND EFFICIENCY

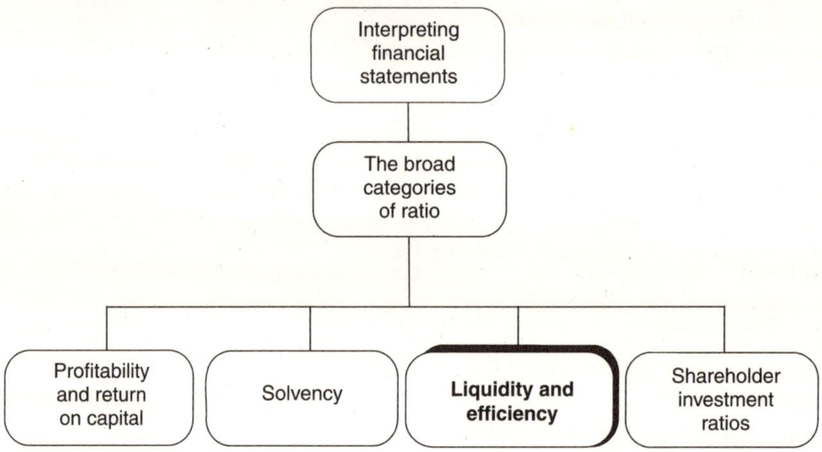

Profitability is of course an important aspect of a company's performance and **solvency** (debt or gearing) is another. Neither, however, addresses directly the key issues of **liquidity** and efficiency.

Definitions

Liquidity is the amount of cash a company can put its hands on quickly to settle its debts (and possibly to meet other unforeseen demands for cash payments too).

Efficiency relates to how well the company is managing its working capital (current assets and liabilities).

Liquid funds consist of:

(a) Cash

(b) Short-term investments for which there is a ready market

(c) Fixed-term deposits with a bank or building society, for example, a six month high-interest deposit with a bank

(d) Trade debtors (because they will pay what they owe within a reasonably short period of time)

In summary, **liquid assets** are current asset items that will or could soon be **converted into cash, plus cash itself**. Two common definitions of liquid assets are:

(a) All current assets without exception
(b) All current assets with the exception of stocks

A company can obtain liquid assets from sources other than sales, such as the issue of shares for cash, a new loan or the sale of fixed assets. But a company cannot rely on these at all times, and in general obtaining liquid funds depends on making sales and profits. Even so, profits do not always lead to increases in liquidity. This is mainly because funds generated from trading may be immediately invested in fixed assets or paid out as dividends. You should refer back to Chapter 10 on cash flow statements to examine this issue.

The reason why a company needs liquid assets is so that it can **meet its debts when they fall due**. Payments are continually made for operating expenses and other costs, and so there is a cash cycle from trading activities of cash coming in from sales and cash going out for expenses. This is illustrated by Figure 11.1.

4.1 The cash cycle

To help you to understand liquidity ratios, it is useful to begin with a brief explanation of the cash cycle. The cash cycle describes the flow of cash out of a business and back into it again as a result of normal trading operations.

Cash goes out to pay for supplies, wages and salaries and other expenses, although payments can be delayed by taking some credit. A business might hold stock for a while and then sell it. Cash will come back into the business from sales, although customers will delay payment by taking some credit themselves.

Figure 11.1 The cash cycle

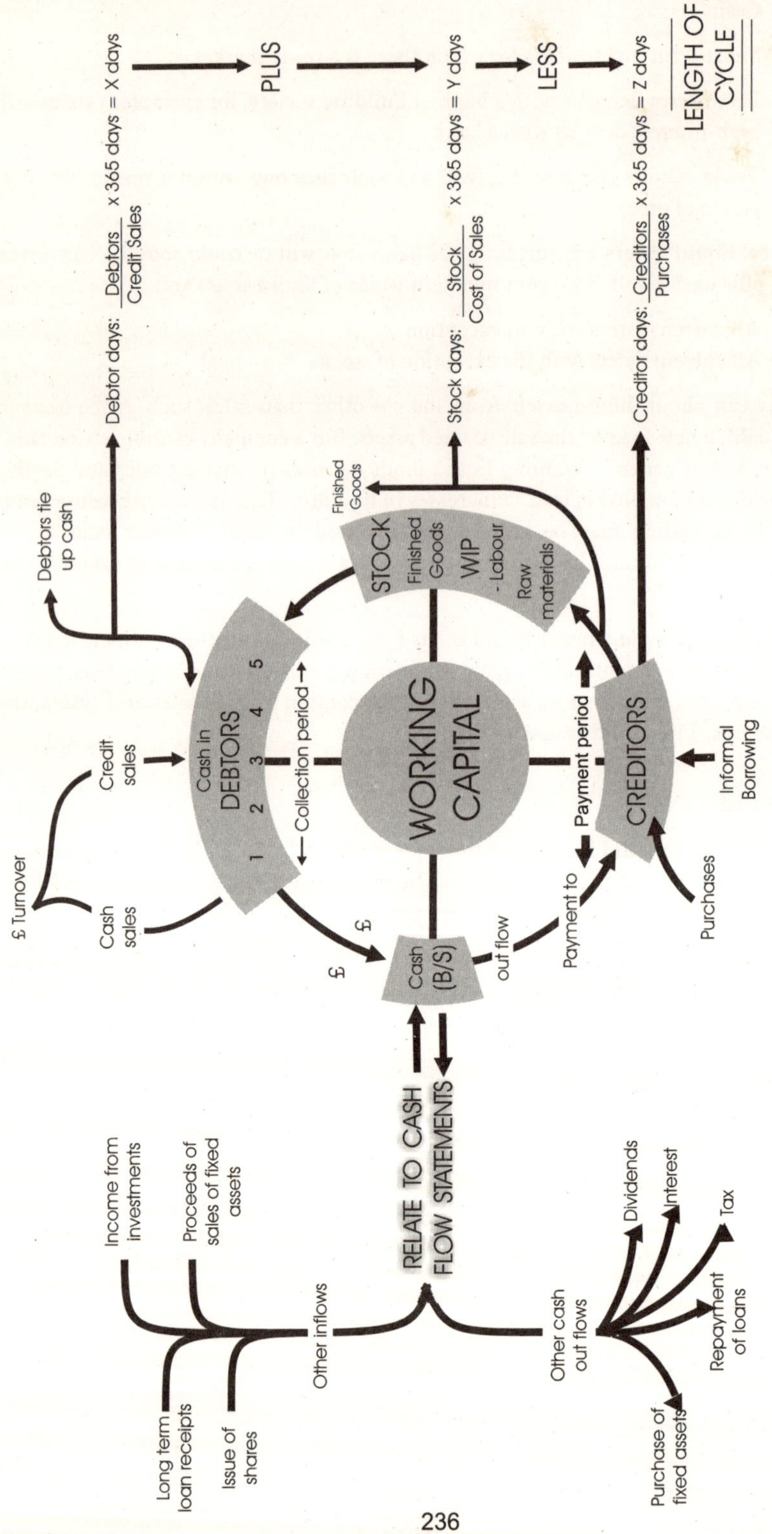

The main points about the cash cycle are as follows.

(a) The timing of cash flows in and out of a business does not coincide with the time when sales and costs of sales occur. Cash flows out can be postponed by taking credit from creditors. Cash flows in can be delayed by having debtors.

(b) The delay between making a purchase and making a sale also affects cash flows. If stocks are held for a long time, the delay between the cash payment for stocks and cash receipts from selling them will also be a long one.

(c) Holding stocks and having debtors can therefore be seen as two reasons why cash receipts are delayed. Another way of saying this is that if a company invests in working capital, its cash position will show a corresponding decrease.

(d) Similarly, taking credit from creditors can be seen as a reason why cash payments are delayed. The company's liquidity position will worsen when it has to pay the creditors, unless it can get more cash in from sales and debtors in the meantime.

Liquidity ratios and working capital ratios are used to analyse a company's liquidity, length of cash cycle, and investment in working capital.

4.2 Liquidity ratios: current ratio and quick ratio

The 'standard' test of liquidity is the **current ratio**. It can be obtained from the balance sheet, and is calculated as follows.

Definition

$$\textbf{Current ratio} = \frac{\text{Current assets}}{\text{Current liabilities}}$$

The idea behind this is that a company should have enough current assets that give a promise of 'cash to come' to meet its commitments to pay off its current liabilities. Obviously, a **ratio in excess of 1** should be expected. Otherwise, there would be the prospect that the company might be unable to pay its debts on time. In practice, a ratio comfortably in excess of 1 is expected, but what is 'comfortable' varies between different types of businesses.

Companies are not able to convert all their current assets into cash very quickly. In particular, some manufacturing companies might hold large quantities of raw material stocks, which must be used in production to create finished goods stocks. Finished goods stocks might be warehoused for a long time, or sold on lengthy credit. In such businesses, where stock turnover is slow, most stocks are not very 'liquid' assets, because the cash cycle is so long. For these reasons, we calculate an additional liquidity ratio, known as the **quick ratio** or **acid test** ratio.

Definition

The **quick ratio**, or **acid test ratio**: $\dfrac{\text{Current assets less stocks}}{\text{Current liabilities}}$

This ratio should ideally be at least 1 for companies with a slow stock turnover. For companies with a fast stock turnover such as a supermarket, a quick ratio can be comfortably less than 1 without suggesting that the company should be in cash flow trouble.

Both the current ratio and the quick ratio offer an indication of the company's liquidity position, but the absolute figures should not be interpreted too literally. It is often theorised that an acceptable current ratio is 1.5 and an acceptable quick ratio is 0.8, but these should only be used as a guide.

EXAMPLE: FOOD RETAILING V MANUFACTURING

Different businesses operate in very different ways. A supermarket group for example might have a current ratio of 0.5 and a quick ratio of 0.2. The supermarket has low debtors (people do not buy groceries on credit), low cash (good cash management), medium stocks (high stocks but quick turnover, particularly in view of perishability) and very high creditors (it buys its supplies of groceries on credit).

Compare the supermarket ratios with a manufacturing and retail organisation which has a current ratio of 1.4 and a quick ratio of 1.00. Such an organisation operates with liquidity ratios closer to the standard.

What is important is the **trend** of these ratios. From this, one can easily ascertain whether liquidity is improving or deteriorating. If the supermarket had traded for the last ten years (very successfully) with current ratios of 0.5 and quick ratios of 0.2 then it should be supposed that the company can continue in business with those levels of liquidity. If in the following year the current ratio were to fall to 0.4 and the quick ratio to 0.1, then further investigation into the liquidity situation would be appropriate. It is the relative position that is far more important than the absolute figures.

Don't forget the other side of the coin either. A current ratio and a quick ratio can get bigger than they need to be. A company that has large volumes of stocks and debtors might be over-investing in working capital, and so tying up more funds in the business than it needs to. This would suggest poor management of debtors (credit) or stocks by the company.

4.3 Efficiency ratios: control of debtors

A rough measure of the average length of time it takes for a company's debtors to pay what they owe is the 'debtor days' ratio, or **debtors' payment period**.

Definition

$$\textbf{Debtors' payment period} = \frac{\text{Trade debtors}}{\text{Sales}} \times 365 \text{ days}$$

The figure for sales should be taken from the P & L account. Trade debtors are not the total figure for debtors in the balance sheet, which includes prepayments and non-trade debtors; instead it will be itemised in an analysis of the debtors total, in a note to the accounts.

The estimate of debtor days is only approximate.

(a) The balance sheet value of debtors might be abnormally high or low compared with the 'normal' level the company usually has.

(b) Sales in the P & L account are exclusive of VAT, but debtors in the balance sheet are inclusive of VAT. We are not strictly comparing like with like.

Sales are usually made on 'normal credit terms' of payment within 30 days. Debtor days significantly in excess of this might be representative of poor management of funds of a business. However, some companies must allow generous credit terms to win customers. Exporting companies in particular may have to carry large amounts of debtors, and so their average collection period might be well in excess of 30 days.

The trend of the collection period (debtor days) over time is probably the best guide. If debtor days are increasing year on year, this is indicative of a poorly managed credit control function (and potentially therefore a poorly managed company).

EXAMPLE: DEBTOR DAYS

The debtor days of three companies – a supermarket, a combined manufacturing and retail organisation, and a manufacturer – were as follows.

Company	*Current year* *Trade debtors / Sales*		*Debtor days (×365)*	*Previous year*		*Debtor days (×365)*
Supermarket	$\frac{£5{,}016K}{£284{,}986K}$	=	6.4 days	$\frac{£3{,}977K}{£290{,}668K}$	=	5.0 days
Manufacturing/ retail	$\frac{£458.3m}{£2{,}059.5m}$	=	81.2 days	$\frac{£272.4m}{£1{,}274.2m}$	=	78.0 days
Manufacturer	$\frac{£304.4m}{£3{,}817.3m}$	=	29.3 days	$\frac{£287.0m}{£3{,}366.3m}$	=	31.1 days

The differences in debtor days reflect the differences between the types of business. The supermarket has hardly any trade debtors at all, whereas the manufacturing companies have far more. The debtor days are fairly constant from the previous year for all three companies.

4.4 Efficiency ratios: stock

Another ratio worth calculating is the **stock turnover period**, or **stock days**. This is another estimated figure, obtainable from published accounts, which indicates the average number of days that items of stock are held for. Like debtor days, it is only an approximate, estimated figure, but one which should be reliable enough for comparing changes year on year.

Definitions

Stock days: $\dfrac{\text{Stock}}{\text{Cost of sales}} \times 365$

Stock turnover ratio: $\dfrac{\text{Cost of sales}}{\text{Stock}}$

Stock turnover ratio is a measure of how vigorously a business is trading.

A lengthening stock turnover period for stock days from one year to the next indicates:

(a) A slowdown in trading

(b) A build-up in stock levels, perhaps suggesting that the investment in stocks is becoming excessive

If we add together the stock days and the debtor days, this should give us an indication of how soon stock is convertible into cash. Both debtor days and stock days therefore give us a further indication of the company's liquidity.

EXAMPLE: STOCK TURNOVER

Returning once more to our first example, the estimated stock turnover periods for the supermarket were as follows.

Current year $\dfrac{\textit{Stock}}{\textit{Cost of sales}}$	*Stock turnover period (days × 365)*	*Previous year*
$\dfrac{£15{,}554K}{£254{,}571K} \times 365 =$	22.3 days	$\dfrac{£14{,}094K}{£261{,}368K} \times 365 = 19.7$ days

---

Activity 4 **(20 minutes)**

Bingo Ltd, a manufacturer, buys raw materials on six weeks credit, holds them in store for three weeks and then issues them to the production department. The production process takes two weeks on average, and finished goods are held in store for an average of four weeks before being sold. Debtors take five weeks credit on average.

Calculate the length of the cash cycle.

Activity 5 **(15 minutes)**

During a year a business sold stock which had cost £60,000. The stock held at the beginning of the year was £6,000 and at the end of the year it was £10,000.

What was the annual stock turnover ratio?

4.5 Efficiency ratios: creditors

Definition

Creditors' payment period is calculated by the formula:

$$\frac{\text{Trade creditors}}{\text{Purchases or cost of sales}}$$

It is rare to find purchases disclosed in published accounts and so cost of sales serves as an approximation.

The creditors' payment period often helps to assess a company's liquidity; an increase in creditor days is often a sign of lack of long-term finance or poor management of current assets, resulting in the use of extended credit from suppliers, increased bank overdraft and so on.

EXAMPLE: LIQUIDITY AND EFFICIENCY RATIOS

Calculate liquidity and efficiency ratios from the accounts of the BET Group, a business which provides service support (cleaning etc) to customers worldwide.

	20X4	*20X5*
Sales	2,176.2	2,344.8
Cost of sales	1,659.0	1,731.5
Gross profit	517.2	613.3
Current assets		
Stocks	42.7	78.0
Debtors (note 1)	378.9	431.4
Short-term deposits and cash	205.2	145.0
	626.8	654.4
Creditors: amounts falling due within one year		
Loans and overdrafts	32.4	81.1
Corporation taxes	67.8	76.7
Dividend declared	11.7	17.2
Creditors (note 2)	487.2	467.2
	599.1	642.2
Net current assets	27.7	12.2
Notes		
1 Trade debtors	295.2	335.5
2 Trade creditors	190.8	188.1

Solution

	20X4	*20X5*
Current ratio	$\frac{626.8}{599.1} = 1.05$	$\frac{654.4}{642.2} = 1.02$
Quick ratio	$\frac{584.1}{599.1} = 0.97$	$\frac{576.4}{642.2} = 0.90$
Debtors' days	$\frac{295.2}{2{,}176.2} \times 365 = 49.5$ days	$\frac{335.5}{2{,}344.8} \times 365 = 52.2$ days
Stock days	$\frac{42.7}{1{,}659.0} \times 365 = 9.4$ days	$\frac{78.0}{1{,}731.5} \times 365 = 16.4$ days
Creditors' payment period	$\frac{190.8}{1{,}659.0} \times 365 = 42.0$ days	$\frac{188.1}{1{,}731.5} \times 365 = 40.0$ days

BET Group is a service company and hence it would be expected to have very low stock and very short stock days. The similarity of debtors' and creditors' days means that the group is passing on most of the delay in receiving payment to its suppliers.

BET's current ratio is a little lower than average but its quick ratio is better than average and very little less than the current ratio. This suggests that stock levels are strictly controlled, which is reinforced by the low stock turnover period. It would seem that working capital is tightly managed, to avoid the poor liquidity which could be caused by high debtor days and comparatively high creditors.

5 SHAREHOLDER INVESTMENT RATIOS

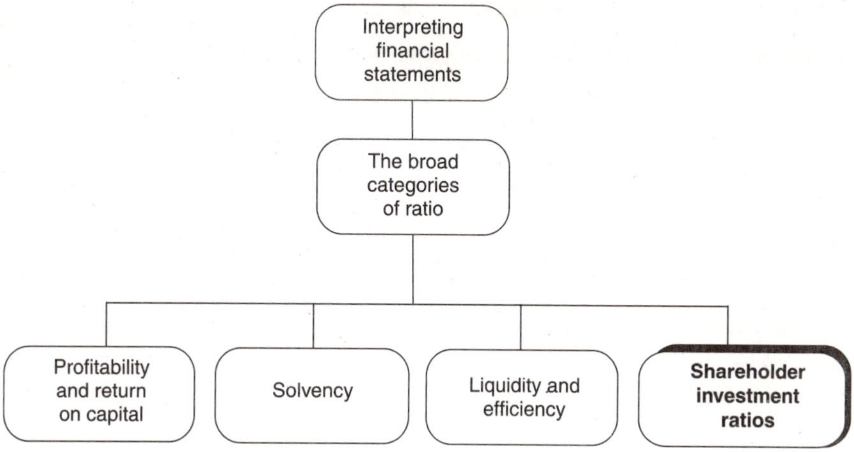

Shareholders' investment ratios help equity shareholders and other investors to assess the value and quality of an investment in the ordinary shares of a company.

They are:

(a) Earnings per share (EPS)
(b) Dividend per share (DPS)
(c) Dividend cover
(d) P/E ratio
(e) Dividend yield
(f) Earnings yield

The value of an investment in ordinary shares in a listed company is its **market value**, and so investment ratios must have regard not only to information in the company's published accounts, but also to the current market price. The fourth, fifth and sixth ratios all involve using the share price.

5.1 Earnings per share (EPS)

Definition

> **Earnings per share (EPS)**: the return on each ordinary share in the year =
>
> $$\frac{\text{Earnings for period}}{\text{Number of ordinary shares in issue}}$$

Earnings are profits after tax and preference dividends, which can either be paid out as a dividend to ordinary shareholders or retained in the business.

EXAMPLE: EARNINGS PER SHARE

Suppose that Draught Ltd reports the following figures:

PROFIT AND LOSS ACCOUNT FOR 20X4 (EXTRACT)

	£
Profit before interest and tax	120,000
Interest	(20,000)
Profit before tax	100,000
Taxation	(40,000)
Profit after tax	60,000
Preference dividend	(1,000)
Profit available for ordinary shareholders (= earnings)	59,000
Ordinary dividend	(49,000)
Retained profits for the year	10,000

The company has 80,000 ordinary shares and 20,000 irredeemable preference shares.

Calculate earnings per share for Draught Ltd in 20X4.

Solution

$$\text{EPS is } \frac{£59{,}000}{80{,}000} = 73.75 \text{ pence}$$

5.2 Dividend per share and dividend cover

Definitions

$$\textbf{Dividend per share (DPS)} = \frac{\text{Total ordinary dividend}}{\text{Number of ordinary shares in issue}}$$

$$\textbf{Dividend cover} = \frac{\text{EPS}}{\text{DPS}}$$

Dividend cover shows how much of the profit on ordinary activities for the year that is available for distribution to shareholders has been paid, and hence what proportion will be retained in the business to finance future growth. A dividend cover of 2 times would indicate that the company had paid 50% of its distributable profits as dividends, and retained 50% in the business to help to finance future operations. Retained profits are an important source of funds for most companies, and so the dividend cover can in some cases be quite high.

A significant change in the dividend cover from one year to the next would be worth looking at closely. For example, if a company's dividend cover were to fall sharply between one year and the next, it could be that its profits had fallen, but the directors wished to pay at least the same amount of dividends as in the previous year, so as to keep shareholder expectations satisfied.

5.3 P/E ratio

Definition

> The **P/E ratio** is the ratio of a company's current share price to the earnings per share: $\frac{\text{Market price per share}}{\text{EPS}}$

A high **P/E ratio** indicates strong shareholder confidence in the company and its future, eg in profit growth, and a lower P/E ratio indicates lower confidence.

The P/E ratio of one company can be compared with the P/E ratios of:

(a) Other companies in the same business sector
(b) Other companies generally

5.4 Dividend yield

Definition

> **Dividend yield** is the return a shareholder is currently expecting on the shares that he holds in the company:
>
> $$\text{Dividend yield} = \frac{\text{DPS}}{\text{Market price per share}} \times 100\%$$

Shareholders look for both dividend yield and capital growth in the market value of each share. Dividend yield is therefore an important aspect of a share's performance.

> **Activity 6** **(10 minutes)**
>
> In the year to 31 December 20X8, DPP Holdings plc declared an interim ordinary dividend of 5p per share and a final ordinary dividend of 11p per share. Assuming a market share price of 432 pence, what is the dividend yield?

5.5 Earnings yield

Earnings yield is a performance indicator that is not given the same publicity as EPS, P/E ratio, dividend cover and dividend yield.

Definition

> **Earnings yield** is measured as the earnings per share as a percentage of the current share price: $\frac{\text{EPS}}{\text{Market price per share}}$.

It indicates therefore what the dividend yield could be if the company paid out all its profits as dividend and retained nothing in the business.

Earnings yield attempts to improve the comparison between investments in different companies by overcoming the problem that companies have differing dividend covers. Some companies retain a bigger proportion of their profits than others, and so the dividend yield between companies can vary for this reason.. Earnings yield overcomes the problem of comparison by assuming that all earnings are paid out as dividends.

Earnings yield = dividend yield × dividend cover.

$$\frac{\text{EPS}}{\text{Market price per share}} = \frac{\text{DPS}}{\text{Market price per share}} \times \frac{\text{EPS}}{\text{DPS}}$$

Activity 7 **(1 hour)**

	Company P		*Company Q*	
	£m	£m	£m	£m
Profit on ordinary activities after tax		41.1		5.6
Dividends				
Preference	0.5		–	
Ordinary	20.6		5.4	
		21.1		5.4
Retained profits		20.0		0.2

	Company P	*Company Q*
Number of ordinary shares	200m	50m
Market price per share	285p	154p

Required

Compare the dividend yield, dividend cover and earnings yield of the two companies.

Chapter roundup

- Ratio analysis involves comparing one figure against another to produce a ratio, and assessing whether the ratio indicates a weakness or strength in the company's affairs.
- This lengthy chapter has gone into quite a lot of detail about basic ratio analysis. The ratios you should be able to calculate and/or comment on are as follows.

Profitability ratios

- return on capital employed (ROCE)
- net profit as a percentage of sales (net margin)
- asset turnover ratio
- gross profit as a percentage of sales (gross margin)

Debt and gearing ratios

- debt ratio
- capital gearing ratio
- debt/equity ratio
- interest cover
- cash flow ratio

Liquidity and efficiency ratios

- current ratio
- quick ratio (acid test ratio)
- debtor days (average debt collection period)
- stock days
- stock turnover ratio
- creditors' payment period

Ordinary shareholders' investment ratios

- earnings per share (EPS)
- dividend per share (DPS)
- dividend cover
- P/E ratio
- dividend yield
- earnings yield

Quick quiz

1. Apart from ratio analysis, what other information might be helpful in interpreting a company's accounts?
2. What is the usual formula for ROCE?
3. ROCE can be calculated as the product of two other ratios. What are they?
4. Define the 'debt ratio'.
5. In a period when profits are fluctuating, what effect does a company's level of gearing have on the profits available for ordinary shareholders?
6. What is a company's cash flow ratio?

7 What is earnings per share?

8 What is the P/E ratio?

Answers to quick quiz

1 Various other items and notes in the publicised accounts.

2 $\dfrac{\text{PBIT}}{\text{Capital employed}}$

3 Profit margin × asset turnover = ROCE

4 $\dfrac{\text{Debts}}{\text{Total assets}}$

5 See Section 3.4.

6 $\dfrac{\text{Net cash inflow}}{\text{Total debts}}$

7 The amount of net profit that is attributable to each ordinary share.

8 $\dfrac{\text{Current share price}}{\text{EPS}}$

Answers to activities

1 $\text{ROCE} = \dfrac{\text{PBIT}}{\text{Capital employed}}$

$\text{PM} = \dfrac{\text{PBIT}}{\text{Sales}}$

$\text{AT} = \dfrac{\text{Sales}}{\text{Capital employed}}$

It follows that ROCE = PM x AT, which can be rearranged to the form given in option D.

2 Interest charges should be taken gross, from the note to the accounts, and not net of interest receipts as shown in the P & L account.

	20X8	*20X7*
$\dfrac{\text{PBIT}}{\text{Interest charges}}$	$\dfrac{360{,}245}{18{,}115}$	$\dfrac{247{,}011}{21{,}909}$
	= 20 times	= 11 times

Furlong plc has more than sufficient interest cover. In view of the company's low gearing, this is not too surprising and so we finally obtain a picture of Furlong plc as a company that does not seem to have a debt problem, in spite of its high (although declining) debt ratio.

3

	20X8	20X7
	£	£
Operating profit	359,501	244,229
Depreciation	151,107	120,147
Profit on disposals	(66,500)	(25,200)
Change in stocks:		
20X8: 76,550 – 44,422	32,128	
20X7: 58,149 – 76,550		(18,401)
Change in debtors:		
20X8: 853,441 – 1,002,701	(149,260)	
20X7: 807,527 – 853,441		(45,914)
Change in creditors:		
20X8: 881,731 – 912,456	(30,725)	
20X7: 912,456 – 905,637		6,819
Cash inflow from operating activities	296,251	281,680
Total debts:		
20X8: 881,731 + 100,000	981,731	
20X7: 912,456 + 100,000		1,012,456
Cash flow ratio	30.2%	27.8%
Increase in cash flow ratio	8.6%	

4 The cash cycle is the length of time between paying for raw materials and receiving cash from the sale of finished goods. In this case Bingo Ltd stores raw materials for three weeks, spends two weeks producing finished goods, four weeks storing the goods before sale and five weeks collecting the money from debtors: a total of 14 weeks. However, six weeks of this period is effectively financed by the company's creditors so that the length of the cash cycle is eight weeks.

5 $$\text{Stock turnover ratio} = \frac{\text{Cost of sales}}{\text{Average stock}} = \frac{£60{,}000}{(10{,}000 + 6{,}000)/2} = 7.5 \text{ times}$$

6 The net dividend per share is (5 + 11) = 16 p

$$\frac{16\text{p}}{432\text{p}} \times 100 = 3.70\%$$

7

	Company P	Company Q
	£m	£m
Profit on ordinary activities after tax	41.1	5.6
Preference dividend	(0.5)	–
Earnings	40.6	5.6
Number of shares	200m	50m
EPS	20.3p	11.2p
DPS (ordinary dividends)	10.3p	10.8p
Dividend cover	$\frac{20.3}{10.3}$	$\frac{11.2}{10.8}$

	Company P £m	*Company Q* £m
	= 1.97 times	= 1.04 times
Dividend yield	$\frac{10.3}{285} \times 100\%$	$\frac{10.8}{154} \times 100\%$
	= 3.6%	= 7.0%
Earnings yield	$\frac{20.3}{285} \times 100\%$	$\frac{11.2}{154} \times 100\%$
	= 7.1%	= 7.3%

The dividend yield of Company Q is much higher, but the dividend cover of Company P is greater. (The dividend cover of Q is only just greater than 1. Company Q has just about managed to pay its dividend out of profits made in the year.)

Index

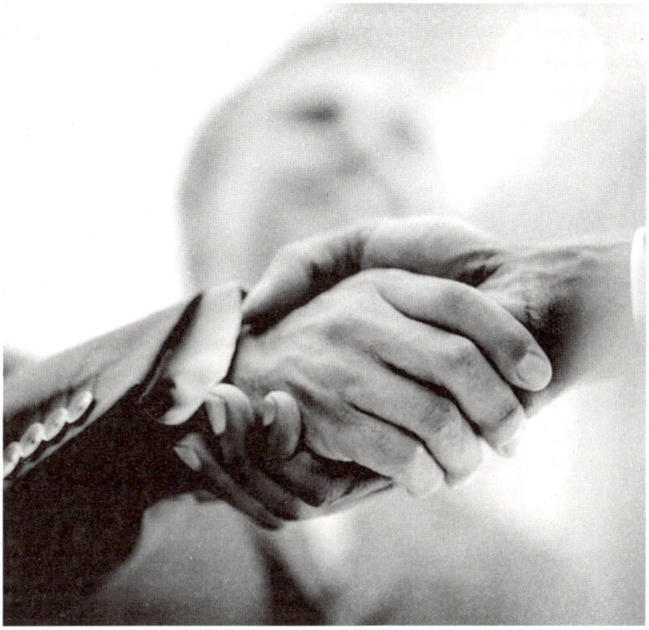

Definitions are highlighted in **bold**